WORLD WAR I

AN ILLUSTRATED HISTORY

by Lloyd Clark Royal Military Academy Sandhurst
with an introduction by Gary Sheffield Joint Services Command and Staff College

Foreword by
Lt Gen Sir Roderick Cordy-Simpson KBE, CB
President of The Royal British Legion

Helicon

Helicon Publishing Ltd
42 Hythe Bridge Street
Oxford OX1 2EP
e-mail: admin@helicon.co.uk
Web site: http://www.helicon.co.uk

Designed and typeset by Mark-making Design Ltd

Picture credits:
p20 © Billie Love Collection
p186 © AKG London
p26, 28, 105, 144, 229 © Syndication International
All other photos with special thanks to © The Imperial War Museum

Reprographics by Hilite Design and Reprograhics Ltd, Southampton

Printed and bound by Mateu Cromo, Madrid, Spain
ISBN 1-85986-338-8

British Cataloguing in Publication Data
A catalogue record is available from The British Library

Papers used by Helicon Publishing Ltd are natural recyclable products made from wood grown in sustainable forests.
The manufacturing processes of both raw materials and paper conform to the environmental regulation of the country of origin.

Editorial Director
Hilary McGlynn

Managing Editor
Elena Softley

Project Editor
Caroline Broughton

Text editors and proofreaders
Stephen Delany
Ruth Collier

Indexer
Drusilla Calvert

Picture research
Sophie Evans
Caroline Broughton

Page design
Mark-making Design Ltd

Production Manager
John Normansell

Cartography
Olive Pearson

To Catriona, Freddie, and Charlotte with all my love.

May they know only peace.

Contents

List of Maps

General Map Key

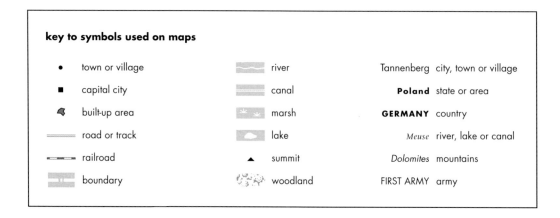

Patron Her Majesty The Queen

The Royal British Legion
48 Pall Mall
London SW1Y 5JY

Legion*line* (Helpline) 08457 725 725
www.britishlegion.org.uk

World War I was one of the defining events of the 20th century. Thirteen million men lost their lives in a war that was unprecedented in scale. Never before had so many men from so many different countries lost their lives in a single conflict; never before had commanders had to rethink so drastically their battle tactics in the face of such huge technological advances in munitions.

This book aims to convey the experience of World War I, as it was for the soldiers, civilians, and commanders of the time. Through narrative, quotes, maps, and photographs it provides a chronological record of the conflict, on land, sea, and in the air, not just within Europe, but internationally.

World War I provides us with some of our most enduring images of the horror of war, but the collection of photos in this book also aims to reveal other aspects; the bravery, comradeship, and day-to-day reality of trench warfare and the world at war.

The Royal British Legion grew out of a world changed forever by World War I and exists, then as now, to care for those who served their country and to commemorate the sacrifice of all those who gave their lives. In remembering in particular the horrors of World War I, I hope we can help to ensure that such devastation does not happen again.

LIEUTENANT GENERAL SIR RODERICK CORDY-SIMPSON KBE, CB
NATIONAL PRESIDENT

Safeguarding the welfare, interests and memory of those who have served in the Armed Forces.
A Registered Charity. Charity No. 219779.

INTRODUCTION
THE IMPORTANCE OF WORLD WAR I

World War I was the defining event of the 20th century. It marked the abrupt and brutal end of a distinct period in history, the so-called 'Long Nineteenth Century', that stretched from the outbreak of the French Revolution in 1789 to the assassination of Archduke Franz Ferdinand in Sarajevo in 1914. World War I (also called the Great War) heralded the beginning of what historians now call the 'Short Twentieth Century' - a bloody cycle of conflicts and confrontations that encompassed the two global conflagrations of 1914–18 and 1939–45 as well as the Cold War, and which ended only with the collapse of Soviet communism in 1989–91. Without an understanding of World War I, the 20th century cannot be fully comprehended. Yet today, in Britain and the USA, World War I is habitually described as 'futile'. But was World War I really pointless? Does it matter that Britain, France, and the USA won, and the Central Powers of Germany and Austria-Hungary lost? What sort of world would have resulted from a German victory?

If we play the game of counterfactual history - of 'what ifs' and 'might have beens' - we can imagine that World War I does not break out in 1914, and that peace endures between the Great Powers. Would the Russian Revolution, which historically broke out in 1917, have happened? Even without the challenge of war in 1914, Imperial Russia was facing severe problems in the second decade of the 20th century. Defeat at the hands of Japan in 1904–05 had triggered an abortive revolution, and rapid industrialization brought massive unrest in its wake.

Yet in 1914 the Imperial system and the tsar retained some credibility. The system had shown its willingness to undertake reform, albeit limited, and Nicholas II retained the affection of the bulk of his people. Arguably, it was military defeat in 1914–16, and the shattering of the tsar's credibility when he unwisely assumed direct responsibility for the conduct of the war, that destroyed the Imperial system. Moreover, the appalling pressures faced by Russia in 1914–17 could have only resulted from a conflict on the scale of World War I. It is entirely possible that, without the war, Imperial Russia could have reformed itself sufficiently to avert the prospect of violent revolution. The degree of change involved may well have amounted to a revolution that was more-or-less peaceful. Even if there had been a violent and successful revolution in a warless Russia (a big 'if'), the chances are that it would not have been led by Vladimir Ilyich Lenin. Without the unique circumstances created by the war, Lenin is unlikely to have been in a position to launch his Bolshevik revolt. In 1924 he would have died in Switzerland, an embittered exile, rather than revered as the founder of the world's first workers' and peasants' state. And without Lenin's October Revolution, there would have been no Stalin, no Great Terror, and, possibly, no Cold War.

World War I also diverted Germany brutally onto another journey. By 1914, the government of Kaiser Wilhelm II was in an immensely stronger position than that of his cousin Tsar Nicholas II. Imperial Germany was a bizarre mixture of ancient and modern – a monarchy tending towards absolutism, combined with some of the trappings of a modern democracy. Although there was a strong socialist movement, the Left relied mainly on constitutional means, and the fabric of Wilhelmine society was reasonably cohesive. However, as early as 1894, a senior German official had warned that Wilhelm's was 'an operetta regime, but not one that a European nation at the end of the 19th century will put up with'. That being said, it is unlikely in the extreme that if World War I had not happened, Imperial Germany would have collapsed as quickly as it did. That monumental collapse was the direct result of military defeat in 1918. However, demands for moves towards greater democracy might have become a problem for the Kaiser's regime in the 1920s and 1930s (he lived until 1941), for they certainly conflicted with Wilhelm's concept of himself as an absolute ruler. The most significant change in German history – had the Great War not happened – would have been that Adolf Hitler would have been far less likely to become dictator.

In 1914 Hitler lived on the margins of German society. A citizen of Austria-Hungary who had fled to Germany to avoid military service, Hitler was eking out a miserable living. As for so many people in many different countries, the outbreak of war in August 1914 changed Hitler's life for the better. It is not surprising that a photograph captures him in a public square in Munich celebrating the announcement of war. Hitler proved to be a brave and resourceful soldier who won the Iron Cross twice. At the end of the war, bewildered and disgusted by Germany's defeat, Hitler seized the opportunity to enter radical right-wing politics. Had he done so in the conditions that pertained before August 1914 (or in our counterfactual universe), Hitler and his National Socialist German Worker's Party would have got nowhere. In the conditions of the early 1920s, when Germany was coping simultaneously with defeat, humiliation, rampant inflation, and the transition to democracy, Hitler came to prominence. His accession to power was aided by the repercussions of the 1929 Wall Street Crash, but also by considerable luck and the miscalculations of his rivals. Without World War I, Hitler would have remained a small-time agitator and failed artist. World War II would not have happened – or at least, not in the form it actually took.

The absence of World War I would have had a less spectacular impact on British history than would have been the case for Russia or Germany, but no less profound. For one thing, the British Empire would have survived much longer than it actually did. One by-product of the Great War was the emergence of the 'White Dominions' – Australia, New Zealand, and Canada – as nations in their own right; they were no longer simply overseas appendages of Great Britain. The Anzacs fought at Gallipoli in 1915 and the Canadians on Vimy Ridge in 1917 – battles that proved to be defining symbols of their emerging nationhood. This process was by no means complete in 1918, and indeed the ties had been loosening for some years before the outbreak of war, but nonetheless the Great War was a watershed in the history of the British Empire. If there had been no 1914–18 conflict, at the very least this process would have been retarded.

Also, the unravelling of the African and Asian elements of the British Empire would not have been so rapid. Here we get into some very muddy waters. An important consequence of the war was that Japan increased its power and influence in the Far East at the expense of its nominal ally, Britain. Peace from 1914 to 1918 would have at the very least delayed this process, and may have curbed Japan's expansionist ambitions in the 1930s. If this is so, and we also assume that war does not break out in Europe in 1939, we reach a situation where Japan does not attack European colonial possessions in Asia. Alternatively, if they do, the Europeans and the USA are strong enough to fight off the Japanese. Thus the spectacle of a non-white power defeating Europeans and Americans in 1941–42 does not happen, and the myth of white invincibility, a crucial element in the maintenance of colonial rule in what is now called the developing world, remains intact a little longer. Consequently, the great surge of decolonization that occurred in the two decades following the end of World War II, one of the major developments in global history, is postponed. The word 'postponed' is appropriate, since a movement towards decolonization was in any event inevitable – but possibly in the 21st century rather than the 20th.

As far back as the mid-19th century, a French observer, Alexis de Tocqueville, recognized that the USA had the potential to become a superpower. The problem came in converting US *potential* – in population, economic resources, and industrial strength – into political and military power. The USA has had a peculiar history. It was born as a result of a rebellion against a colonial power; a country peopled largely by emigration from overseas, blessed by accidents of history and geography, with weak states on its frontiers and two vast oceans separating it from potential foes. Its peculiar history led to two important factors that helped to determine US policy. The first was isolationism, a determination to stay out of European affairs, combined with a suspicion of the concept of the 'balance of power'. The second was a reluctance to spend money on its armed forces. The result was that in 1914 the USA was an economic giant that punched well *below* its weight on the international stage. It was not a serious player in the July crisis that led to the outbreak of war in 1914, although it became one very soon afterwards.

If World War I had not happened, would the USA have remained an isolationist, sleeping giant? The answer is almost certainly yes. As it was, although US industries rapidly geared up to supply the Allied war effort, it took the severe provocation of a German campaign of unrestricted submarine warfare to bring about a declaration of war from President Woodrow Wilson. Only the spectacle of US ships being sunk and US lives being lost brought about this change. And at the end of the war, the USA turned its back on Wilson's experiment in internationalism and returned to isolationism. In our counterfactual world, it is difficult to conceive of anything short of a crisis on the scale of the 'real' 1914–18 war that would have impelled the USA towards internationalism - and only then if US interests had been directly threatened. Without World War I, then, the USA is likely to have remained a sleeping giant, unwilling to flex its muscles on the international stage.

Many other counterfactuals could be considered. The strains of World War I led directly to the rise of fascism in Italy. Without the war, would Mussolini have come to power in 1922? Or if he had, what would have been the character of the regime led by this renegade socialist? By 1914 France was coming to terms with the loss of Alsace and Lorraine to Germany in 1871. Could it be that a war of revenge was not inevitable, and that without the Great War some form of Franco-German accommodation could have been reached? One thing that is certain is that in 1918 France, although victorious, was relatively weaker than it had been before the war. Without World War I France's power would have remained stronger for longer. And what about Austria-Hungary, that polyglot empire of myriad nationalities? From today's perspective it seems a ridiculous anachronism that was bound to collapse – yet it is worth pondering on the fact that it proved to be far from a pushover, and it survived four years of total war. Without war, it is conceivable that it could have survived for decades, no doubt with timely concessions made to various nationalities. Much the same points can be made of the Ottoman Empire. If Austria-Hungary and Turkey had survived until the 21st century, the situation in the Balkans in 2001 would have looked very different. That is not to argue that there would not be problems and conflict - but it would be a different type of problem. Moreover, without the defeat of Ottoman Turkey (and World War II) it is unlikely that the state of Israel would have emerged at the time it did, if indeed at all.

We are so accustomed to hearing World War I referred to as a disaster that it is worth considering another counterfactual: what if the war *had* taken place, but Germany and Austria-Hungary had won? There was nothing inevitable about the Allied victory in the Great War. Germany came very close to defeating France and Britain in 1914, and again for a fleeting moment in spring 1918. The activities of the U-boats in the First Battle of the Atlantic in 1917–18 came uncomfortably close to cutting Britain's Atlantic lifeline, and the Central Powers did succeed in defeating

Russia, one of the pillars of the Triple Entente, in 1917–18. One does not have to rearrange historical facts to any great extent to produce a situation in which Germany concedes in the west but emerges victorious, and immensely powerful, in the east. Just suppose that at the end of 1917 the Germans decide to quit while they are ahead. They recognize that their campaign of unrestricted submarine warfare has failed to knock Britain out of the war; instead it has jolted the USA out of its neutrality. As a result, at some point in 1918 or early 1919 vast numbers of US troops will arrive on the Western Front. Instead of opting for the gamble of attacking in the West to defeat the British and French before the US recruits arrive, as happened in reality, the German leadership decide to make peace. An apparently high-minded offer to conclude a peace without annexations, to evacuate Belgium and occupied France would have been calculated to appeal to President Wilson, and might well have split the Americans and the British from the French. A really far-sighted approach would have been to strike a deal with France over the future of Alsace and Lorraine, thus bringing the French on board the peace process.

The Germans could have afforded these concessions – massive as they were – because of the scale of their victory in the east. In the spring of 1918, Russia lay prostrate. Its armies were in ruins, the Kerensky offensive of July–August 1917 having been defeated. Russia was in a state of political chaos, the tsar having been overthrown by the Liberal Revolution of March, and the Bolshevik coup succeeding in November. Germany had occupied the Ukraine, and pushed forward the pre-war frontier by some 960 km/600 mi. In March 1918 Lenin reluctantly accepted the Treaty of Brest-Litovsk, which formalized Russia's losses and Germany's gains. On 9 December 1917 Romania was forced to agree to an armistice, and in May 1918 the Treaty of Bucharest was signed, which in the words of the British official historian 'placed Romania both militarily and economically entirely in the hands of Germany'. Berlin was on the point of realizing in large part the pre-war dreams of 'Mittleuropa', an economic zone dominated by Germany. This enormous increase in German power was a matter of serious concern to Britain, who saw a threat to the Middle East and even Britain's position in India. Had World War I ended in late 1917 or early 1918 on the basis of a return to the status quo *ante bellum* in the west, but Germany retaining her gains in the east, there is no doubt who would have been the real winner.

In the event Germany chose to risk everything on an attack in the west rather than consolidating her conquests in the east. By overstretching themselves, the Germans lost everything, their dreams of an empire in the east being defeated not in Russia but in eastern France and Belgium, on the Hindenburg Line, on the Marne, and around Ypres. Defeated, that is, for the moment; because the continuities between Germany's attempts to gain Mitteleuropa and Hitler's aims of seeking Lebensraum 25 years later are obvious and compelling. The appalling nature of the Third Reich has tended to blind people to the nastiness of the Kaiser's Germany. While it was not on a par with the Nazi regime in terms of pure evil and capacity for genocide, Imperial Germany was authoritarian, militarist, and anti-democratic; Wilhelm's character contained a very unpleasant streak of extreme anti-Semitism. Its behaviour in occupied territories was deeply unappealing, and had it prevailed in 1914–18, the peoples of occupied Europe would have been in for a very hard time. Liberal democracy would have been extinguished from the continent of Europe, and Britain – assuming that it remained unoccupied, even if its armies were defeated in the field – would have been faced with the ultimate nightmare.

British policy had for centuries been to maintain the balance of power – to prevent any one continental power from becoming overmighty. Thus Britain had fought against the France of Louis XIV and Napoleon, and was to fight again against Hitler. A victorious Germany in World War I would have left Britain with a bleak choice. Either it could have acquiesced in its defeat, and become reconciled to being reduced to a second-class power, or Britain could have chosen to fight on, hoping that something – presumably in the form of the USA – would turn up, as actually happened in World War II. Neither option was attractive. World War I is often proclaimed to be 'futile'. The problem is that the less than ideal world of 1919 is usually compared with the allegedly halcyon days before August 1914. This is not a fair comparison. This author believes that the balance of evidence points towards the Central Powers bearing the lion's share of responsibility for the outbreak of the war and the failure to conclude a compromise peace once hostilities commenced. The acid test of the truth of the 'futility' proposition can thus be boiled down to the question: if the Allies had lost World War I, would they have been better or worse off? The answer is clearly 'worse'. For the Western democracies World War I was not a futile conflict; it was a just and necessary war fought against aggressive ideological foes. Imperfect as the world of 1919 was, it was one in which democracy survived in Western Europe, in which militarist autocracies had been defeated. We know that two decades later war broke out again. That was an appalling tragedy. To view the struggle of 1914–18 as 'futile' because an even more terrible war came along 20 years later makes as little sense as denigrating World War II because it was promptly succeeded by 45 years of Cold War. In both 1914–18 and 1939–45 the Allies defeated an immediate threat, and if on either occasion they had lost, the consequences would have been appalling – for the people of that time, and for us, their descendants.

Gary Sheffield
Joint Services Command and Staff College, nr Swindon.

CHAPTER 1
ORIGINS AND PLANNING

The Origins of the War

World War I was a cataclysmic conflict that lasted over four years and resulted in the deaths of as many as 13 million people. The causes of this world-changing event pose questions that countless historians have endeavoured to answer ever since the Treaty of Versailles formally brought the war to an end in 1919. Nevertheless, the origins of the war can be split into two broad areas: historical, or long-term, causes; and immediate causes.

Fighting on the barricades during the Paris Commune of March–May 1871. The Paris Commune was a two-month period during which the working class ruled Paris, resulting from France's disastrous defeat at the hands of the Germans during the Franco-Prussian War.

The proclamation of the German Empire at Versailles, following France's humiliating defeat in the Franco-Prussian War, 1870–71. Following German unification, Chancellor Otto von Bismarck tried to position Germany as a major European force without arousing the suspicions of other powers such as Austria-Hungary and Britain.

Troops in action during the Balkan wars. In the First Balkan War between Serbia and Turkey in 1912, Serbia's success threatened Austria-Hungary's dominance in the Balkans, and also hindered Germany's aim to become the pre-eminent European power in Turkey. In the Second Balkan War of October 1913, Serbia occupied Albania in order to gain access to the Adriatic Sea, but withdrew following an Austro-Hungarian ultimatum.

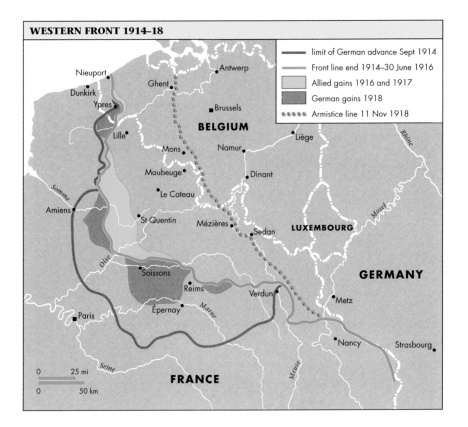

WESTERN FRONT 1914–18

Legend:
- limit of German advance Sept 1914
- Front line end 1914–30 June 1916
- Allied gains 1916 and 1917
- German gains 1918
- Armistice line 11 Nov 1918

Nieuport, Antwerp, Dunkirk, Ghent, Ypres, Brussels, Lille, BELGIUM, Mons, Namur, Liège, Maubeuge, Dinant, Le Cateau, Amiens, St Quentin, Mézières, LUXEMBOURG, Sedan, Soissons, Reims, Verdun, Metz, Paris, Épernay, Nancy, Strasbourg, GERMANY, FRANCE

Rivers: Somme, Oise, Seine, Marne, Meuse, Mosel, Rhine

0 25 mi
0 50 km

'We had to avoid wounding Austria too severely; we had to avoid leaving behind in her any unnecessary bitterness of feeling or design for revenge; we ought rather to reserve the possibility of becoming friends again with our adversary of the moment, and in any case to regard the Austrian state as a piece on the European chessboard and the renewal of friendly relations as a move open to us. If Austria were severely injured, she would become the ally of France and of every other opponent of ours; she would even sacrifice her anti-Russian interests for the sake of revenge on Prussia.'
Otto von Bismarck, 'Memoirs' from 1866.

The historical causes of World War I can be traced back at least as far as the unification of Germany after the Franco-Prussian War of 1870–71. The humiliating defeat of France and its loss of Alsace and Lorraine began a fraught period in European history during which the balance of power began to shift. Germany was at the centre of this dismantling of the established order as its chancellor, **Otto von Bismarck**, began to manoeuvre Germany carefully into a position where it could assert itself and become the pre-eminent state in Europe. The problem was that such a scheme was sure to attract the suspicions of powers anxious to maintain the *status quo*. Bismarck therefore deftly engaged in complex diplomacy in order to allay the fears of these other countries – especially Britain, France, and Russia – and to protect his new-born state. The result of Bismarck's enterprise was an agreement with Austria-Hungary and Italy – the 1882 Triple Alliance – and, in an attempt to pacify the British, a Reinsurance Treaty with Russia. The agreements required careful balancing on Bismarck's part and, while France and many other states remained wary, the chancellor dared not take his eye off the situation lest the whole edifice fell crashing to the ground.

At the same time the European balance of power was shifting in other arenas that were not directly related to German ambitions, but which were set to complicate international relationships even further. In southeastern Europe the Austro-Hungarian empire was in decline, and in its weakened position looked increasingly to the Balkans for future security. The Balkans,

Bismarck, Otto Eduard Leopold von (1815–1898)

As prime minister of Prussia from 1862 to 1890 and chancellor of the German Empire from 1871 to 1890, Otto von Bismarck was keen to create a united German state under Prussian leadership and then develop it into a first-class world power. Having fought wars against Austria in 1866 and France in 1870–71, Prussia did emerge as the dominant German state, and unification under its leadership came in 1871. The complexity of Germany's diplomacy over the next two decades owed much to Bismarck's desire to protect the fledgling German state, by attempting to maintain good relations with all the other major European powers. Nevertheless, the establishment of the Triple Alliance in 1881 (with Austria and Italy) served to upset the status quo, and before long the battle lines for World War I had been drawn. Bismarck was forced to resign in March 1890 after Kaiser Wilhelm II, impatient with his chancellor's constant diplomatic manoeuvrings, decided upon a more overtly aggressive foreign policy.

Dreadnought

The *Dreadnought* was a class of battleship built for the British navy in the last days of the naval arms race with Germany. HMS *Dreadnought* was launched in 1906 and was far superior in terms of speed and armaments to anything then afloat. Based on the designs of Admiral Fisher, the *Dreadnought* was the basis of battleship design for more than 50 years. The German Nassau class was established in 1907, and by 1914, the USA, France, Japan, and Austria-Hungary all had battleships of a similar class to the *Dreadnought*.

HMS Dreadnought *was the first of a powerful line of big-gun vessels. Despite being equipped with armour plating that was 30 cm/1 ft thick, steam-turbine propulsion (a first for a large warship) provided a top speed and range that easily bettered any existing ship.*

however, were a volatile region that would emerge from the 1912–13 war against the Ottoman Empire with greater nationalistic tendencies, aided by the sympathies of a Slavic Russia keen to extend its own influence in the region.

The problems inherent in such delicate international situations were constantly on Bismarck's mind as he made his diplomatic calculations, but unfortunately for him, his days in power were numbered. When Kaiser Wilhelm II came to the throne in 1888, he followed an increasingly bellicose *Weltpolitik* (world policy) which upset Bismarck's diplomatic strategy and, in 1890, made the chancellor's position untenable. During the years that followed his resignation, much of Bismarck's diplomatic work was clumsily undone. The Reinsurance Treaty, for example, fell into abeyance, which allowed an alliance between Russia and France that made Germany look uneasily to the east as well as to the west.

Weltpolitik, in overtly challenging the established balance of power in Europe, engendered in Russia, France, and Britain the disagreeable feeling that their interests were being threatened. All three states felt challenged by Germany's growing economic strength, found its flagrant militarism distasteful, and feared the consequences of its desire for colonies. The naval arms race that Germany provoked with Britain – then the world's greatest imperial power – came about as a direct result of Germany's new-found strength and territorial ambitions. The Navy Laws of 1898 and 1900 represented clear challenges by the Kaiser and the German secretary of the navy, Admiral Alfred von Tirpitz, to the British command of the seas. While Germany failed to produce sufficient vessels to achieve its naval ambitions, it did succeed in raising British hackles.

The 1904 Entente Cordiale between Britain and France, and the subsequent establishment of a triumvirate with the inclusion of Russia three years later, reflected the

Signatures from the 1831 treaty (ratified in 1839) that guaranteed the neutrality of Belgium. The breaking of this treaty by Germany in August 1914, and its failure to withdraw from Belgium in response to a British ultimatum, was an immediate cause of the outbreak of World War I.

EASTERN FRONT 1914–18

0 — 100 mi
0 — 200 km

L. Peipus

Baltic Sea

Riga

Daugavpils

Königsberg

East Prussia

Niemen

Masurian Lakes

GERMANY

RUSSIA

Vistula

Warsaw

Brest-Litovsk

Pinsk

Pripyat

Lodz

Poland

Kiev

Dnieper

Cracow

Przemysl

Lemberg

Dniester

AUSTRIA-HUNGARY

——— limit of Russian advances 1914–15
——— limit of German advances 1915–16
[ ] territory gained by Russians June–Aug 1916
[ ] territory gained by Germans 5 Sept 1917
- - - - limit of German advances 3 Mar 1918

ROMANIA

Danube

Black Sea

Archduke Franz Ferdinand with his wife and children. Franz Ferdinand (the heir to the Hapsburg Empire) and his wife were assassinated on a visit to the Bosnian capital, Sarajevo, on 28 June 1914, precipitating the outbreak of World War I five weeks later. The timing of the visit was unfortunate, if not provocative, falling as it did on Serbia's national day and the anniversary of a humiliating Serbian defeat by the Turks at the Battle of Kosovo in 1347.

intensity of international alliances at the dawn of the new century. Nations that had been old commercial and colonial competitors during the previous century were drawn together against those perceived as posing an even greater threat to their interests. The battle lines of Europe were being drawn – all that was required for war was the opportunity to start one.

The immediate cause of the war was the assassination of Archduke Franz Ferdinand and his wife in the Bosnian town of Sarajevo on 28 June 1914. The murder of the heir to the Habsburg throne at the hands of Gavrilo Princip, a young Serb nationalist, exacerbated pre-existing tensions in the area and triggered a chain reaction of events that was to lead to violent conflict. The Austrians perceived the event as a Serb challenge to Habsburg rule in a country that they had annexed in 1908. With the

The start of the war (1914)

28 June: Assassination of the archduke of Austria by a Serb nationalist.

23 July: Austria, perceiving the assassination as a challenge to Austrian rule over Serbia, issues Serbia with an ultimatum, which is ignored because of its unreasonable demands.

28 July: Austria declares war on Serbia.

30 July: Russia mobilizes in support of Serbia.

1 August: Germany, having promised Austria support in its ultimatum, declares war on Russia.

2 August: Germany, wanting to move through Belgium in order to pre-emptively attack France (due to France's alliance with Russia), issues an ultimatum to Belgium. Passage is refused.

3 August: Germany invades Belgium, Luxembourg, and France.

4 August: Britain declares war on Germany in response to its failure to withdraw from Belgium.

Grey, Viscount Edward (1862–1933)

Edward Grey was foreign secretary in the British Liberal administration from 1905 to 1916. During his period in office, Grey helped to establish the Triple Entente (Britain, France, and Russia) and backed France against Germany in the Agadir Incident of 1911. Grey worked tirelessly to avoid war in 1914, but unsuccessfully proposed that a European conference be held in the wake of the assassination of Franz Ferdinand. During the war, Grey succeeded in maintaining good relations with the USA, but his negotiations over the Treaty of London in April 1915 (in which Italy agreed to join the Entente Powers) and his support for a US plan to convene a European conference in 1916 (an attempt to end the war) were less successful. When David Lloyd George became prime minister in December 1916, Grey's long tenure at the Foreign Office came to an end, and he retired from political life.

Viscount Edward Grey was British foreign secretary from 1905 until Lloyd George became prime minister at the end of 1916. He explored every avenue in attempting to avert war in the summer of 1914; however, once hostilities had begun, he warned that a German victory must be prevented as it would jeopardize the independence of Belgium, Holland, and Denmark, and possibly even of Norway and Sweden.

Habsburg Empire in a parlous state and Germany, having promised support, actively encouraging Vienna to provoke a crisis, Serbia was issued with an ultimatum on 23 July. This made such unreasonable demands on Serbia that Belgrade dismissed it out of hand – and so began a series of ultimatums, war declarations, and invasions. The Austrians declared war on Serbia on 28 July and two days later Russia mobilized in support of Serbia. On 1 August, Germany declared war on Russia, and on the following day issued an ultimatum to Belgium. On 3 August, Germany and France declared war upon each other as the Kaiser's troops invaded their old enemy along with Belgium and Luxembourg. Finally, on 4 August, Britain declared war on Germany in response to the failure of its army to withdraw from Belgium.

Thus, 'The nations slithered over the brink into the boiling cauldron of war without any trace of apprehension or dismay,' as David Lloyd George later wrote in his *War Memoirs*. It must be remembered that the states that went to war in August 1914 did so for the same reason that they had made their alliances: because they felt that it was necessary. That did not mean that every nation looked forward to the prospect. Standing at a Foreign Office window watching the lamps being lit in St James's park, **Sir Edward Grey** remarked to a friend: 'The lamps are going out all over Europe; we shall not see them lit again in our lifetime.'

Railway communications developed rapidly during World War I. In 1914, German forces had been severely hampered by the lack of a usable railway system to reinforce the front effectively.

Women telegraphists of the Queen Mary's Army Auxiliary Corps (QMAAC) at the Signals Office in Boulogne later in the war. The increase in mechanization and the much greater troop mobility in World War I meant that hand-signalling on the battlefield had become outmoded. The telephone became the main means of communication in the trenches, and between the trenches and headquarters.

The 1914 Military Plans and Opposing Armies

The ability of each European state to wage mass warfare was greater in 1914 than it had ever been before. The size of armies had increased as the European population had grown, and the ability of states to sustain them in the field had increased with the expansion of their economies and administrative infrastructures. By the early 20th century, maturing industries were capable of providing massive numbers of weapons and the necessary ammunitions; organized agriculture could provide plentiful food; railway systems were able to move men and supplies rapidly; and the electric telegraph gave a means of simple command and control. The lethality of weaponry had also increased during the previous 30 years as rate of fire, accuracy, and range had all been enhanced by the invention of breech-loading weapons, magazine-loading rifles, belt-fed machine guns, and quick-firing artillery.

The Industrial Revolution had changed the face of warfare, but far from fearing that this meant it would be more difficult for armies to attain decisive victories in short wars, the continental powers felt confident that their great offensives would deliver their political aims swiftly.

An aerial view of the Krupp's steelworks in Essen, Germany, c.1914. Krupp's manufacturing expertise made it an ideal candidate for converting to weapons and ammunitions production at the outbreak of war.

German infantry advancing across open country in 1914. Once Liège had fallen on 16 August 1914, 1.2 million well-trained German troops poured into Belgium and quickly overran much of the country.

SCHLIEFFEN PLAN 1914

Map legend:
- ▪ fortress
- German army deployments
- – – – German objective 23 Aug
- ····· German objective 1 Sept
- ➤ planned German advances

Schlieffen, Count Alfred von (1833–1913)

Count Alfred von Schlieffen had a passion for both military history and strategy. This, together with his experiences in the Franco-Prussian War (1870–71), was used to great effect during his time as Chief of the Imperial General Staff between 1891 and 1906. His bold plan for knocking France out of a future war in just six weeks – before turning to destroy Russia – took his name, but he died before it could be implemented. Although he left his successor, Helmuth von Moltke, the details of the plan (which in all probability was already fatally flawed), it was altered and failed to achieve its grandiose aims when put into action in 1914.

Count Alfred von Schlieffen.

Count Alfred von Schlieffen developed a German offensive directive just before his retirement as Chief of the Imperial General Staff in late 1905. Schlieffen gave his name to a plan that aimed to achieve a decisive victory over France in just six weeks, before Germany then turned east to defeat the Russians. The main thrust of this bold plan was a strong and rapid advance through Belgium and the Netherlands, followed by a southerly wheel to the west of Paris. With Paris surrounded, the Kaiser's troops would then strike out towards the Franco-German border, where they would crush a French army pinned in position by other German formations. Although fraught with logistical difficulties, some of them so great that it might well have been impossible for the offensive ever to succeed, the original version of the Schlieffen Plan was far more daring than the version actually used by Schlieffen's successor, **Helmuth von Moltke**. The new and diluted plan demanded increased troop numbers in the east (to await the Russians) and the strengthening of the pinning formations in Alsace and Lorraine in order to repel the French. Schlieffen's dying words had been, 'Keep the right wing strong,' but von Moltke weakened it and, in addition, created a potential bottleneck for his attacking troops around Liège by his decision not to infringe upon Dutch neutrality.

Moltke, Helmuth von (1848–1916)

Moltke took over as Chief of the Imperial General Staff from Schlieffen in 1906. The nephew of Field Marshal Helmuth von Moltke, the mastermind of the Prussian victory over the French in 1871, Moltke 'the younger' – already in bad health – had the unenviable task of putting Schlieffen's plan into action in August 1914. The failure of the plan that he diluted resulted in the German defeat at the Battle of the Marne and his sacking on 14 September 1914. Although he was appointed deputy Chief of Staff at the end of the year, he was dogged by illness in the final years of his life and died in 1916.

Kaiser Wilhelm II with Gen Helmuth von Moltke (right), who succeeded Alfred von Schlieffen as Chief of the Imperial General Staff in 1906. A grandson of Queen Victoria – a fact that still surprises many people today – Kaiser Wilhelm II retained his titles of British Field Marshal and Admiral of the Fleet until the day World War I broke out.

The Schlieffen Plan asked much of the German army, but its commanders had confidence in the strength of its 87 infantry and 25 cavalry divisions. With an efficient general staff providing the necessary direction and focus, well-versed staff officers ensuring good local organization, a strong officer corps, and troops that were well trained and confident with their equipment, Germany had a fearsome force.

The French Plan XVII was developed by their army commander-in-chief, **Joseph Joffre**, in April 1913. An offensive across the Franco-German border was designed to seize Alsace and Lorraine and was then to be followed by an attack to push the Germans back to the Rhine. If the Germans attacked through Belgium, there was also an option to swing north to cut their lines of communication. However, although Joffre had believed that the Germans would move through Belgium, he had not anticipated the strength of such an attack. Thus, Plan XVII played right into German hands, leaving the French weak at exactly the point where Moltke sought to pass his main force: the north.

The French army consisted of 62 infantry divisions and 10 cavalry divisions, and had for decades been mesmerized by an offensive philosophy to the detriment of its general flexibility. Offensive demands dominated strategy, tactics, organization, and equipment – no aspect of the army was left untouched by it. But the French army had worked hard to repair the damage it had suffered during the 1870–71 war with Prussia and, despite this great flaw, was generally competent in most areas.

A French infantry battalion on parade. The infantry suffered heavy losses within days of the outbreak of war. A disastrous bayonet charge against nine German battalions at Rossignol on 22 August 1914 forced an immediate change in military tactics; Chief of the General Staff Joseph Joffre ordered that future attacks were to be preceded by artillery bombardment, in order to weaken enemy fire and to reduce the distance the infantry had to advance.

German troops head for the front in August 1914 in a railway wagon bedecked with bullish slogans. 'Ausflug nach Paris (going to Paris)' already indicates a clear ambition, while the wagon's origin (Elsaß–Lothringen, or Alsace–Lorraine) is ironic in the light of that territory's much-disputed (and certainly not forgotten) transfer from France to Germany in 1871.

Russia's offensive action was encapsulated in its Plan 19. Facing enemies on two fronts – Germany and Austria-Hungary – Russia decided not to deal with them piecemeal, but to attack both simultaneously. While Germany was working its way through Belgium and France, Russian forces were to attack Germany in East Prussia and Austria-Hungary in Galicia. This daring plan would test the rather backward Russian infrastructure and army to the full. The strength of the Russian army was debatable for, despite its great size – 114 infantry divisions and 36 cavalry divisions – its troops were poorly organized, badly led, and insufficiently equipped. The 'Russian steam-roller' was not all it might have been, and has been aptly described as a 'clumsy giant'. But the Tsar's army was slowly improving and, because of its size and resource potential, clearly posed a great threat.

Joffre, Joseph Jacques Césaire (1852–1931)

Joseph Joffre was one of France's most experienced soldiers in 1914, having taken part in the Franco-Prussian War (1870–71) and numerous colonial actions. Appointed Chief of the General Staff in 1911, Joffre prepared the French army to undertake offensive action, as in his Plan XVII, but soon after the German invasion began in August 1914 his troops were required to take defensive positions around Paris. Taking advantage of German over-stretch during the Battle of the Marne in September 1914, however, Joffre managed to push the Germans back to the Aisne. However in the following year he revealed that he lacked the flexibility needed to cope with the new challenges presented by trench warfare and this, together with the shock of Verdun, led to his replacement by Nivelle. Despite his demotion, 'Papa' Joffre remained an important symbolic figure for the French people throughout the war, and he went on to serve as president of the Supreme War Council in 1917.

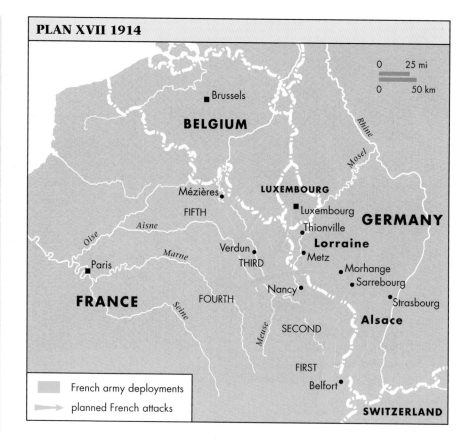

PLAN XVII 1914

Left to right: Gen Joseph Joffre, President Raymond Poincaré, King George V, Gen Ferdinand Foch and Field Marshall Sir Douglas Haig on the terrace of Haig's headquarters at Beauquesne in August 1918.

Like Russia, Austria-Hungary planned a simultaneous offensive against two enemies. Conrad von Hötzendorff, the Austro-Hungarian commander-in-chief, sought not only to deliver a mortal blow to Serbia (a perceived threat to the Dual Monarchy) by striking across the Danube and occupying Belgrade, but also to defeat the Russians by driving into northern Poland. The Habsburg army was hardly a culturally unified force, however, as the troops of its 74 infantry divisions were just one quarter ethnic Hungarian, less than one quarter German, and more than half were a mixture of Czechs, Slavs, and Italians. Thus, although it was a competent army, its lack of homogeneity posed serious questions concerning its future political reliability.

Britain, meanwhile, had no great offensive plan largely due to its small army, large navy, and the existence of the English Channel. The British army was primarily a colonial police force made up of volunteers, rather than conscripts. Thus, the British Expeditionary Force (BEF), some six infantry divisions and one-and-a-half cavalry divisions strong, could be expected to do little more on reaching the continent than strengthen the left flank of the French army. However, despite its size – the Kaiser is said to have called it a 'contemptible little army' – it was, man for man, as good as any of its European counterparts by 1914. Flexibility and experience were on the side of the BEF, but few of its officers had ever commanded large formations.

Russian general Aleksei Brusilov attends divine service with his troops. In one of Russia's first major successes of the war, Brusilov's army broke through Austro-Hungarian defences into Austrian Galicia on 18 August 1914, mostly as a result of the massive forces under his command – 35 infantry divisions.

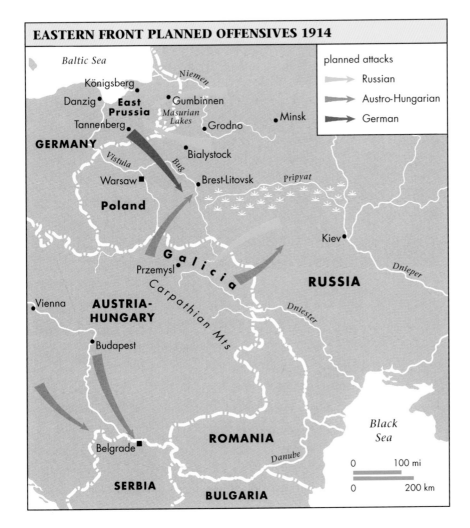

EASTERN FRONT PLANNED OFFENSIVES 1914

planned attacks

Russian

Austro-Hungarian

German

Baltic Sea

Königsberg

Danzig

East Prussia

Tannenberg

Niemen

Gumbinnen

Masurian Lakes

Grodno

Minsk

GERMANY

Vistula

Bug

Bialystock

Warsaw

Brest-Litovsk

Pripyat

Poland

Kiev

G a l i c i a

Przemysl

Carpathian Mts

RUSSIA

Dnieper

Vienna

AUSTRIA-HUNGARY

Dniester

Budapest

Black Sea

ROMANIA

Danube

0   100 mi

0   200 km

Belgrade

SERBIA

BULGARIA

The British were going to have to learn how to cope with mass armies as the offensive plans employed by the continental powers were to lead to great battles involving huge numbers of troops.

A good deal of preparation had gone into readying these men for action and, by early August 1914, it was time to put them to the test.

Austro-Hungarian troops prepare to leave Prague for the front in 1914. The well-defined national borders of pre-1914 Europe disguised some significant territorial restlessness – for example, land-locked Serbia was seeking access to the Adriatic Sea, while several of the ethnic minorities reluctantly joined under the Dual Monarchy of Austria-Hungary wanted to link with a neighbouring state or even to gain some measure of independence. With the onset of war, Austria-Hungary planned to curb Serbia's designs.

CHAPTER 2
HOME FRONTS AT THE OUTBREAK OF WAR

Civilian Attitudes to the War

In each capital city, the declarations of war were greeted by enthusiastic crowds gathering in public places to sing their national anthems, wave flags, and acclaim their government's decision to fight. While it would be wrong to imply that all sectors of society welcomed the onset of war, in general, anti-war feeling was extremely limited; what feeling there was soon drowned under the tidal wave of approval enveloping the nations. Positive attitudes to the outbreak of war temporarily healed internal political and social divisions that had blighted the main protagonists in peacetime, and aided the period of mobilization that followed.

Cheering crowds outside Buckingham Palace, London, on the outbreak of war in 1914. Few people expected the war to last beyond the end of the year.

Kaiser Wilhelm II appears on the balcony of his palace in Berlin following the mobilization order on 1 August 1914. Germany had failed to reply to a communication from Britain asking whether they would respect Belgian neutrality.

Crowds gather at the Nevsky Prospect in St Petersburg, Russia, on the announcement of partial mobilization on 29 July 1914. The tsar withdrew a full-mobilization order having been encouraged by the Kaiser's telegram that claimed he was urging the Austro-Hungarians to arrive at an accommodation with Russia.

Citizens in Budapest read the Austro-Hungarian mobilization order in the newspaper in July 1914. Austria-Hungary had delivered a 15-point ultimatum to Serbia that the latter effectively agreed to, therefore giving Austria-Hungary little real reason for going to war with Serbia.

When war broke out, Britain, France, and Germany were all in the midst of dealing with important political challenges. One could even argue that war provided a welcome diversion from such difficulties, and that the nations were persuaded to unite in the cause of armed conflict. In Britain, although notions of duty, King and Country, and empire were still strong, they were being increasingly challenged by an ever-more-vocal 'working class' formed primarily from workers in the manufacturing and agricultural sectors. This social stratum and the political movements representing it drew attention to social, political, and economic inequalities, and forced the scrutiny of class privilege, workers' rights, and female suffrage. Divisive issues such as these, together with the question of Irish home rule, were at the top of the political agenda of **Herbert Asquith's** Liberal government in 1914. The outbreak of a European war, however, diminished their importance and the nation united (apart from a few members of the government, a section of the liberal press, and a few pacifists) in the face of the common German enemy.

Something similar happened in France despite the deep political fissures there. Labour unrest, a lack of political continuity (there were ten ministries between 1909 and 1914), and weak national leadership had beset the nation in the early years of the 20th century. Nevertheless, under the presidency of **Raymond Poincaré**, France united as her old enemy, Germany, thrusted westwards.

Even Germany itself, under the chancellorship of **Theobold von Bethmann-Hollweg**, had internal problems. Following unification in 1871, the nation had industrialized at an astonishing rate, giving rise to a whole new social stratum – the urban proletariat – which, as in Britain and France, began to challenge the status quo. Thus on the eve of war, as the Kaiser's troops marched into Belgium and Luxembourg, a great socialist anti-war rally was being held in Berlin. Despite such unrest, the war papered over internal political cracks, and the population paraded in front of its enemies as one.

Why did these nations unite on their declarations of war? The answer to this complex question lies in the middle of the 19th century, and involves the relationship between society and the state, national values, and the

Poverty was a problem in Britain's cities before World War I. Despite loyalty to King and Country remaining strong, an increasingly vocal 'working class' began effectively to draw attention to social, political, and economic inequalities.

Herbert Asquith, British prime minister from 1908 to 1916.

Henley Regatta before the outbreak of war in 1914. An apparent sense of normality belies the horror of the conflict to come, but few people believed that if war came it would last beyond Christmas.

Poincaré, Raymond (1860–1934)

Raymond Poincaré had served as both prime minister and minister of foreign affairs before the war and was elected president of the French Third Republic in 1913. Despite having a largely ceremonial role as head of state, Poincaré sought to be influential, but also understood that others must run the war. In November 1917, when the nation was in crisis, he called upon Clemençeau to form a government but soon found his own position undermined by this appointment. The friction between the two men continued long after the armistice, and at the Paris Peace Conference Clemençeau rejected the president's demands for harsher peace terms to be imposed upon Germany. Poincaré remained president until early 1920 and eventually re-entered politics and became prime minister again in 1922. Having presided over the French occupation of the Rhine, Poincaré formed three more coalition governments in the 1920s and died in 1934.

A poverty-stricken family in Russia during World War I. Poverty was one of the major causes of the social unrest that increasingly threatened the autocratic rule of Tsar Nicholas. In an attempt to stave off such challenges, he agreed to implement a liberal constitution in 1905, but it was to prove to be too little, too late.

President Raymond Poincaré of France (centre) with the mayor of Lille and Gen W R Birdwood to his right at one of the gates of Lille on 21 October 1918.

The poor queue by the Freibank in Germany before the outbreak of war. Despite having huge resources to engage in a costly arms race in the lead-up to World War I, Germany had its share of poverty-stricken citizens.

social and cultural conditioning of the population. At the outbreak of war the populations of the major protagonists could be described as patriotic – possessing a heightened sense of duty – and this was also true of their working classes. Thanks to the mental 'conditioning' of the times, citizens were convinced that their own country held the moral high ground in international affairs and that their country's political aims were just. Neither the church nor intellectual opinion contradicted these beliefs in August 1914.

The German socialist Karl Liebknecht, speaking at a peace demonstration organized by the Sozialistische Partei Deutschland (SPD) in September 1911. A deputy in the German Reichstag (parliament), Liebknecht was the only member to vote against an August 1915 motion sanctioning unlimited resources to pursue the German war effort. The following year he was expelled from the Reichstag and sentenced to two years' hard labour for urging soldiers not to fight.

The church found itself able to justify the use of violence in pursuit of national political aims in all the major belligerent countries. There were many reasons for this, not least the fact that the patriotic clergy were themselves an important part of the status quo. But more than this, the clergy's fervent defence of the decision to go to war was a necessary result of their pastoral duties. For the first few weeks of the fighting, the clergy provided moral support for families as their menfolk went off to fight, but as soon as casualties started to be suffered and the names of the dead became known, they had the difficult task of comforting the bereaved. Intellectually the clergy might have wished to preach the need for enemies to be reconciled, but their hearts told them that the population wanted to hear that the war was necessary and just. The Bishop of London, Arthur Winnington-Ingram, summed up the church's position in a sermon:

> '[The war is being fought to]...save the freedom of the world, to save Liberty's own self, to save the honour of women and the innocence of children, everything that is noblest in Europe, everything that loves freedom and honour, everyone that puts that principle above ease and life itself beyond mere living, are banded in a great crusade – we cannot deny it – to kill Germans: to kill them not for the sake of killing, but to save the world... .'

Intellectuals supported the war in the same vein, for they too were largely from the privileged classes with a vested interest in the status quo, and they too were patriotic. The German novelist, Thomas Mann, wrote, 'Only the enemies of the spirit opposed the war which would leave Germany stronger, prouder, freer, happier.' Moreover, some intellectuals

Bethmann-Hollweg, Theobold von (1856–1921)

Theobold von Bethmann-Hollweg became German chancellor in 1909 at a time when domestic political problems were high on the political agenda. Although he had little experience of foreign affairs, he had to spend an increasing amount of time dealing with international relations, and worked hard to reduce the strength of the Triple Entente. Although he ultimately failed in these attempts, he was successful in his bid to convince the German public that they were fighting a defensive war in 1914. Bethmann-Hollweg endeavoured to entice the Allies with several peace initiatives during the war, but was not helped in this by the German high command demanding unreasonable terms. It was against Bethmann-Hollweg's advice that unrestricted submarine warfare was unleashed in 1917 and, as he predicted, it brought the USA into the war. By 1917 Bethmann-Hollweg had lost the support of all political groups and, with Hindenburg and Ludendorff demanding his dismissal, he retired in July of that year.

German chancellor Theobald von Bethmann-Hollweg (left) converses with the German foreign secretary and vice chancellor. Bethmann-Hollweg initiated several peace attempts during the conflict, and correctly anticipated America's entry into the war if Germany conducted unrestricted submarine warfare against its shipping.

With the outbreak of war, anti-German feelings ran high – shops owned by Germans or even people with German-sounding names became targets for angry mobs.

An Italian military chaplain. In the early days of World War I, in all countries involved in the conflict, the Church was able to justify the need to go to war – particularly as the Church was so inextricably linked to the state. However, once casualties started being reported in large numbers within weeks of the outbreak of hostilities, priests had a major task on their hands to comfort bereaved families.

undoubtedly enjoyed their new-found common bond with the masses after a lifetime of marginalization, but more importantly many also believed that war would be a catalyst for much-needed change – a spiritual revolution perhaps – or maybe an opportunity to reassess old morals and values. The intellectuals had high hopes of the war, and they found it as captivating as the rest of the population did. Many contemporary accounts relate how easily individuals were caught up in the tide of popular enthusiasm for the fighting. The Austrian writer Stefan Zweig, for example, said, 'I must acknowledge that there was a majestic, rapturous, and even seductive something [in the air and] … in spite of all my hatred and aversion for war, I should not like to have missed the memory of those first days.'

In many major towns and cities this 'seductive something' merged into xenophobia as 'spies' were interned and foreigners were hounded. In London the premises of many German businesses (and even businesses with German-sounding names) were vandalized, and foreign street names in Paris were changed. Nevertheless, despite such extremism, the passage from peace to war was generally a smooth one, and as nations mobilized, their populations watched and waited.

ARMÉE DE TERRE ET ARMÉE DE MER

ORDRE
DE MOBILISATION GÉNÉRALE

Par décret du Président de la République, la mobilisation des armées de terre et de mer est ordonnée, ainsi que la réquisition des animaux, voitures et harnais nécessaires au complément de ces armées.

Le premier jour de la mobilisation est le ~~Dimanche 2 Août 1914~~

Tout Français soumis aux obligations militaires doit, sous peine d'être puni avec toute la rigueur des lois, obéir aux prescriptions du **FASCICULE DE MOBILISATION** (pages coloriées placées dans son livret).

Sont visés par le présent ordre **TOUS LES HOMMES** non présents sous les Drapeaux et appartenant :

1° à l'**ARMÉE DE TERRE** y compris les **TROUPES COLONIALES** et les hommes des **SERVICES AUXILIAIRES**;

2° à l'**ARMÉE DE MER** y compris les **INSCRITS MARITIMES** et les **ARMURIERS** de la **MARINE**.

Les Autorités civiles et militaires sont responsables de l'exécution du présent décret.

Le Ministre de la Guerre.   *Le Ministre de la Marine.*

IMPRIMERIE NATIONALE — 2.148.1914.

A French poster announcing a full mobilization of forces on 2 August 1914. The decree orders the requisition of all animals, cars, and equipment needed by French forces in order to mobilize effectively.

The 'Call To Arms'

On the continent, conscription immediately came into force with the declaration of war, and men rushed to their mobilization points. The fact that so many conscripts turned up surprised many military men (in France only 1% failed to comply), but at least they had massive military machines that could lurch into life. The British army was tiny by comparison. While Germany could call upon 4.3 million trained men in August 1914 – 1.5 million of whom were deployed on the western front within two weeks of mobilization – the British Expeditionary Force (BEF), consisting of only regular troops, amounted to a mere 150,000 men. Before long, heavy casualties were being suffered by all sides, and from Whitehall the BEF looked increasingly vulnerable. Thus, **Lord Kitchener**, secretary of state for war, decided to raise a 'New Army' – in excess of 1 million men – from volunteers who would enlist for the duration. It was this campaign that led to the famous Alfred Leete poster of a uniformed and impressively moustachioed Kitchener declaring, 'Your Country Needs You!'.

Kitchener's success in raising this army can be seen in the number of men who volunteered for service in the first few months of war. On 7 August 1914, Kitchener called for 100,000 volunteers between the ages of 19 and 30 and he got them within three weeks. Raising the upper limit to 35 soon after, 761,824 men had volunteered by early October and the millionth man volunteered well before the end of the year. This volunteering phenomenon, what Winston Churchill called one of 'the

Field Marshal Horatio Kitchener was one of the first government officers to understand that the war was likely to be a long, drawn-out affair, and accordingly he planned for a three-year conflict.

Recruiting army volunteers in Trafalgar Square, London, in 1914. In order to boost the professional forces of the British Army, Lord Kitchener made a public call on 7 August 1914 for 100,000 volunteers – within four days, men were swearing the Oath of Allegiance at the rate of one hundred every hour in London.

Recruits to the British Army take the Oath of Allegiance in 1914. Although the British Army was relatively small at the outbreak of war, it was a highly trained force and the only professional army among the Allies. Within eight weeks of war breaking out, Kitchener's appeals for volunteers had resulted in over 750,000 men joining up.

Australian Recruitment

When Britain went to war, so did the Empire. Australian prime minister Joseph Cook said on 30 July 1914, 'Remember that when the Empire is at war, so is Australia at war.' Shortly after that he declared that if the United Kingdom went to war, 'Australians will stand beside our own to help and defend her to our last man and our last shilling.' Just as in Britain, Australians answered the 'Call to Arms' in great numbers, and this trend continued until April 1915. By the end of 1915, however, enlistment rates had fallen to such a low level that there were not even enough men to replace casualties, and new administrative structures had to be established to induce men to volunteer. Heavy Australian casualties during the Battle of the Somme meant that there was still a lack of volunteers, and the new Australian prime minister, W M Hughes, considered introducing conscription. The public rejected the idea of conscription in a referendum, but about half of Australia's eligible men did volunteer to serve in the war; of these, four-fifths (roughly 412,000 men) served overseas, and one-fifth died, and about half were wounded.

While Alfred Leete's famous poster entitled 'Your Country Needs You' was aimed at the domestic recruiting effort, similar campaigns were directed towards men from the British Empire. At least 60,000 Canadians, 59,000 Australians, 49,000 Indians, and 16,000 New Zealanders died while fighting for the Allies in World War I.

wonders of the time', can be explained only partly by excitement at the outbreak of war. Future officers – more often than not members of the upper classes, and upholders of the status quo – had the most to lose if the war were lost, but other factors in their decision to join up were the ideals of honour, glory, and self-sacrifice that had been learned at school.

Rupert Brooke's '1914', a poem written without the author having witnessed the horrors of war, could be said to reflect the attitude of this sector of British society:

> If I should die, think only this of me:
> That there's some corner of a foreign field
> That is for ever England. There shall be
> In that rich earth a richer dust concealed;
> A dust whom England bore, shaped, made aware,
> Gave, once, her flowers to love, her ways to roam,
> A body of England's, breathing English air,
> Washed by rivers, blest by suns of home.

Such words would seem to befit an 'innocent' generation that had been educated since childhood to believe in chivalry and duty, and for whom the war constituted an opportune test.

The ranks of Kitchener's Army, meanwhile, were filled largely with the working classes and those from the middle classes who had not grown up in the English 'public school' system (called private schools in the USA). These men enlisted for a greater variety of reasons than those of the

Brooke, Rupert Chawner (1887–1915)

English war poet Rupert Brooke was born in Rugby, Warwickshire, and took up a fellowship at King's College, Cambridge, in 1913 after suffering a nervous breakdown at the age of 24. Later that year he toured the USA, New Zealand, and the South Seas, and in 1914 became an officer in the Royal Naval Volunteer Reserve. After fighting at Antwerp, Belgium, he sailed for the Dardanelles, but died of blood poisoning on the Greek island of Skyros and was buried there. Brooke's poetry was untouched by the horrors of war, and caught the prevailing early wartime spirit of splendid and selfless patriotism. Brooke stands as a symbol of the World War I 'lost generation'.

An extract from a letter written by the war poet Rupert Brooke to Walter de la Mare on 20 November 1914. Brooke was one of the few war poets to have established a reputation for his work before the outbreak of hostilities, and his letter compliments de la Mare on his own war poem that had been published in The Times *newspaper in August.*

potential officers, for they had not been influenced in the same way while growing up. Thus, while they too might have had ideas of honour and glory in their heads as they signed their attestation forms, they just as likely sought a brief sojourn from their dull jobs – for few believed that the war would be protracted – or even submitted to unbearable peer pressure. It is certainly true that some vacillated before journeying to the recruiting station for fear of what would happen to their family, finances, and job while they were serving. For the majority of young men in Britain, however, the outbreak of war was not a disaster, but a great opportunity.

Recruits to the Lincolnshire Regiment undergo rifle training in September 1914. The speed of enlistment caught the authorities by surprise, and basic equipment (such as boots and uniforms) was in short supply. In October, Britain sent an emergency force of 8,000 troops to help the Belgians defend Antwerp. Two-thirds of them had only just begun their training, and some had never even fired a rifle before.

However, the flood of volunteers added to the problems that Britain had in turning these civilians into soldiers. The sheer numbers of men enlisting – 30,000 a day in mid-September and 2.46 million in all by the end of 1915 – quickly overwhelmed the existing administrative system and led to a lack of barracks, billets, and even the most basic military equipment, including boots and uniforms. For the best part of a year, Kitchener's volunteers had to make do with the limited resources available to them, and that meant living in tented camps, wearing civilian dress, and training themselves. Meanwhile, the BEF fought gallantly with their allies in France and Belgium in order to ensure that the war lasted long enough for the 'New Army' to see action.

'On August 5th, 1914, I reported to my regimental depot, being an Army Reservist. What a meeting of old friends! All were eager to take part in the great scrap that every pre-war soldier had expected. At the depot all was bustle, but no confusion. In the mobilization stores, every reservists' arms and clothing were ticketed, and these were soon issued, with webbing equipment. About 300 men were then selected and warned to hold themselves in readiness to proceed to the South Coast to make up the war strength of their battalion stationed there. There was great competition to go with this draft, the writer being one of the lucky ones to be selected.'
Private R G Hill, 'An Old Contemptible at Le Cateau', August 1914.

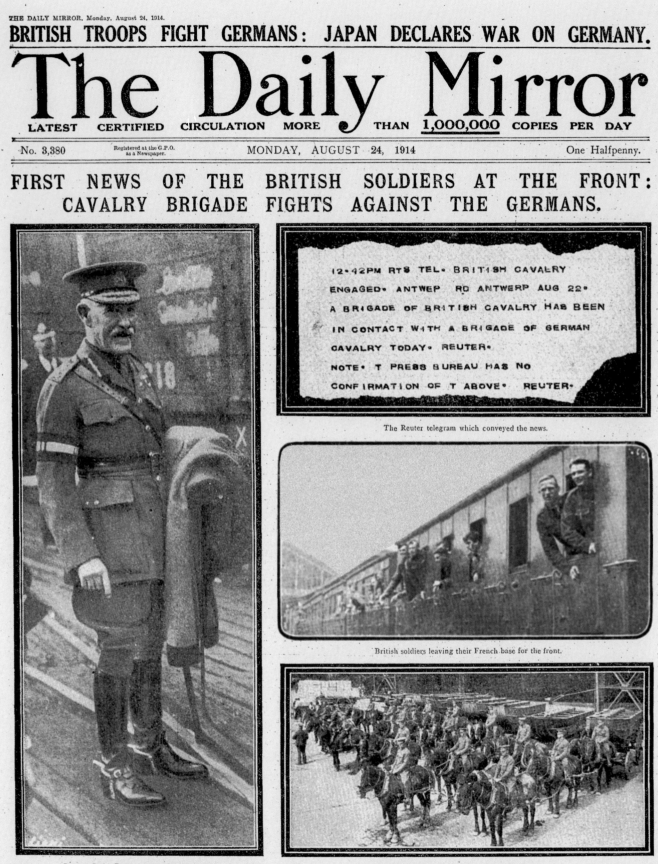

THE DAILY MIRROR, Monday, August 24, 1914.

BRITISH TROOPS FIGHT GERMANS: JAPAN DECLARES WAR ON GERMANY.

The Daily Mirror

LATEST CERTIFIED CIRCULATION MORE THAN 1,000,000 COPIES PER DAY

No. 3,380 — Registered at the G.P.O. as a Newspaper. — MONDAY, AUGUST 24, 1914 — One Halfpenny.

FIRST NEWS OF THE BRITISH SOLDIERS AT THE FRONT: CAVALRY BRIGADE FIGHTS AGAINST THE GERMANS.

12·42PM RTS TEL· BRITISH CAVALRY ENGAGED· ANTWEP RD ANTWERP AUG 22· A BRIGADE OF BRITISH CAVALRY HAS BEEN IN CONTACT WITH A BRIGADE OF GERMAN CAVALRY TODAY· REUTER· NOTE· T PRESS BUREAU HAS NO CONFIRMATION OF T ABOVE· REUTER·

The Reuter telegram which conveyed the news.

British soldiers leaving their French base for the front.

General Smith-Dorrien leaves for the front.

Soldiers and pontoons safely landed at Boulogne.

"When shall we get some news of our men at the front?" "Have our men done any fighting yet?" To ask questions which no one can possibly answer seems to be a habit that men drop into in war time, and these are typical of the queries that everybody has been asking everybody else. Yesterday a telegram reached London stating that British and German cavalry had been fighting, the first news of their movements since they landed on French soil.

CHAPTER 3
THE OPENING MOVES
AND DEADLOCK

The Failure of the Offensive Plans – The Western Front

The year 1914 was one of failed offensive plans, a year in which one million men died, and a year in which both the Western and Eastern Fronts settled into the routine of deadlock.

The German Schlieffen Plan was launched on 4 August when five armies attacked and began to engage the small Belgian army. Although Liège held out until 16 August, the fall of this fortress opened the floodgates for 1.2 million German troops to swarm over Belgium and push the defenders back towards Antwerp, Brussels, and Namur.

German troops advance through the Belgian city of Liège in early August 1914. The Germans' initial attack on 5 August failed to capture any of the city's 12 forts, thanks to stiff resistance from 35,000 garrison troops, but the central citadel succumbed two days later. However, it took another five days for German forces to capture all twelve.

THE DAILY MIRROR, Friday, September 11, 1914.

THE KAISER'S HUNS STILL PURSUED BY THE BRITISH.

The Daily Mirror

LATEST CERTIFIED CIRCULATION MORE THAN 1,000,000 COPIES PER DAY

No. 3,396.   Registered at the G.P.O. as a Newspaper.   **FRIDAY, SEPTEMBER 11, 1914**   One Halfpenny.

THE GERMANS' DASTARDLY WORK: BELGIAN WOMAN WHOSE HOME IS BURNT DOWN FORCED TO BEG FOR BREAD.

This is a picture which will excite the pity and sympathy of everyone who is not a "cultured" German, but it is calculated to send the Kaiser and his ghoulish officers into transports of delight. The arch-bully Wilhelm is making Europe run with blood to satisfy his overweening ambition and is torturing women and children for a pastime. This heart-rending scene is but one example of his fiendish work. It shows a poor woman who has been forced to beg for money to buy food for her tiny children sitting weeping before the ruins of her burnt-out home. To Belgium brutal and unspeakable vindictiveness has been displayed because she declined to put a price upon her honour, a word meaningless to a nation taught by a cruel and cynical military caste that it is the right of the strong to bully the weak.—(*Daily Mirror* photograph.)

Although a substantial part of Belgium was quickly overrun, tenacious local resistance – combined with early German difficulties with their lines of communication – did slow the advance, including that of the 580,000 men of Kluck's and Bülow's First and Second armies that formed the 'strong right arm' of the attack. Any time the Allies could gain was crucial, as it gave them the opportunity to deploy their meagre resources against the coming onslaught.

A large crowd of Belgian refugees greets the Archbishop of Malines (Cardinal Mercier) outside Westminster Cathedral, London, in September 1914. Belgian forces had launched a major counterattack on the village of Weerde following the German retreat from the Marne, but the Germans held the village and used it as a launchpad for occupying the town of Malines and then for an assault on Antwerp, the last significant city in Belgium still under Belgian control.

'London, August 30 – I left Brussels on Thursday afternoon and have just arrived in London. For two hours on Thursday night I was in what for six hundred years has been the city of Louvain. The Germans were burning it, and to hide their work kept us locked in the railway carriages. But the story was written against the sky, was told to us by German soldiers incoherent with excesses; and we could read it in the faces of women and children being led to concentration camps and of citizens on their way to be shot.'
New York Tribune, August 31, 1914, Reported from Louvain by Richard Harding Davis.

'It is not true that Germany is guilty of having caused this war. Neither the people, the Government, nor the 'Kaiser' wanted war .... It is not true that our troops treated Louvain brutally. Furious inhabitants having treacherously fallen upon them in their quarters, our troops with aching hearts were obliged to fire a part of the town, as punishment. The greatest part of Louvain has been preserved .... '
From the 1914 'Manifesto of the 93 German Intellectuals to the Civilized World'. Signatories to the document included Professor Paul Ehrlich, Max Planck, Professor of Physics, Berlin, and Wilhelm Roentgen, Professor of Physics, Munich.

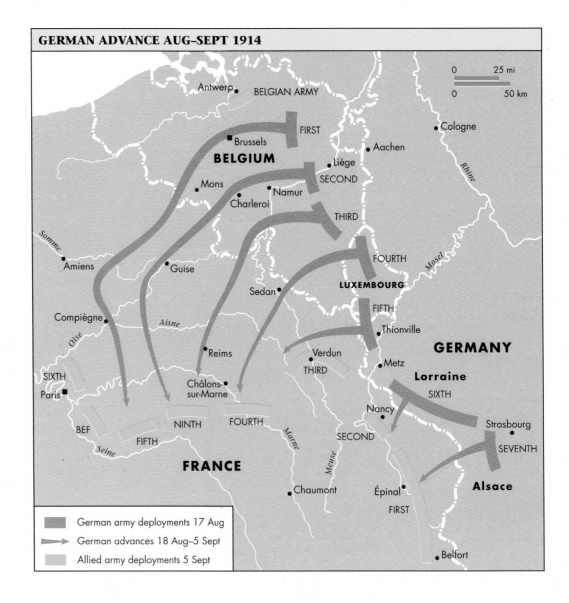

GERMAN ADVANCE AUG–SEPT 1914

German army deployments 17 Aug

German advances 18 Aug–5 Sept

Allied army deployments 5 Sept

'We embarked for France and landed at Boulogne on the morning of August 23rd. What a contrast between us and the slip-shod undersized French territorials who were guarding the docks! In their baggy red trousers and long blue coats, they looked like comic-opera soldiers.'
Private R G Hill, 'An Old Contemptible at Le Cateau', August 1914.

These resources included the single French army at Joffre's disposal, and Gen Charles Lanrezac's Fifth, which was deployed at Charleroi with the BEF on its left at Mons. The rapidly developing crisis in the north was not the only situation demanding Joffre's attention, however, for by the time Brussels fell on 20 August, his own Plan XVII was in deep trouble.

The French plan to liberate Alsace and Lorraine and push to the Rhine began on 14 August, and was conducted by four armies. Although German border outposts were swiftly overrun, the operation quickly began to go awry and the French lost their advantage. The German armies in this area had spent considerable time and energy organizing their defences in an attempt to thwart enemy advances, but Plan XVII's failure was largely due to French ineptitude. Great offensive spirit and garish uniforms did little to offset the problems caused by a lack of accurate intelligence, weak command, and poor supply. Joffre was forced to learn about the rigours of modern warfare the hard way. German counterattacks hit the French hard, and defeats at Morhange and Sarrebourg on 20 August sent them reeling back. In the space of just two weeks a dazed French army suffered over 300,000 casualties (including an estimated 10% of their pre-war officer class) and had been forced to withdraw back past their original lines in most areas. Had the Germans been capable of exploiting these victories by following up and routing the French army, European history might have been very different. However, Joffre was given a valuable breathing space, so while Plan XVII died, the French army did not.

As Joffre reassessed the strategic situation during late August, his attention was immediately drawn to German progress through Belgium. On 23 August, Kluck's First Army was checked by the BEF at Mons and then at Le Cateau three days later. Bülow's Second Army, meanwhile, was impeded

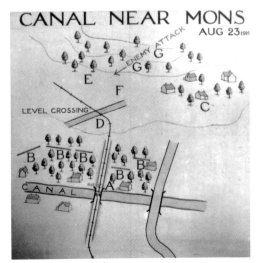

Diagram showing the position of British and French forces by the Mons Canal on 23 August 1914. The Battle of Mons was the first major armed clash involving British forces on the Western Front. German forces emerged from a wood, and were fired on by British troops, who eventually withdrew after a prolonged exchange of fire.

British cavalry withdrawing during the retreat from Mons, August 1914. At first, British commander Sir John French intended to maintain his position at Mons, but on hearing of the French Fifth Army's withdrawal at Namur, he realized that the British forces could be cut off. At midnight on 23 August, he ordered the British Expeditionary Force (BEF) to retreat southward towards the French frontier.

August 31st
'We marched instead, staggering about the road like a crowd of gypsies. Some of the fellows had puttees wrapped round their feet instead of boots; others had soft shoes that they had picked up somewhere; others walked in their socks with their feet all bleeding. My own boots would have disgraced a tramp, but I was too frightened to take them off, and look at my feet. Yet they marched until they dropped, and then somehow got up and marched again.'
Cpl Bernard John Denore, in action at the Battle of and Retreat from Mons, 23 August to 5 September, 1914.

French troops advance through a village during the Battle of the Marne in September 1914. The battle ended with the Germans retreating a total of 96 km/60 mi from their positions at the start of the battle.

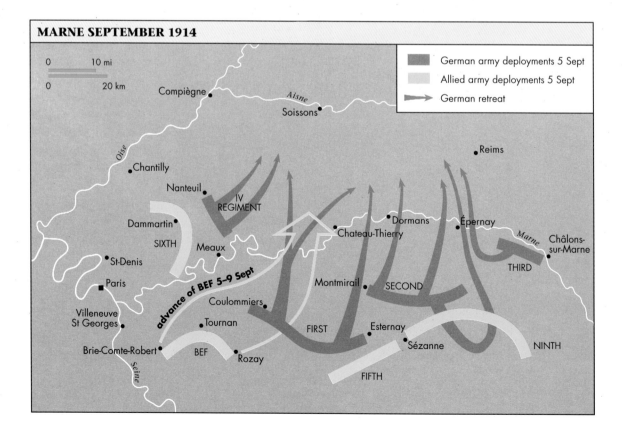

MARNE SEPTEMBER 1914

0 10 mi	German army deployments 5 Sept
0 20 km	Allied army deployments 5 Sept
	German retreat

Compiègne

Aisne

Soissons

Reims

Oise

Chantilly

Nanteuil

IV
REGIMENT

Dammartin

Dormans

Épernay

Marne

Châlons-
sur-Marne

SIXTH

Meaux

Chateau-Thierry

THIRD

St-Denis

Paris

advance of BEF 5–9 Sept

Montmirail

SECOND

Villeneuve
St Georges

Coulommiers

Tournan

FIRST

Esternay

Brie-Comte-Robert

BEF

Rozay

Sézanne

NINTH

Seine

FIFTH

by Lanrezac's Fifth Army at Guise on 29 August. These vital delaying actions began to open a gap between the two German armies, and forced Kluck to turn to the east of Paris (rather than heading to the west as planned) in order to keep in contact with the Second Army.

By early September the Allies had formed a new front line east of Paris just south of the River Marne; this included troops redeployed from Joffre's southern front and a Sixth Army, commanded by Gen Maunoury, that had been hastily cobbled together from reserve troops. For its part the German army was over-extended and exhausted after nearly a month on the

The church at Dickebusch was used as a hospital by the French at the first Battle of Ypres in Belgium in Oct–Nov 1914. This battle was a taste of things to come on the Western Front later in the war – more than 5,000 British and 5,000 German soldiers had been killed, and the Germans had failed in their attempt to break through to the port of Calais on the English Channel.

Falkenhayn, General Erich (1861–1922)

Falkenhayn was appointed minister of war in 1913 after a conventional career as a Prussian officer. He replaced Moltke as chief of staff in 1914, combining this new job with his old one for six months. In early 1915, having stabilized the German army on both fronts, Falkenhayn launched an offensive that led to the breakthrough at Gorlice-Tarnow in May, and the capture of Poland. In 1916 he sought decisive victory on the Western Front with his plan to 'bleed the French white' at Verdun. This failure led to his removal and demotion to field command in Romania and the Middle East. Falkenhayn was replaced in early 1918 after Jerusalem fell to the British, and he ended the war in an unimportant job in Lithuania.

The Austrian Archduke Frederick at Hermannstadt Station (Hungary) in November 1916 with Gen von Falkenhayn, commander of the German Ninth Army fighting against the Romanians.

offensive – a situation exploited by Joffre, who counterattacked with some success. In the Battle of the Marne on 5–10 September, Maunoury struck at Kluck's exposed right flank, while the BEF and the French Fifth and Ninth Armies endeavoured to engage the enemy head on. The attack was a success, and between 10 and 13 September the Germans withdrew to defensive positions on the high ground around the River Aisne. Although

The Christmas Truce

There was an unofficial cessation of hostilities between Allied and German troops on the front lines during Christmas 1914. In a war that had already been marked by great acts of brutality and massive casualties, enemies shook hands in No Man's Land, exchanged cigarettes, swapped food, and even played football. 'Just you think,' one British soldier wrote home, 'that whilst you were eating your turkey I was out talking with the very men I had been trying to kill a few hours before!' Although this fraternizing is well known in much of the British sector, there were also similar cease-fires in the French and Belgian sectors.

English and German troops fraternize with each other in Belgium on Christmas Day 1914. In one of the most extraordinary events of any war, soldiers from both sides exchanged souvenirs and food, and also arranged joint burial services for those who had died. British commanders put a stop to such displays of friendship when they became known.

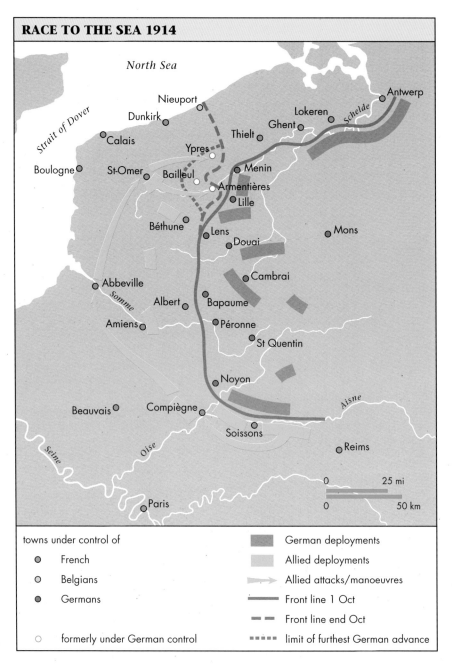

RACE TO THE SEA 1914

towns under control of

- ⊙ French
- ○ Belgians
- ● Germans
- ○ formerly under German control

▬ German deployments

▬ Allied deployments

⟶ Allied attacks/manoeuvres

— Front line 1 Oct

– – Front line end Oct

····· limit of furthest German advance

the Allies pursued the retreating Germans, they did not have the resources to maintain the pressure and so, after digging in opposite their enemy, stalemate ensued.

The German retreat from the Marne marked the demise of the Schlieffen Plan, and with it the end of Moltke's career as Chief of the Imperial General Staff. While deadlock set in south of the Aisne to the Swiss border during the autumn of 1914, it was **Eric von Falkenhayn** who sought to circumvent the problem. The 'Race to the Sea' saw both the Allies and Germans mount a series of outflanking manoeuvres with the

'I was sergeant, and was told to take and hold a certain part of the trench where the occupants had just been driven out. On rushing the trench, and leaping into it, I found that the dead were lying three deep in it. After taking bearings, I told the men to keep under cover and detailed one man, Ginger Bain, as 'look out'. After what seemed ages Ginger excitedly asked, 'How strong is the German Army?' I replied, 'Seven million.' 'Well,' said Ginger, 'here is the whole bloody lot of them making for us.' Sergent J F Bell, 'The First Battle of Ypres', October 1914.

A rifle gallery in a German front-line trench in 1914. Trenches became a major feature of World War I, particularly on the Western Front. They were eventually a complex network of deep channels with parallel lines of trenches extending rearwards for a considerable distance behind the front line – even if the front-line trench was overrun, the difficulty of penetrating the second- and third-line trenches often prevented further advance by an attacking force.

Russian soldiers on the march, with their bicycles folded on their backs. Bicycles were used extensively on the Eastern Front as an ideal form of transport for soldiers on patrols to reconnoitre enemy positions.

Ludendorff, General Erich von (1865–1937)

Ludendorff was one of the most influential figures of World War I, and his rise through the military ranks was rapid. Having helped seize Liège in mid-August 1914, Ludendorff was appointed chief of staff of the Eighth Army (commanded by Hindenburg) in East Prussia. A successful partnership grew from their victory at Tannenberg, and when Hindenburg became commander of the German army on the Eastern Front, Ludendorff became his chief of staff with the rank of lieutenant general. When Hindenburg replaced Falkenhayn as Chief of the Imperial General Staff in 1916, Ludendorff was promoted to first quartermaster-general and increasingly dominated the team. He resumed offensive action after the Brusilov Offensive in 1917 and was actively involved in the return of Lenin to Russia. The Russian Revolution and subsequent closure of the Eastern Front meant that more German forces were available for Ludendorff's great offensive in the West in March 1918. This attack, which developed into a series of offensives lasting until July, took considerable ground but failed operationally and strategically. The Allied offensives that followed persuaded Ludendorff to argue for armistice, but on 26 October he was forced to resign and fled to Sweden. After the war he took part in the Nazi uprising in Munich in 1923 and sat in the Reichstag as a right-wing Nationalist.

Soon after my arrival at Warsaw in 1914, Vyrebov . . . came to me and proposed that we visit the Warsaw-Vienna station, where there were about 17,000 men wounded in the battles at Lodz and Berezini. At the station we found a terrible scene: on the platforms in dirt filth, and cold, in the rain, on the ground, even without straw, an unbelievable quantity of wounded, who filled the air with heartrending cries, dolefully asked: 'For God's sake, order them to dress our wounds, for five days we have not been attended to.' M V Rodzianko, 'Krushenie Imperii,' Arkhiv Russkoi Revoliutsii (Berlin, 1926), XVII, 82-85, translated by J S Curtiss, in The Russian Revolutions of 1917.

aim of getting into the enemy's rear areas to cut its lines of communication. Exhaustion, a lack of resources, and the strength of the defence all combined to defeat these offensive measures, and by mid-October, the line of trenches had spread north and had reached the coast at Nieuport in Belgium. The fighting continued, however, as commanders demanded one last push before the end of the year.

On 20 October, for example, the Germans attacked around Ypres in Belgium, attempting to reach the channel ports of Calais and Dunkirk. Outnumbered and outgunned, the BEF suffered very heavy casualties, but once again the strength of the defence – combined with German over-extension – led to the attack being repulsed. Joffre also attacked in Champagne and the Vosges, a bloody offensive that continued to the end of the year. Thus, while the famous **Christmas truce** of 1914 took place in some sectors, fighting continued in appalling weather conditions in others. The stalemate was not broken and the Christmas goodwill did not last for long.

TANNENBERG AND GERMAN ADVANCE 1914

territory occupied by Russians 20–23 Aug
German advances 26–30 Aug
territory occupied by Russians 1 Sept
Russian retreat 1 Sept
German advances 1–13 Sept

Serbian troops and equipment pass through the city of Skopje. Austria-Hungary hoped that defeat of Serbia might make peace with Russia possible, ending the war and leaving much of the structure of Europe intact.

German soldiers repairing telegraph wires. Communications technology developed apace during the war – manual signalling had become outmoded due to the pace of battle, and radio was still in an embryonic stage of development, so the usual method of communication was by telephone.

1914 Western Front

4 August:	German Schleiffen Plan launched with an advance through Belgium.
14 August:	French Plan XVII to liberate Alsace and Lorraine and push to the Rhine is begun.
16 August:	German army brings down Liège, Belgium, and advances through Belgium.
20 August:	Brussels falls. German army defeats the French at Morhange and Sarrebourg.
23 August:	German army is checked by the British army at Mons.
26 August:	German army is checked by the British army at Le Cateau.
29 August:	German army is impeded by the French army at Guise.
5–10 September:	German defeat at the Battle of the Marne.
10–13 September:	German army withdraws to defensive positions on the high ground around the River Aisne.

Hindenburg, Field Marshal Paul von (1847–1934)

Born in Posen of a Prussian Junker family, Paul von Hindenburg joined the army in 1866 and fought in both the Austro-Prussian and Franco-Prussian Wars. Although he retired as a lieutenant general in 1911, World War I provided him with new opportunities. Hindenburg commanded the Eighth Army in East Prussia at the time of the Russian offensive in 1914, and he received the credit for defeating the Russians at Tannenberg. In November 1914 he became commander of German forces on the Eastern Front and attained the rank of field marshal. In August 1916, Hindenburg replaced Falkenhayn as supreme commander of German forces and, with Erich Ludendorff, practically directed Germany's policy until the end of the war. His strategy for the Western Front was to strengthen German defences and the 'Hindenburg Line' was constructed to this end. In the east, however, he launched a number of offensives that ended in the Treaty of Brest-Litovsk. The German 'spring offensives' of 1918 were not successful, and the Allied attacks that followed led to the Armistice. Hindenburg remained in command of the army until July 1919, despite the German defeat, and became president of the Weimar Republic from 1924 to 1934.

Field Marshal von Hindenburg with Gen Ludendorff on his 70th birthday on 2 October 1917. Hindenburg replaced Falkenhayn as supreme commander of German forces in August 1916, and he and Ludendorff effectively formed a German military dictatorship almost until the war ended.

The Failure of the Offensive Plans – The Eastern Front

The fighting on the Eastern Front was also destined for deadlock but, as in the west, there was considerable movement at the outset when offensive plans were put into action. Germany was certainly ill-prepared to meet the Russian onslaught into East Prussia that began on 17 August. The Germans were concentrating on the West and, having banked on a slow mobilization by Russia, had left only one army (commanded by Gen von Prittwitz) defending East Prussia. In a surprise move, the Russian First and Second armies, commanded by generals Rennenkampf and Samsonov, advanced and achieved considerable early success. However, the German withdrawal to Königsberg after their defeat of 19 and 20 August at Gumbinnen exposed an over-stretched and poorly equipped Russian army, and their advance slowed.

The chance to counterattack was seized, but not by Prittwitz, who was replaced by the formidable team of **Gen Paul von Hindenburg** and his chief of staff, **Maj-Gen Erich von Ludendorff**. Hindenburg's retaliation sought to exploit the lack of cooperation between the two Russian armies, and he was helped by their transmission of unencoded signals, and by supply problems. Thus, when a huge gap opened up between the two armies centred on the Masurian Lake, the better-organized Germans were quick to strike. By cleverly concentrating the bulk of his forces against Samsonov in the south, Hindenburg fought a series of actions between 26 and 31 August that have become known as the Battle of Tannenberg. During that fighting, Samsonov's force was caught in a double envelopment and, having been cut off from resupply and reinforcement, surrendered; Samsonov himself committed suicide. Rennenkampf's army suffered defeat at the First Battle of the Masurian Lakes and quickly withdrew, and East Prussia was evacuated by 10 September. The episode cost the Russians 300,000 casualties, and German territory was not to be occupied again by hostile forces during the war.

Having achieved this success, Hindenburg would have liked the opportunity to transfer his forces south in order to attack the right-hand side of the other Russian offensive in Galicia. But, while Hindenburg was busy despatching the Russians from East Prussia, Austria-Hungary was suffering. The forces of Gen Conrad, Austrian chief of the general staff, had conducted an offensive against Serbia and had successfully occupied Belgrade. However, Serb counterattacks had liberated the capital and, despite attempts to retake it, the city remained in enemy hands.

The Austrian plan to drive into northern Poland had also faltered. This attack had begun on 23 August, and involved three Austrian armies advancing north and east from Lemberg on a 200-mile front. The defending Russian forces of Gen Ivanov's Southwestern Army Group were engaged at the northern end of the front, and during the last week of

A Russian artillery battery in action in a wooded area. The Russians were often desperately short of guns and ammunition in World War I, the consequent lack of artillery support being a significant cause of the huge number of casualties that Russia suffered.

August the Austrians gained the upper hand. Meanwhile, the Russian Third and Eighth Armies attacked from the southern sector of the front. In this push, the Austrian Third Army and elements of the Second Army were defeated at Zlotchow on 26 August and were forced to retreat back to Lemberg. Following up their success, the Russians maintained pressure on Conrad's beleaguered Austrian troops, and achieved a breakthrough on 1 September to the north of Lemberg. A series of sustained Russian counterattacks along the entire front eventually forced the Austrians to withdraw to within 80 km/50 mi of Cracow and by the end of September nearly all of Galicia had been surrendered.

With Conrad's forces pushed back the prospects did not look good for Germany's ally, and this explains why Falkenhayn was moved to help shore up the front, to stop the Russians from breaking through to Silesia. In all, four German corps were moved from East Prussia to Poland and into a newly constituted German Ninth Army – commanded by Hindenburg – that was deployed on the Austrian left flank near Cracow in the last week of September. With this boost to their combat strength, the Central Powers went on the offensive once more.

Hindenburg advanced on Warsaw on 28 September but the Austrian attack, despite relieving Przemysl on 9 October, petered out eight days later. The new turn of events forced the Russians to reassess their options rather rapidly, and they decided to move some troops from Galicia and redeploy them against Hindenburg's open left flank. As a result of the renewed Russian offensives the Central Powers were forced to withdraw once again, and by the end of the month the Germans had been pushed back to their start line and had sustained over 40,000 casualties. At this point the Russians suspended their operations for, although they had been effective, their great offensive efforts had severely weakened them and they needed time to reorganize, recuperate, and resupply. However, the Germans did not wish to wait to be attacked by Russia and so Hindenburg, the newly appointed commander of German forces on the Eastern Front, decided to attack in a southeasterly direction towards Warsaw on 11 November. The Ninth Army covered 50 miles in four days as it pushed between the Russian First and Second armies, but just three

1914 Eastern Front

17 August:	Russian onslaught into East Prussia.
19 and 20 August:	German defeat at Gumbinnen by Russian First and Second Armies; withdrawal to Königsberg.
23 August:	Austrian armies attempt to drive into northern Poland, and have to fight defending Russian armies.
26 August:	Austrian armies are defeated by Russian forces at Zlotchow and are forced to retreat to Lemberg.
26-31 August:	Battle of Tannenberg – German army defeats Russian First and Second Armies.
1 September:	Russian armies break through Austrian troops to the north of Lemberg.
28 September:	The German Ninth Army advances on Warsaw, but renewed Russian offensives cause German forces to withdraw back to their start line.
11 November:	Hindenberg, leading the German forces, attacks once again in a southeasterly direction towards Warsaw.
14 November:	Russian Fifth Army counterattacks into Silesia.
16 November:	The plight of the Russian Second Army, forced by German advances back to Lodz, is so severe that Russia pulls the Fifth Army out of attack in Silesia and into defence around Lodz.
6 December:	Russia withdraws from Lodz in order to protect Warsaw.

Conrad von Hötzendorf, Franz, Count (1852–1925)

Conrad was Austrian chief of the general staff from 1906, and was largely responsible for modernizing and reorganizing the Austro-Hungarian army prior to World War I. He supported the aggressive policies towards Italy and Serbia and the diplomatic moves that set the war in motion. Although he was a good organizer and strategist, his record in the field was poor and he lost territory to the Russians in 1914. Conrad was increasingly forced to accept that Germany dominated the Central Powers, and this undermined his own power base. He failed in his attempt to deliver a fatal blow to the Italians in the Trentino Offensive in 1916, and this served to weaken his position further. In March 1917, Conrad was dismissed from his post and was sent to command the Trentino Front. He was relieved of this command as well, following the failure of his great offensive in June 1918.

Count Conrad von Hötzendorf, the Austrian chief of general staff from 1906 until his dismissal in March 1917.

days later the Russian Fifth Army counterattacked into Silesia. The advancing German army forced the Russian Second Army back to Lodz, where they suffered heavy losses. Indeed, the plight of the Second Army was so desperate that the Russians pulled the Fifth Army out of attack on 16 November and into defence around Lodz. The Germans continued to exert pressure on the Russians for another month, but on 6 December the Tsar's forces withdrew from the city in order to straighten their line and protect Warsaw.

These manoeuvres were the last major actions on the Eastern Front in 1914 and, in worsening weather, the fighting came to an end and stalemate set in. In the vast open spaces of the Eastern Front, there had been a great deal of manoeuvre and counter-manoeuvre – a situation that was to be repeated in following years by commanders unhampered by continuous lines of trenches. Nevertheless, on the Eastern Front (as on the Western Front) the offensive plans of 1914 failed to achieve the decisive victory that they sought and, as a result, fighting continued into 1915.

CHAPTER 4
REALITY DAWNS: 1915

The failure of offensive plans in 1914 forced the belligerents to reassess their strategy in early 1915 and fight in circumstances that had not been anticipated. While aggressive offensive action was pursued on both fronts at various times during the year, the difficulties inherent in obtaining decisive victory, and even in restoring mobility in the West, became increasingly apparent. In 1915 the realities of 'the Great War' began to

German forces entering the Galician fortress of Przemysl. Russian troops had taken Przemysl on 22 March 1915, capturing 120,000 Austrian prisoners and 700 heavy guns. However, having advanced further west, by the last week of May the Russians were being pushed back, and Austro-German soldiers retook Przemysl on 3 June.

The Eastern Front and Prospects for Mobility

While trench deadlock dominated the Western Front from late 1914 to early 1918, the same was not true in the east. The reason was that far fewer troops were deployed in the east than in the west, relative to the length of front. In the early months of 1915, for example, 100 German divisions faced 110 Entente divisions in France and Flanders, while in the east – a front that was over twice the length of the Western Front – just 80 Central Powers divisions faced 83 Russian divisions. When combined with the ease of resupply and reinforcement in the west as a result of the superior road and rail network, this meant that it was very difficult to break the enemy's line and advance into open country. Indeed, as the attackers moved forward, they found it increasingly difficult to resupply as they advanced away from their railheads and over churned-up battlefields. Meanwhile, the retreating enemy profited from shortened lines of communication and an improvement in their ability to deploy reinforcements quickly. Thus, prior to the German offensive of March 1918, many battles on the Western Front simply became slogging matches, with very little ground taken relative to the resources expended.

'The fall of Przemysl is the most striking example so far of the general demoralization of the Austrian army and monarchy.
The troops, instead of being all Hungarians, were of various Austrian nationalities; and there is good reason to think that the conditions of defence led to feuds, brawls and, in the end, open disobedience of orders.'
Bernard Pares, March 1915.

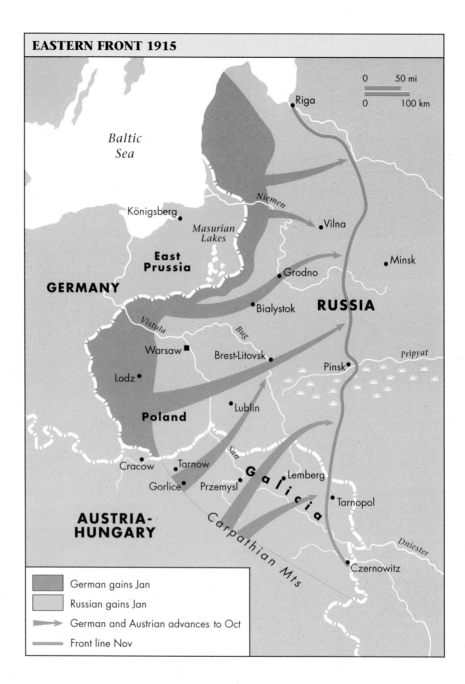

EASTERN FRONT 1915

Baltic Sea

Riga

Königsberg

Masurian Lakes

East Prussia

GERMANY

Niemen

Vilna

Minsk

Grodno

Bialystok

RUSSIA

Vistula

Bug

Warsaw

Brest-Litovsk

Pripyat

Lodz

Pinsk

Poland

Lublin

San

Cracow

Tarnow

Gorlice

Przemysl

Lemberg

Galicia

Tarnopol

AUSTRIA-HUNGARY

Carpathian Mts

Dniester

Czernowitz

German gains Jan

Russian gains Jan

German and Austrian advances to Oct

Front line Nov

reveal themselves, forcing the generals to revise their fighting methods and the belligerent states to prepare for a protracted struggle with many sacrifices.

1915: The Eastern Front

The decision made by both sides to continue the war into 1915 brought many problems for the generals at the fighting fronts. Although many welcomed another opportunity to get to grips with the enemy, it was not necessarily obvious to them where and when to launch operations, nor what fighting methods might be appropriate in the extraordinary circumstances in which they found themselves.

Germany had a particular problem. Faced by enemies on two fronts but unable to launch major offensives on both, the German high command had to prioritize. Although Falkenhayn was adamant that final victory could be won only in the west, he was flexible enough to understand that the east provided far greater opportunity for mobility. He therefore decided to concentrate his offensive efforts on the Russian army

German soldiers on patrol in deep snow on the Russian Front. Despite being more used to the severe conditions, even the Russians were not immune to the effects of the cold – in early April 1916, for example, 12,000 Russian soldiers died from frostbite on the Eastern Front near Lake Naroch.

Russian prisoners-of-war await treatment at a German dressing station following the recapture of Przemysl in June 1915. Right from the start of the war, Russian casualties preferred to be treated in German field hospitals because of the insanitary conditions and primitive treatment on offer from their own medical service.

while remaining on the defensive against France and Britain. Offensives in the east also had the added advantage of taking some pressure off the troubled army of Austria-Hungary which, after its performance in 1914, looked capable of achieving little without German support.

Having redeployed a large proportion of their reserves to the east over the winter of 1914–15, the Central Powers were in a position to attack early in the new year. The Austrian attack in the Carpathians began on 23 January and sought to relieve 120,000 of Conrad's troops besieged in Przemysl. However, in common with so many offensives on both fronts during the war, within a few days the terrain and weather brought them to a grinding halt. Attempts to re-establish momentum failed during the spring

A German 8-in mortar being fired on the Russian front in August 1915. On 5 August, the German army entered Warsaw, the first time for exactly a century that Russia had not had control of the Polish capital. Flushed by this success, Germany now set its sights on taking Finland, which Russia had controlled for even longer.

Russian forces sustained huge losses against armies of the Central Powers on 8 June 1915 at Skaudville Manor near Bubic. Having attacked on three sides, they were repulsed by the defending forces.

despite attempts by both sides. The expenditure of resources required to sustain this fighting affected the fighting abilities of both the Austro-Hungarians and the Russians. Having suffered 520,000 casualties (including the 120,000 prisoners taken by the Russians when the Przemysl fortress fell in late March), Conrad's army was exhausted and became even more reliant upon the support of its German ally. The Russians also lost heavily in early 1915 – 400,000 casualties in all – and were extremely short of both munitions and equipment, which not only had an obvious negative impact upon operations, but also severely affected the morale of the troops.

The German attack began north of the Masurian Lakes on 7 February. The surprise it achieved owed much to the awful weather that greeted the opening shots, but it proved very difficult to exploit this initial success. A 112-km/70-mi advance by two German armies did lead to the surrender of the Russian XX Corps on 21 February, but logistic difficulties made it impossible to turn this into something fatal for the Russians. Nevertheless, with the Germans having taken so much ground, inflicted 100,000 casualties upon the enemy (in return for slight losses themselves), and taken a further 100,000 Russian prisoners, the offensive had long-term mental and physical repercussions for the tsar's forces in terms of their ability to sustain such massive blows.

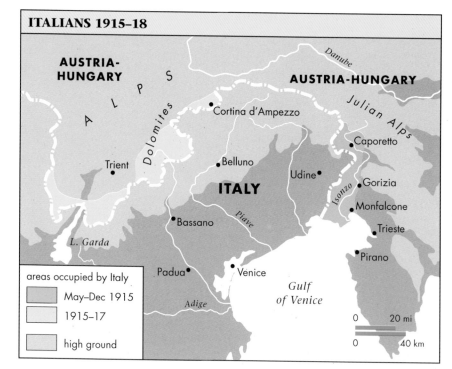

ITALIANS 1915–18

AUSTRIA-HUNGARY

AUSTRIA-HUNGARY

ALPS

Danube

Julian Alps

Dolomites

Cortina d'Ampezzo

Trient

Belluno

Caporetto

Udine

Gorizia

ITALY

Isonzo

Monfalcone

Bassano

Piave

Trieste

L. Garda

Pirano

areas occupied by Italy

May–Dec 1915

1915–17

high ground

Padua

Venice

Gulf
of Venice

Adige

0   20 mi

0   40 km

An official Italian photograph of observers ascending the precarious ladders to an observation post in the Trentino in Austria to the north of Lake Garda. In May 1915, the Austrians launched a huge offensive and drove the Italians from the mountains, taking 30,000 prisoners.

The German success in the Masurian offensive would have been far sweeter, however, had Falkenhayn not had great concern for the well-being of Conrad's forces to his south. Clearly, German advances in the north would count for little if the Russians were able to destroy the Austro-Hungarian army and drive onwards. The rapid establishment of a new Eleventh Army under Gen August von Mackensen in the Carpathians was an acknowledgement of the much-feared growing disparity in the region. The secret deployment of this force between the towns of Gorlice and Tarnow not only went some way towards redressing that imbalance, but also allowed the Germans to launch a major new offensive. Starting on 2 May, this attack achieved immediate success, with the enemy front line being overrun and deftly-employed reserves maintaining the momentum. The Russians fell back and were given no time to reorganize; Galicia was cleared and by 15 May the Central Powers had reached the River San. Once again logistic difficulties and exhaustion tempered success, but this impressive breakthrough cost the Russians more ground and another 412,000 casualties.

Further pain was inflicted on the Russians by Hindenburg's attack from East Prussia during the summer of 1915. This attempt to dilute the Russian forces further went well and led to an advance of some 480 km/300 mi. Although the simultaneous thrust by the Austro-Hungarian army further to the south was a failure and cost 200,000 casualties, 1915 campaigning had cost the Russians 2 million men.

A sentry patrols on the Cima Lana, high up in the Italian Dolomite mountains to the east of Bolzano. Such picturesque terrain was in sharp contrast to the often flat, featureless, muddy, and tree-shattered landscape of the Western Front a few hundred miles to the northwest.

Serbian cavalry cross the River Drin during the retreat to Albania in November 1915. Bulgarian forces had captured the Serbian city of Nis, once more giving Germany a direct rail link from Berlin to Constantinople. Serbian forces and civilians numbering 200,000 retreated across the mountains to the safety of Albania.

There was another twist to the fighting on the Eastern Front in 1915 when the Italians entered the war on 23 May on the side of the Entente. This decision spread the Central Powers' fighting strength even more thinly, because although it did not possess a particularly efficient or effective fighting force, Italy still had to be contained. The terrain along the Austro-Italian border was conducive to defensive operations, however, as only a 32 km/20 mi stretch of it was not mountainous. Thus, when **Gen Luigi Cadorna** (the Italian commander-in-chief) attacked on 23 June 1915, his options were rather limited and he soon found that the enemy had taken up strong defensive positions on the high ground some distance from the border. This attack (along with three others over the course of the year) was subsequently smashed on the rocks of the Isonzo plateau. These offensives cost the Italians 125,000 men and the Austrians around 100,000.

As the outcome of the Isonzo offensives reveals, the fighting on the Eastern Front during 1915 was having a detrimental impact upon the resources of the Central Powers. But while these allies could ill afford to mount major offensives without thinking carefully about their ability to hold the front, Serbia remained a potential threat. The offensive conducted in the autumn by Germany, Austria-Hungary, and Bulgaria (the newest member of the Central Powers) – a combined force of some 300,000 men – sought to destroy this threat once and for all. As the attack began on 6 October, a combined Franco-British force began to deploy in Salonika in an attempt to bolster the 200,000-strong Serb army, but it was too late. Despite the failure of the Central Powers to encircle their enemy, Belgrade fell quickly and the Serbs were driven back to the Adriatic where, in late November, they had to be evacuated by the naval forces of the Entente. Serbia had been defeated.

Cadorna, General Luigi (1850–1928)

Luigi Cadorna joined the army at the age of 16 and rose to become Chief of the Italian General Staff between June 1914 and November 1917. Although he took over an army that was poorly equipped, badly led, and had low morale, within a year he had made a number of changes that allowed them to undertake offensive action in 1915. However, the huge losses sustained by the Italians in a dozen offensives on the Isonzo Front between 1915 and 1917 did little to engender high morale. The last of these battles – the Italian defeat at Caporetto in November 1917 – cost Cadorna his job. Although he managed to stabilize the line on the River Piave after a general retreat, Cadorna was blamed for his lack of preparation and was replaced by Gen Diaz.

Gen Luigi Cadorna, appointed Italian chief of staff in 1914.

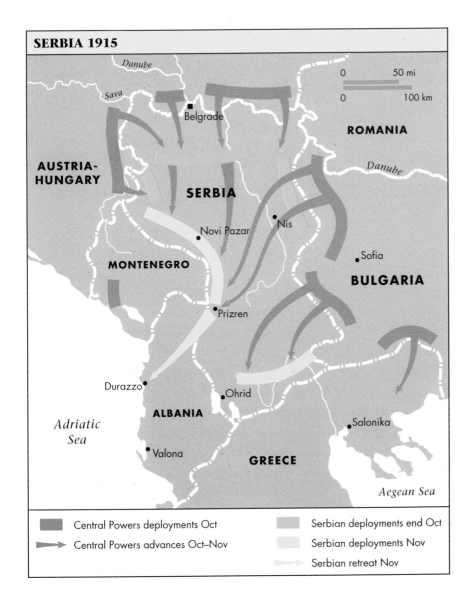

SERBIA 1915

Key:
- Central Powers deployments Oct
- Central Powers advances Oct–Nov
- Serbian deployments end Oct
- Serbian deployments Nov
- Serbian retreat Nov

Campaigns such as those conducted in the Balkans reveal the mobile nature of the war in this region (and on the Eastern Front more generally) during 1915, but despite this movement there was still no decisive breakthrough in that year. The problems of exploiting and sustaining success over vast distances caused huge problems that were not easily overcome. Indeed, the mobile nature of the war on the Eastern Front disguised the true character of the fighting in this area; in reality it mirrored the attritional conflict developing in the west more closely than might be apparent simply by looking at arrows on maps.

The Western Front

With the German desire to stay on the defensive in the west until Russia had been knocked out of the war, 1915 was a year of unrelenting Allied attacks – apart from one brief offensive foray by the Germans in April. However, in their deadlocked environment, the great problem facing the British and French high commands was how to restore mobility to the front

A French machine gun being pressed into service as an anti-aircraft gun, mounted on the top of Hazebroucke church tower in March 1915.

'The nature of the gases carried by the German asphyxiating shells remain a mystery. Whatever gas it is, it spreads rapidly and remains close to the ground. It is believed not to be specially deadly – one that rather overpowers its victims and puts them hors de combat *without killing many. Its effect at Bixschoote may have been due to panic caused by the novelty of the device.'* Will Irwin, correspondent from the *New York Tribune*, April 25, 1915.

'The British casualties exceeded 2,000 out of 50,000 men engaged on that occasion. This was due to the impetuosity of the new troops and of some officers who misunderstood the object of the attack, advanced too quickly and too far, and thus uselessly exposed their men to the effects of the severe counterblows which the Germans, with their accustomed thoroughness, did not fail to deliver. There also was confusion in the matter of bringing up re-enforcements.' Count Charles de Souza, on the Battle of Neuve Chapelle, 1915.

German shells bursting just behind the British front-line trenches to prevent reinforcements being brought up at the Battle of Neuve Chapelle, 10–14 March 1915. The British tried to break through the German trenches at Neuve Chapelle to capture the nearby village of Aubers, but poor communications and a failure to cut the German wire on one sector resulted in disastrous casualties – in one attack, every one of almost 1,000 attackers became a casualty.

Soldiers of 19 Brigade of the 2nd Battalion Argyll and Sutherland Highlanders don some of the first gas masks to be used as protection against German poison-gas attacks. Respirators for protection against poison gas were first issued to the battalion on 3 May 1915.

The Use of Gas

Although the French used tear gas from August 1914, poisonous gas was not seen on the battlefield until the Germans experimented with it at Ypres on 22 April 1915. The chlorine gas used on that day was released from over 500 cylinders in the German front line and blew on the wind towards the Allies. In this attack some 5,000 troops died after inhaling the substance, and a further 10,000 were wounded. The psychological effect was considerable, and the Germans could have taken advantage of this had the high command been more enthusiastic about its potential. However, an opportunity did not readily present itself again, as protective devices were quickly introduced and continually developed throughout the war to combat the effects of new gases. By July 1915 gas was being accurately delivered in artillery shells, with the choking phosgene and the deadly mustard gas (which was highly toxic, odourless, and virtually colourless) following. Gas was not a war-winning weapon in itself, but it did decrease the fighting effectiveness of troops encumbered by masks – a fact quickly picked up on by the Allies, who also started to use gas in 1915. This weapon caused at least one million casualties during the war.

and overcome the strength of the defence. The offensives of 1915 did not provide the solution, but they did provide both operational and tactical clues.

The offensives began on 10 March with the BEF conducting its first independent attack, in which Gen Sir Douglas Haig's First Army was charged with eliminating the Neuve Chapelle salient before advancing to Aubers Ridge. In an attempt to overcome the strong German defences in the area, the plan was for the artillery to provide an intensive 35-minute 'hurricane' bombardment in order to neutralize the enemy and cut their wire, while a standing barrage would also be laid down to prevent German reinforcements from reaching the front line. In the event the artillery plan worked well on two-thirds of the front, and the infantry managed to break in to the German line; however, communications and reinforcement problems (which were to become chronic) meant that no break-out took place. In a battle that lasted until 13 March and cost the British 12,000 casualties, Neuve Chapelle was taken but Aubers Ridge remained in enemy hands. There were many lessons to be learned from this experience – for example, that surprise could be created by a brief, but intense bombardment. But war fighting does not allow for reflection at leisure, and this lesson was sadly forgotten soon after an increase in shell production allowed for protracted preliminary bombardments.

An improvised alarm to warn of gas attack in the trenches in the Ypres Salient, 1915. The Germans used poison gas for the first time in April 1915, while it was another six months before British forces deployed this devastating weapon.

Flame-throwers

The flame-thrower was a weapon that emitted a stream of burning liquid that could be directed against troops or strongpoints. A useful tactical accessory (like gas), it was first used by the Germans at the Battle of Hooge in July 1915. It consisted of a backpack with a reservoir of compressed nitrogen and a tank containing about 10 litres/18 pints of 'flame liquid' – usually a mixture of coal tar and benzine. A hose ran from the fuel tank to a nozzle with an ignition device fitted to it. On pressing the trigger, gas forced the liquid through the nozzle, and at the same time the ignition device fired the liquid. The gas pressure was sufficient to give the flaming liquid a range of about 47 m/50 yd.

A French staff officer crawls in trenches just 73 m/80 yd from German lines at the foot of the opposite bank, near the village of Souchez near Lens on 15 May 1915.

An official German photograph of a flame-thrower in use. The flame-thrower produced a powerful jet of burning liquid, and was designed for use against troops or strongholds. The Germans used the flame-thrower for the first time against French trenches near Verdun in February 1915.

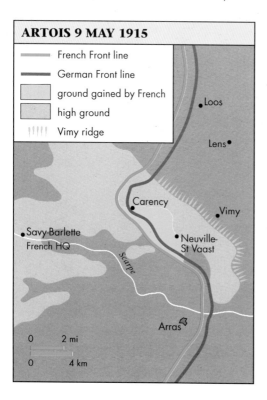

ARTOIS 9 MAY 1915

———	French Front line
———	German Front line
▭	ground gained by French
▭	high ground
⏐⏐⏐⏐	Vimy ridge

Loos

Lens

Carency

Vimy

Savy-Barlette French HQ

Neuville-St Vaast

Scarpe

Arras

0   2 mi

0   4 km

The constant refinement of older weapons technology such as artillery, and the development of new and appropriate tactics for it, was an ongoing concern throughout the war – huge resources were poured into it by all sides in an attempt to overcome the deadlock. The use of new weaponry was also a feature of the fighting. The first use of **poison gas** by the Germans at Ypres in 1915, for example, led only to minor tactical gain but taught them much about the strengths and weaknesses of such a weapon. The same could be said of the introduction of the **flame-thrower** (also by the Germans at Ypres in 1915), and such arms – although not war-winners – became important tactical accessories as the war progressed.

The lesson-learning continued with Joffre's Artois offensive, which began on 9 May 1915. Centred on Vimy Ridge, this assault began after a massive artillery bombardment from 1,200 guns (which included 300 heavy guns), and saw the French advance 4 km/2.5 mi to a point where they overlooked the vast Douai Plain. However, once again communication difficulties and the maldeployment of the reserve – which was 11.2 km/7 mi away – gave the Germans time to stabilize the line, and the fleeting opportunity for French exploitation passed. The battle continued with little success until mid-June, and eventually cost the French 100,000 casualties and the Germans 75,000.

The ruins of Loos near Lens in October 1915. The British advanced against the German Sixth Army at Loos from 25 September to 14 October, while the French conducted another attack in the Second Battle of Champagne. This battle marked the first occasion on which the British used poison gas – which could swiftly immobilize large numbers of enemy soldiers, as long as the wind was blowing in the right direction.

The Vimy Ridge experience revealed to the French the clear need to conduct a reappraisal of certain facets of their offensive methods – the British thought the same after their failure to take Aubers Ridge as part of the larger offensive that began on the same day. Therefore the Battle of Artois was a defining moment in the Allied bid to overcome trench deadlock; indeed, many of the lessons learned during this period were to have vital implications for future battles. But while it was clear to Allied generals that new fighting methods would have to be developed to cope with the conditions encountered on the Western Front, they also

The village of Souchez near Lens, France, in ruins in November 1915. Souchez had been recaptured by the French on 26 September, having been the scene of bitter hand-to-hand fighting in May–June 1915.

increasingly believed that a war of attrition – a deliberate attempt to soak up the enemy's human and material resources – would be required before they could achieve a breakthrough.

Consequently, the Allied offensives of late September 1915 – while seeking to break the German lines – were also regarded by the high command as crucial in the ongoing development of fighting methods, and

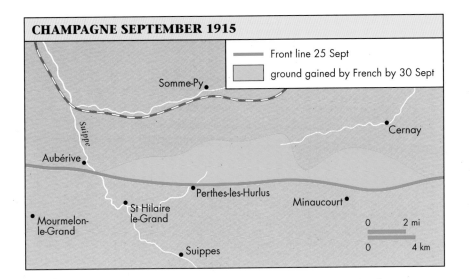

CHAMPAGNE SEPTEMBER 1915

Front line 25 Sept

ground gained by French by 30 Sept

Somme-Py

Cernay

Suippe

Aubérive

Perthes-les-Hurlus

Minaucourt

St Hilaire le-Grand

Mourmelon-le-Grand

0   2 mi

0   4 km

Suippes

vital to the creation of disparity. Therefore simultaneous offensives in Artois (where 18 French and 12 British divisions attacked) and Champagne (where 35 French divisions were involved) were not the mere futile gestures of incompetent and unimaginative generals.

The attacks commenced on 25 September. In Champagne, the strength of the German Second Line and the outrunning of the artillery support almost inevitably led to failure, although a section of the enemy front line was overrun where the wire had been cut. The slogging match that ensued continued for four days, but no more ground was taken. Meanwhile, in Artois the French pressed towards Vimy Ridge once more. However, the failure of the artillery preparation here caused a lethal combination of uncut barbed wire and undamaged machine guns that immediately led to the attack faltering. Although the French briefly took the crest of Vimy Ridge, the strength of German defence in the area quickly resulted in the French part of the attack being halted after very heavy losses.

In the BEF sector, some divisions were initially successful – although they were both helped and hindered by the use of gas and a smoke screen – and the German front line was taken on a 6.4-km/4-mi front, including the village of Loos and the outskirts of Lens. However, the already-common problem of being able to make a lodgement in the enemy line – but then being unable to exploit it – was to stifle success here. The dreadful decision by **Sir John French** (commander-in-chief of the BEF) to keep the reserve under his personal command some 25.6 km/16 mi from the front line during the break-in phase not only exacerbated an already difficult position, but also revealed the poor relationship he had with some of his subordinates. Thus, although the reserves went up the line that night, by the time they attacked, the British had missed their opportunity. The ill-considered attacks that followed over the next couple of days without

French, John Denton, 1st Earl of Ypres (1852–1925)

An experienced soldier, French had been Chief of the Imperial General Staff just before the war and commanded the BEF from August 1914 to December 1915. Although the retreat of the BEF to the River Marne in 1914 was a success, he controlled his two corps poorly as they passed through the Forest of Mormal, and allowed them to separate. Becoming pessimistic about the chances of his force being able to rebuff the German advance, French seriously considered taking his men out of the line and withdrawing to St Nazaire to recuperate. The timely arrival of Kitchener in France on 1 September dissuaded him from carrying out this move, so the BEF continued to fight with French forces down towards Paris. Indecisiveness and lethargy also blighted his attack between the German First and Second Armies during the Battle of the Marne, and he exhibited further ill judgement during the Battle of Loos in September 1915, when his deployment of the reserve was highly detrimental to the BEF's ability to exploit its initial lodgements in the German line. French was removed from command in December 1915, and was replaced by Sir Douglas Haig.

Field Marshal Sir John French (centre, in overcoat) inspects troops of the Machine Gun Corps in February 1915. French was one of the commanders who put an immediate stop to any future fraternization between British and German troops, as had happened spontaneously at Christmas the previous year.

'The shell-fire was deafening enough, but the clatter that commenced with our further advance was abominable. It was as if the enemy were attacking with a fleet of motorcycles – it was the hellish machine guns ... How heavily we had suffered could be gauged by the bleeding mass of men that lay in the shelter of the roadside.'
W Walker, 'The Battle Of Loos', 1915.

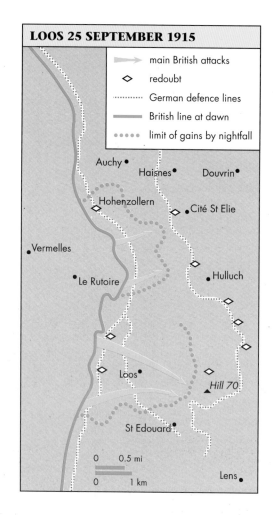

LOOS 25 SEPTEMBER 1915

→ main British attacks
◇ redoubt
.... German defence lines
——— British line at dawn
••••• limit of gains by nightfall

Auchy
Haisnes
Douvrin
Hohenzollern
Cité St Elie
Vermelles
Le Rutoire
Hulluch
Loos
Hill 70
St Edouard
0   0.5 mi
0   1 km
Lens

artillery support merely added more casualties to an already-substantial list. For the BEF, the Battle of Loos was a turning point – not just as a result of what it could learn from the fighting, but also due to the fact that most of its original members had already become casualties. As for Gen Sir John French, he was sacked in December and was replaced by Sir Douglas Haig.

The Artois–Champagne offensives cost the British 60,000 casualties, the French 250,000 and the Germans 140,000 by the time the fighting had petered out in early November. Although not inconsiderable for the Germans, these casualty figures revealed to the Allies that while they had been educating themselves in the art of attack, their enemy had been working to perfect the art of defence. With such developments taking place, it became clear (if it had not already become so) that it was going to take some considerable time to break the trench deadlock.

CHAPTER 5
THE GLOBAL CONFLICT

The Expanding War

World War I began in Europe and its origins were European, but within a few short days of hostile action starting in Belgium, the conflict began to take on global dimensions. The possession of colonies by each of the

Japanese infantry outside Port Arthur. On 23 August 1914, as a British ally, Japan declared war on Germany, and a month later Japanese forces joined with those from Britain and Australia to mop up German resistance in the countless islands and ports that Germany had acquired in its imperialist phase leading up to World War I.

protagonists led to the rapid expansion of the war as powers sought to protect their interests and, crucially, deny their opponents access to important territories and resources. The increasingly global nature of the war naturally affected strategic thinking and, to some decision-makers, victory was best sought through the fighting of 'peripheral' campaigns.

'Easterners' versus 'Westerners'

The strategic debate concerning the focus of Allied strategy began with the establishment of trench deadlock on the Western Front at the end of 1914. The idea of diverting resources away from the west was anathema to the French, with the Germany army still on their soil. However, in Britain some men of influence thought that the available resources might be used more effectively if they were employed in attacks upon German allies and resources in other theatres. Such ideas were given even greater credence by the failure of the Allied spring offensives on the Western Front in 1915. At this time David Lloyd George, the chancellor of Exchequer (and soon to be minister of munitions), and **Winston Churchill**, the First Lord of the Admiralty, were articulate advocates of the 'indirect approach'. However, there was strong opposition to their strategic thinking – especially among the military – and French, Haig, and **Robertson** (who was appointed Chief of the Imperial General Staff in November 1915) all thought that the best policy was to use all available resources to attack the main enemy on the main front. Indeed, they also argued that a diversion of Allied resources away from the west was exactly what Germany was looking for in order to mount her own major offensive in the west, with potentially catastrophic repercussions for the Entente powers. The debate raged throughout the war and both Haig (as commander-in-chief of the BEF) and Lloyd George (as prime minister) spent a considerable amount of time defending their positions and attacking those of their opponents.

Africa

The 'Easterner' versus 'Westerner' debate had not even begun to divide the decision-makers in London when, at the outbreak of war, the British asked their colonies to do all that they could to seize German overseas territories. The response from both Australia and New Zealand was as swift as it was successful, and by October Samoa, New Guinea, and the islands of Bismarck Archipelago had all been taken. However, it was not so easy to achieve similar success on the African continent, where Britain, France, and Germany all had colonies.

Although the German colony of Togoland was overrun by British troops in less than a month, Germany's other West African territory, Cameroon, proved more of a challenge. In a campaign that highlighted their ability to remain mobile in inhospitable terrain, the well-equipped German forces (commanded by Col Zimmermann) evaded capture by a Franco-British

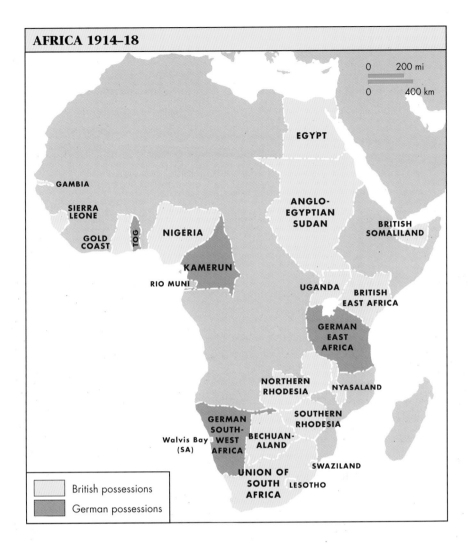

AFRICA 1914–18

0 — 200 mi
0 — 400 km

GAMBIA
SIERRA LEONE
GOLD COAST
TOG
NIGERIA
KAMERUN
RIO MUNI
EGYPT
ANGLO-EGYPTIAN SUDAN
BRITISH SOMALILAND
UGANDA
BRITISH EAST AFRICA
GERMAN EAST AFRICA
NORTHERN RHODESIA
NYASALAND
SOUTHERN RHODESIA
GERMAN SOUTH-WEST AFRICA
Walvis Bay (SA)
BECHUAN-ALAND
SWAZILAND
UNION OF SOUTH AFRICA
LESOTHO

British possessions
German possessions

Churchill, Sir Winston Spencer (1874–1965)

Born at Blenheim Palace in Oxfordshire, England, Winston Churchill joined the army in 1895 and, in the dual role of soldier and military correspondent, served in the Spanish-American War in Cuba, India, Egypt, and South Africa. After entering Parliament as a Liberal member in 1900, Churchill held a number of ministerial appointments including home secretary, First Lord of the Admiralty, and chancellor of the Exchequer (1924–29). Although he spent a number of years in the political 'wilderness' during the 1930s, he returned to lead a coalition government as prime minister in May 1940 and served in this capacity throughout World War II. He led a Conservative government from 1951 to 1955 and remained a Member of Parliament until 1964. During the last years of his life, Churchill devoted much of his time to writing, and produced a four-volume *History of the English-Speaking Peoples* (1956–58).

Winston Churchill advocated improvements to the land campaign and a resumption of naval bombardments in the Gallipoli campaign from May 1915, but his advice was ignored. When he was frozen out of a five-man War Council of the British government in November 1915, he immediately resigned his minor ministerial post and went to the Western Front as a battalion commander.

force for a year and a half in a colony that was larger than Germany itself. The Allies did make some progress towards engaging their enemy, but as they deployed, Zimmermann slipped his troops over the border into neutral Spanish Guinea. Isolated German outposts continued to resist until February 1916, by which time the campaign had soaked up some 24,000 Allied troops.

There were protracted campaigns in other areas of Africa as well. When the British asked South Africa to seize German Southwest Africa, for example, although two wireless stations on the coast were taken on 10 August 1914, nothing further could be done until Louis Botha and Jan Smuts had crushed an anti-British rebellion in South Africa

Field Marshal Jan C Smuts, the South African leader. As a general, Smuts was a member of the British War Cabinet, and in June 1917 he strongly advocated an urgent British offensive against the Germans on the Western Front to break their spirits.

German East Africa was the scene of a prolonged guerrilla campaign, doggedly waged by German forces under Gen von Lettow-Vorbeck (seen here enjoying the trappings of senior rank). He managed to hold numerically superior Allied forces at bay for much of the conflict – even earning the admiration of his enemies.

British Colonies

4 August 1914 (outbreak of war):
Britain asks colonies in Australia, New Zealand, and Africa to seize German territories.

10 August 1914: two wireless stations on the coast of German Southwest Africa are taken by South African British colonies.

27 August 1914: German colony of Togoland surrenders.

October 1914: Samoa, New Guinea, and the islands of Bismarck Archipelago have all been taken by British colonies.

January 1915: British troops are sent in to deal with the one small German garrison remaining in Southwest Africa. A series of German raids on British forces over German East Africa and into adjacent territories including British East Africa begins four years of guerrilla warfare in East Africa.

9 July 1915: German Southwest Africa falls to the South African British colony.

February 1916: German forces finally driven out of Cameroon after protracted fighting.

23 November 1918: German troops at last retreat from German East Africa, when news of the armistice reaches them.

itself. Troops were eventually sent to deal with the small German garrison that remained in the country in January 1915, but the colony only fell to the South Africans on 9 July after its defenders decided that it was impossible to evade capture in the desolate terrain in which they were seeking refuge.

However, the most protracted African campaign took place in German East Africa, a colony about the size of France. In this area Col (later Gen) Paul von Lettow-Vorbeck, who was commanding a German force numbering 14,000 men (including 11,000 African soldiers), worked hard to ensure that he tied up as many Allied resources as possible. In early 1915, after a disastrous British attack on the initially small German contingent in the previous year, Vorbeck launched a series of raids over the colony and into adjacent territories including British East Africa – and so began four years of guerrilla warfare. Although the British had some success in naval actions during 1915, the forces required for an offensive did not become available until the following year. These troops, mainly from South Africa,

Grass and small branches spread on a track near Chikukwe Swamp to make it easier for motorized vehicles to move about during the German East Africa campaign, January 1918. The Germans waged a protracted guerrilla campaign against Allied forces throughout the war.

peaked at 350,000 men and were commanded by Gen Jan Smuts in the spring of 1916 when they sought to surround Vorbeck's force. This attempt failed – along with another in 1917 – with the enemy's acclimatization to and knowledge of the terrain giving them several key advantages, and allowing them to escape. By living off the land, Vorbeck's highly mobile force was incredibly difficult to track down, and it remained at large until news of the armistice reached them on 23 November 1918. Vorbeck was the last German commander of the war to surrender. This long and resource-heavy campaign led to the deaths of some 80,000 British and African troops and, if nothing else, sapped much of South Africa's military strength. Much the same could be said for the impact of the Gallipoli campaign on other Allied resources.

Robertson, Field Marshal Sir William Robert (1860–1933)

Having enlisted as a trooper in the cavalry in 1877, William Robertson rose through the ranks to become a field marshal in 1920, the only man in the British army ever to achieve such a feat. He was both quartermaster-general of the BEF and its chief of staff before being appointed Chief of the Imperial General Staff in late 1915. In this role Robertson advised the Cabinet on strategy, but although he worked well with Haig, as a committed 'Westerner' his relationship with prime minister David Lloyd George (a leading 'Easterner') was often fraught. Disagreements over strategy and, among other things, the establishment of the Supreme War Council, led Lloyd George to become increasingly dissatisfied with Robertson and in February 1918, after the failure of the Third Battle of Ypres, he was replaced by Sir Henry Wilson.

Gen Sir William Robertson (right) and the French general Fayolle inspect a Scottish regiment in Cologne. Robertson was Chief of the Imperial General Staff for much of World War I, but was replaced in February 1918, and commanded British forces on the Rhine after the war.

Soldiers of the King's African Rifles march along the banks of the Rufiji river in January 1917, in the east of the country now called Tanzania. At the end of the war, the vast majority of German East Africa was transferred to Britain as a territory called Tanganyika.

Gallipoli

The Turkish entry into the war on the side of the Central Powers on 29 October 1914 provided the 'Easterners' with a great opportunity to demand the opening of a new fighting front in the spring of 1915. Winston Churchill was certainly keen to exploit the many weaknesses evident in a state that had been ruled since 1909 by Enver Pasha, but had only a tenuous hold on the remnants of the old Ottoman Empire in the Balkans and Middle East. However, the Turkish army was competently trained and led by German officers under the command of Gen Liman von Sanders. This fact served only to convince the First Lord of the Admiralty

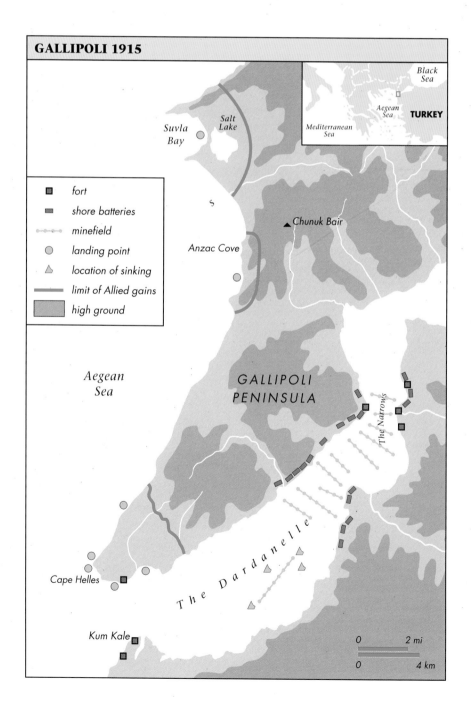

GALLIPOLI 1915

Black Sea

Aegean Sea

Mediterranean Sea

TURKEY

Suvla Bay

Salt Lake

S

▲ Chunuk Bair

Anzac Cove

■ fort
▬ shore batteries
minefield
○ landing point
△ location of sinking
━━ limit of Allied gains
high ground

Aegean Sea

GALLIPOLI PENINSULA

The Narrows

The Dardanelle

Cape Helles

Kum Kale

0   2 mi

0   4 km

that sea power would be the best asset to use in the circumstances, and so when Grand Duke Nicolas asked Kitchener for Allied assistance in October 1914 to help relieve pressure on his forces in the Caucasus, Churchill got to work. His plan was to use expendable battleships to force the Dardanelles straits (connecting the Mediterranean with the Black Sea) and then to threaten Constantinople. Churchill argued that this would at least force Pasha to limit his campaigning, and might even force him to sue for peace. Kitchener was certainly impressed by a plan that could have great strategic implications for minimal risk, and so in January 1915 he agreed to the naval action going ahead.

The naval bombardment of the forts protecting the straits on 19 February was a failure. The guns that were destroyed during this period were done so by various Royal Marine landing parties (who later reported a very limited number of Turks in the area at the time), and not naval firepower. The naval attack achieved little other than alerting the enemy to the possibility of future large-scale landings. Indeed, the Turks had already prepared the defence of the 59-km/37-mi long straits competently; in addition to the large guns in the forts, they had also deployed shore batteries and a minefield. The obvious strength of these defensive preparations led to the decision to launch another attack in order to destroy the forts and provide an opportunity for the mines to be swept. However, this renewed attack on 18 March was a disaster, with one-third of the naval force either sunk or severely damaged.

In the light of the actions of mid-March, it is instructive to reflect upon two of the plan's advantages that Kitchener immediately latched on to when he agreed to the scheme: that attack was unlikely to prove costly; and, that if everything did go wrong, the operation could simply be stopped. The decision not only to continue the action, but actually to expand it into a

Hamilton, Gen Sir Ian (1853–1947)

Ian Hamilton was a very experienced soldier by the time he took command of the Mediterranean Expeditionary Force in March 1915: he had served in numerous colonial wars, and had been chief of staff to Lord Kitchener in the Anglo-Boer War (1899–1902). It was Hamilton to whom Kitchener turned to command the MEF and force the Dardanelles straits after the failure of the naval campaign. Although his plan was a major factor in the Gallipoli failure, it was probably the best that could have been devised in the circumstances, and his failure to intervene in the battle had more to do with his training than a lack of flair. In the event, one could argue that Hamilton was the scapegoat for a poorly conceived campaign which, although designed in reaction to the stalemate on the Western Front, eventually ended up being very much like it. Hamilton was relieved of his command on 14 October 1915 and was replaced by Sir Charles Monro.

V Beach from the bridge of the collier SS River Clyde *at Cape Helles on the Gallipoli Peninsula on 25 April 1915. The* River Clyde, *containing 2,000 Allied troops, was deliberately run aground at V Beach, and a series of lighters placed end to end to provide a bridge to the shore. Fierce machine gun fire caused heavy casualties among the soldiers who tried to land.*

peninsula landing of some 70,000 troops without the benefit of surprise, was bold – to say the least. The man appointed by Kitchener to command this Mediterranean Expeditionary Force (MEF) – a mixture of British, French, Australian, and New Zealand troops – and the officer who was eventually to do most of the planning with very little assistance, was Gen **Sir Ian Hamilton**.

The Gallipoli landings took place on 25 April with the government in London anxiously awaiting news. Diversionary attacks were made by the French, who landed on the Asiatic side of the straits near Kum Kale, and a British division that demonstrated at Bulair. Meanwhile, the main British force landed at Cape Helles in the south in order to destroy the forts defending the Narrows, while the Anzacs (Australian and New Zealand Army Corps) – employed for the first time at Gallipoli – attacked the western coast to facilitate an advance across the peninsula that was designed to cut the enemy's lines of communication and prevent reinforcement. Awaiting them were 84,000 Turks.

The landings on the peninsula were not a success. The British landed at five points at Cape Helles while the Anzacs landed at Ari Burnu (soon to become known as Anzac Cove) one mile north of their intended point. Although Hamilton's plan successfully confused the Turkish defenders as to the MEF's intentions thanks to the spread of the landing forces, this was not exploited, despite a lack of opposition in some areas. In other areas,

Gen Townshend, a veteran of the North West Frontier in India, was in command of British and Indian forces when they surrendered to the Turks at Kut-el-Amara on 29 April 1916. Britain had sent troops to Mesopotamia at the end of 1914 to protect the oil refinery at Abadan, and the eventual outcome was as unsuccessful as the conflict at Gallipoli. This time, however, defeat came at the expense of 9,000 British soldiers being captured – news that was received with shock and disbelief in Britain.

Foreground: wounded soldiers from the Munster Fusiliers on a lighter following the Allied landings at Cape Helles on the southern tip of the Gallipoli Peninsula, April 1915. The ruined fortress of Sedd-el-Bahr is in the background. More than half the soldiers who had landed were either killed or injured, and six men from the Royal Navy were each awarded the Victoria Cross for their bravery at one of the landing beaches on 25 April.

Australian soldiers at Anzac Cove on the Gallipoli Peninsula, 17 December 1915. The possibility of evacuating Allied troops from Anzac and Suvla was first raised by the new British commander, Sir Charles Munro, at the end of October, but the Anzac commander, Gen Birdwood, disagreed with this recommendation because he felt the Turks would claim overall victory. The troops remained on the peninsula for another few weeks.

however, well-deployed defensive troops trapped their attackers on the sand and raked them with gunfire. On 'V' beach, for example, the steamer *River Clyde* (which had been converted into a landing vessel) ran into underwater obstacles and had to disgorge its troops into the water. Turkish machine guns cut down the attackers and thwarted the chances of any forward momentum. The Anzac landing met with limited resistance, but initial confusion caused by the inaccuracy of the landings and poor maps gave the Turks valuable time to recover their poise. Although elements of the force moved quickly inland and up to the high ground of Chunuk Bair, Turkish counterattacks pushed them back on to the beach by dusk. Casualties were very heavy.

Thus, by the time darkness fell on 25 April, the Allies had attained little more than lodgements on the Turkish beaches, and rapidly reorganized defenders took up positions on the high ground to ensure that there would be no further advances inland. A stalemate situation – not too dissimilar to that on the Western Front – soon took hold as both sides dug in. Although Hamilton tried to break it, he soon ran into exactly the same problems as Joffre was experiencing about 1,000 miles away. In just two weeks of

'The water was death; the bully beef was death; everything was death. I was afraid to eat a thing. It terrified me; it made me feel dead. A man would pass me holding his stomach, groaning in agony, and a few minutes later I would take him off to the latrine, dead. The men contracted dysentery and fever every day. The bullets did not take a big toll. It was the death of germs.'
Sgt W H Lench, 'The Evacuation of Suvla Bay', (taken from *True World War I Stories*, Robinson Publishing, 1999).

Allied soldiers being evacuated across Suvla Bay on the Gallipoli Peninsula, in December 1915. The evacuation was conducted in broad daylight, but was never detected by the Turkish or German forces. Ironically, this operation was considered to be the most efficient of the entire Gallipoli campaign.

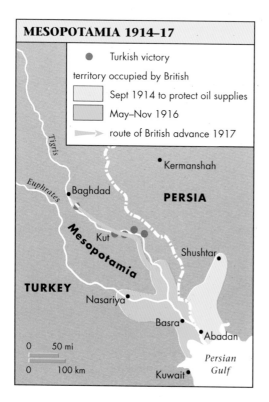

MESOPOTAMIA 1914–17

● Turkish victory

territory occupied by British

☐ Sept 1914 to protect oil supplies

☐ May–Nov 1916

➤ route of British advance 1917

Tigris

Euphrates

Kermanshah

Baghdad

PERSIA

Mesopotamia

Kut

Shushtar

TURKEY

Nasariya

Basra

Abadan

0   50 mi

0   100 km

Kuwait

Persian Gulf

fighting, Hamilton's casualties grew to nearly one third of his force. The response from the British government was to increase the number of troops under his command to nearly 500,000 men – reinforcements that the Western Front could ill afford – and with these men Hamilton mounted another major strike in early August. This attack involved the Anzacs in a night attack to take Chunuk Bair, and a landing at Suvla Bay to create a base from which the northern part of the operation could be supplied. The Anzac push came close to success but was finally defeated by the terrain and exhaustion. In the Suvla operation 25,000 men landed well, but were thwarted when their commander, Sir Frederick Stopford, failed to exploit the opportunity presented to him to outflank the Turks defending at Anzac Cove.

The August failures led to the dismissal of Hamilton, and command of the MEF being given to Sir Charles Monro on 22 October. Monro immediately advised an evacuation of the peninsula – in the words of Churchill, 'He came, he saw, he capitulated,' – and the War Cabinet agreed. Ironically, the evacuation of the peninsula was the most successful

Oil trucks in a railway siding at Black Town. World War I was the first major conflict in which oil played a crucial role in the conduct of war. The increasing mechanization of war in the form of motorized vehicles, aircraft, tanks, and ships meant that oil was now an indispensable commodity.

operation of the campaign, with the troops at both Anzac Cove and Cape Helles being withdrawn by early January 1916 without loss of life. Nevertheless the overall cost of the fighting had been great, with the Allies suffering 180,000 casualties and the Turks many more. The Gallipoli campaign was a failure and, importantly, had diverted over half a million valuable troops away from the Western Front. Haig, the new commander-in-chief of the BEF, did not want to see the situation repeated.

Mesopotamia

The British war against the Turks was not confined to Gallipoli. Indeed, Britain sent troops to Mesopotamia in order to protect the oil refinery at Abadan as early as November 1914. From these small beginnings, a large campaign grew. In April of the following year advances of hundreds of miles were made by Gen Sir John Nixon along the Tigris and Euphrates rivers in order to keep the Turks at bay. The success of these operations led to the seizure of Kut in September, and with it the heady possibility of entering Baghdad. However, when the British continued their offensive, the Turks exploited their overextended lines of communication and launched a successful counterattack that managed to drive Gen Sir Charles Townsend's 13,500-man force back into Kut. The siege of this fortress town lasted from December 1915 until the end of April 1916, when the British forces surrendered as a result of a desperate lack of food and water.

Having failed in their attempts to relieve Kut, the rest of the Mesopotamian army spent most of 1916 reorganizing at Basra under their new commander, Maj Gen Sir Frederick Maude. Reinforced by three extra divisions during this period, Maude launched another attack towards

The Australia medal, issued to commemorate the Gallipoli Landings on 25 April 1915. Australian and New Zealand forces had been diverted from Egypt on their way to the Western Front, with Lord Kitchener judging somewhat complacently that they would suffice for the task of dealing with the Turkish forces in the peninsula.

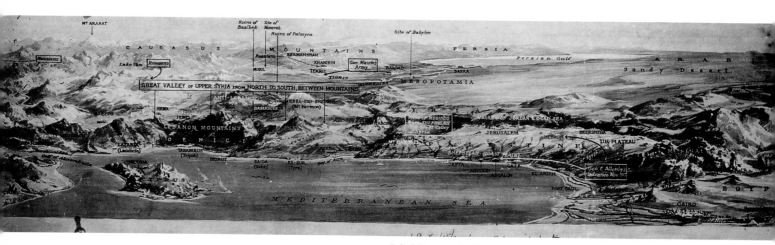

Relief diagram of Palestine from the Mediterranean Sea, indicating the Palestine and Mesopotamia campaigns, and the Russian campaign in the Caucasus mountains beyond.

The ruins of Kut in Mesopotamia in March 1917. Following the disasters of 15 months before – when their forces had to be evacuated from Gallipoli, and Kut fell – Allied fortunes took a turn for the better in 1917. On 24 February, British and Indian forces advanced on Kut, and retook the city along with more than 1,700 prisoners.

Mesopotamia

November 1914: Britain sends troops to Mesopotamia to protect the oil refinery at Abadan against Turkish forces.

April 1915: advances of hundreds of miles are made by Allied forces along the Tigris and Euphrates rivers in order to keep the Turks at bay.

September 1915: seizure of Kut by Allied forces.

December 1915: Turkish counterattack that manages to drive British troops, now trying to advance into Baghdad, back to Kut.

April 1916: British troops, beseiged in Kut, finally surrender. They reorganize at Basra under a new commander, Maj Gen Sir Frederick Maude.

December 1916: another attack towards Baghdad launched.

February 1917: Kut taken by Allied forces.

March 1917: Baghdad taken by Allied forces.

Baghdad in December. The mixture of a slower and more methodical attitude towards attack, helped by numerical superiority, led to a Turkish withdrawal and Kut being taken in late February 1917, with Baghdad falling during the following month. Success had been achieved, but for what and at what price? It is not clear how the taking of Baghdad was meant to help attain Allied war aims; indeed, it could be argued that in diverting nearly half a million troops away from the Western Front, the campaign was detrimental to the Allied cause.

British troops entering Baghdad via the Southern Gate on 11 March 1917. The British mood was in sharp contrast to Gen Townshend's miserable tramp through the same city a year earlier as a prisoner-of-war following his surrender at Kut-el-Amara.

Sinai and Palestine

The Turks in the Sinai and Palestine also managed to pin down valuable British resources some distance from their main enemy. As in Mesopotamia, the initial British involvement was defensive. The Turks attacked the Suez Canal in early 1915 and although this was rebuffed, the British were unable to pursue their enemy across the Sinai. Nevertheless, the Turkish actions frightened the British enough to undertake offensive operations in order to keep the Turks at a safe distance from the canal. This attack began in February 1916 and saw Gen Sir Archibald Murray's force establish a new defensive position 160 km/100 mi east of the waterway by the end of the year. Further similarities with the Mesopotamian campaign can be seen in Murray's next move, as he began to evaluate the possibility of a prestigious British military victory in Palestine. How this would have aided British political aims – other than tying down Turkish resources – is unclear. What is undeniable, however, is that success in Palestine would certainly have been to the advantage of greater British influence in the region after the war.

Murray's first step towards Jerusalem – an attempt to seize Gaza in early 1917 – was unsuccessful. Tenacious Turkish defence led to high British casualties and a new commander, **Gen Sir Edmund Allenby**. Once

Capt the Hon E Cadogan surveys the ruins of the city of Gaza in Palestine following its capture by British troops on 7 November 1917. An Anglo-French offshore naval bombardment had pummelled the city before the British assault – when soldiers entered the city, they discovered that the Turks had looted it before they withdrew.

Lawrence, T E (1888–1935)

Thomas Edward Lawrence was born in Wales and studied at Oxford before becoming an archaeologist. Between 1910 and 1914, Lawrence took part in expeditions to Syria and Mesopotamia, attaining a deep interest in and knowledge of Arab language, culture, and customs. At the outbreak of war he was recalled to England, and was subsequently employed as an intelligence officer in Cairo, producing maps of the Arab regions. When the sheriff of Mecca revolted against the Turks in 1916, Lawrence was given the rank of colonel and went with the British Mission to King Hussein. There he helped reorganize the Arab army, which he then led in guerrilla operations on the flank of the British Army in Palestine between 1916 and 1918. At the end of the war he was awarded the DSO for his services, and became adviser to the Foreign Office on Arab affairs. Disappointed by the failure of the Paris Peace Conference to establish Arab independence, he joined the Royal Air Force in 1922 as an aircraftman under the name Ross, and wrote several volumes about his experiences with the Arabs (including *Seven Pillars of Wisdom*). He was killed in a motorcycle accident in 1935.

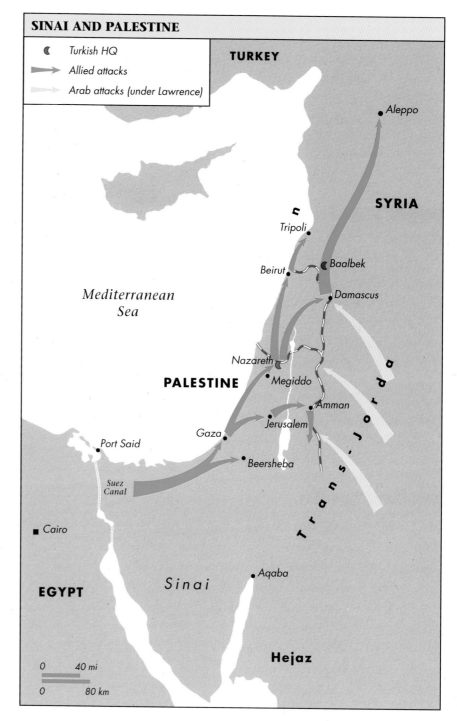

SINAI AND PALESTINE

- ☾ Turkish HQ
- ➤ Allied attacks
- ⟶ Arab attacks (under Lawrence)

TURKEY

SYRIA

Aleppo

Tripoli

Beirut • Baalbek

Mediterranean Sea

Damascus

Nazareth

PALESTINE • Megiddo

Amman

Port Said

Gaza • Jerusalem

Beersheba

Trans-Jordan

Suez Canal

■ Cairo

EGYPT • Aqaba

Sinai

Hejaz

0 ——— 40 mi
0 ——— 80 km

Col T E Lawrence, 'Lawrence of Arabia', in Arab dress in 1917. Lawrence had acquired a deep interest in the Arab language and culture before World War I, and this knowledge was extremely useful to the British in understanding Arab intentions and advising on conduct of the war in desert conditions.

Allenby was in situ, he was to benefit directly from Lloyd George's preference for the 'indirect approach', for just a matter of weeks before major Allied attacks started on the Western Front, he increased the Middle Eastern force to a quarter of a million men. Also providing the campaign with assistance was the Arab revolt against Turkish rule in the Hejaz. Thus, while Allenby was scoring successes at Beersheba and at Gaza, guerrilla activities by Arab forces led by a British officer, **Col T E Lawrence (Lawrence of Arabia)**, threatened the Turkish flank and tied down many of their resources. Allenby entered Jerusalem on 9 December 1917.

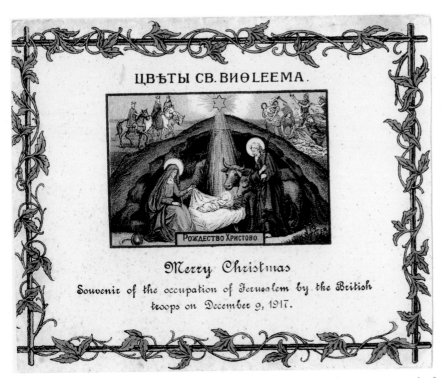

A Christmas card issued to the troops as souvenir of the British occupation of Jerusalem in December 1917.

Allenby, Field Marshal Sir Edmund (1861–1936)

Sir Edmund Allenby commanded a division, a corps, and an army (the Third Army) on the Western Front before taking up the role of commander-in-chief of British forces in the Middle East in 1917. Known as 'The Bull' due to his ferocious temper and great size, Allenby gained a high reputation while in Palestine for the success of his mobile campaign. Against a far weaker and less well-organized army than was to be found in France or Flanders, Allenby nevertheless advanced skilfully and swiftly, and seized Jerusalem in December 1917. After a break in his campaigning, Allenby's forces achieved success in the Battle of Megiddo in September 1918, and eventually entered Damascus just after T E Lawrence in early October.

Plans for further British advances in the Middle East during early 1918 were postponed due to the serious setback caused by the German spring offensives on the Western Front, but Allenby's campaign continued after the BEF had turned the tide, and Haig was gaining offensive momentum of his own. Success at Megiddo in September, together with the continued pressure that Lawrence was exerting in the enemy's rearguard, forced the Turks to fall back on Damascus. However, they had little time to prepare their defences; Allenby reached the city just after Lawrence and the Arabs on 1 October, and the Turkish garrison of 20,000 was taken prisoner. Elsewhere, Beirut was taken on 2 October and Aleppo (320 km/200 mi further north) by 25 October. This succession of defeats led to an armistice with Turkey on 30 October. The campaign in Palestine had cost the British 50,000 casualties.

Sideshows?

The debate is still raging as to whether the 'peripheral' campaigns of World War I helped the Allies win the war, or were simply a waste of resources. What is clear, however, is that while the Allies gained success in some areas relatively cheaply, in others they failed or, at best, gained success at great cost in terms of manpower and other valuable resources. The campaigning against Turkey, for example, cost some 250,000 casualties. It could be argued – as the 'Westerners' did at the time – that had the vast resources required to sustain the 'sideshows' been made available to commanders on the Western Front, they would have had a

'Three telegrams I handled that winter stick in my memory. One from General Allenby to the 60th Divisional General when Jerusalem was taken. It read "Congratulations. Psalm 122, v. 2."

I looked it up. "Our feet shall stand within thy gates, O Jerusalem." I thought it rather decent of Allenby.'

H P Bonser, 'A Sapper in Palestine', (taken from *True World War I Stories*, Robinson Publishing, 1999).

Anti-British graffiti on a street wall in Baghdad. The writer is one of the Turkish defenders attempting to prevent the advancing British troops from taking the city. The British force had marched over 160 km/100 mi in fifteen days.

Gen Allenby's official entry into Jerusalem via the Jaffa Gate on 11 December 1917. The Turkish army had abandoned the city, saving the British forces from having to take it by force. As he had been instructed, Allenby's entry was on foot, avoiding an inevitable comparison with Kaiser Wilhelm's triumphal entry to the city on horseback in 1898.

Salonika

Bulgarian mobilization in September 1915 made the Allies wary of an impending attack on Serbia, and so two divisions (one British and one French) were sent under Gen Sarrail to the Greek port of Salonika. Arriving on neutral soil on 5 October, the force soon moved forward in an attempt to link up with the Serb army. However, it soon became clear to the Allies that a large Bulgarian force blocked their route, and so a retreat back to Salonika was ordered. Numerous inconclusive attacks and counter-attacks occupied the troops in the region over the next couple of years, and by the beginning of 1917, a total of 600,000 Allied troops had been deployed there. The final offensive took place under the command of Gen Franchet d'Espérey in September 1918 when a combined force of some 200,000 Serb, French, British, and Greek troops (the Greeks joined the Allies in 1917) forced an enemy withdrawal. Although Bulgaria eventually signed an armistice on 29 September, Allied casualties in the campaign amounted to 481,000, the vast majority of which were from malaria.

more decisive impact. Indeed, in many cases the 'indirect approach' looked as though the strategic decision-makers were happy to sanction even the most ill-conceived plans in the forlorn hope of side-stepping the deadlock of the Western Front.

The Gallipoli campaign was a case in point. While it was designed as a potential 'shortcut to victory', the concept was fatally flawed by the lack of an achievable military objective. Of course, there were undoubted military successes in the course of these peripheral campaigns, but they tended to be achieved where they had little impact upon the ability of the Allies to overcome their main enemy: Germany. In such circumstances, the fighting that took place away from the Western Front was probably a luxury that the Allies could ill afford.

CHAPTER 6
SUSTAINING WAR

If a belligerent is to have any chance of success, all conflicts require the nation to be able to sustain the war effort (in whatever form that might take) – both on the home front as well as on the fighting front. However, the unexpected length and intensity of World War I tested to the full the ability of combatant nations to mobilize all of their human, economic, and technological resources. There were many ways of attaining total mobilization and sustaining it between 1914 and 1918; indeed, the tools and methods employed during the war revealed much about the social, political, and economic make-up of the individual nations – but there were no second chances, and the cost of failure was immense.

Schoolchildren in Rheims, France, wearing their gas-masks. Gas was used in the trenches by the Germans for the first time on 22 April 1915, and the authorities feared it could eventually be used against civilian populations.

Lloyd George, David (1863–1945)

David Lloyd George was trained as a solicitor and entered Parliament as a Liberal in 1890. By 1908 he was chancellor of the Exchequer, and his radical budget of the following year revealed his desire for social reform and the establishment of a welfare state. During World War I, Lloyd George continued as chancellor of the Exchequer but was later made minister of munitions (1915) and then replaced Asquith as prime minister in December 1916. Lloyd George reinvigorated the war effort, particularly on the home front, and subordinated everything to that end. As a leading 'Easterner' and a politician struggling to restore civilian control to the running of the war, he inevitably had many clashes with the military. He had a particularly difficult relationship with Sir Douglas Haig, as he found the High Command's demand for massive offensives highly unpalatable. Nevertheless, Lloyd George and Haig saw the war through to a victorious conclusion together, both men having attained and maintained their pre-eminent positions. Lloyd George won the post-war election and played a leading role in the Paris Peace Conference. He opposed the hard-line approach towards Germany, and had little enthusiasm for the establishment of the League of Nations. He remained prime minister until 1922.

David Lloyd George on a visit to a trench at Fricourt, September 1916. Having been minister of munitions, Lloyd George became prime minister of a coalition government in December 1916.

Politics and the Economy

The decisions that were made concerning the mobilization of the state depended very much upon the nature of the political system that was in place to fight the war more generally. With the war expected to be short, the military in most belligerent nations took a crucial guiding hand in the running of the war early on – in Britain it was Lord Kitchener, in France it was Joffre, and in Germany it was Falkenhayn. But as the war dragged on, the civilian politicians reasserted their control in the Allied nations, and this helped to ensure that the sustaining of the war was not done without consideration for the needs of those remaining on the home front. This was not the case in the Central Powers, for here the military increased their influence with disastrous consequences for the civilian population.

French police examine civilians' passports in Amiens. At the end of March 1918, a determined German assault saw their forces just over 80 km/50 mi from Paris, but solid British and French defence held the line, and Amiens was saved from being overrun. Had Amiens fallen, the next stop for the Germans would have been the French capital.

In Britain, Kitchener's abrasive manner and leadership style, while continuing to woo the population, served only to alienate his civilian colleagues. His powers were gradually diminished by the elected politicians who were bent on readjusting the power balance. In the politicking that followed, the vigorous and dynamic **David Lloyd George** (who was first chancellor of the Exchequer and then became minister of munitions) managed to oust Asquith as prime minister in December 1916. Although far from cutting the military out of the decision-making process, this move did begin to limit its influence, and helped to

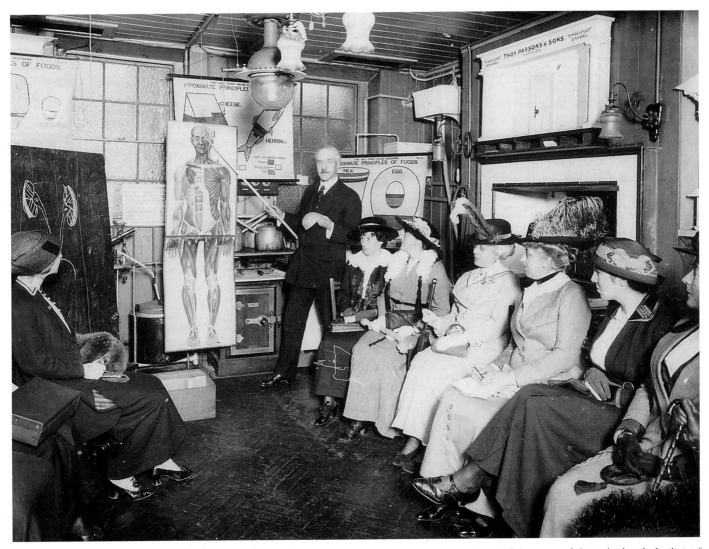

Dr R Murray Leslie is seen lecturing to Red Cross nurses being trained at the Institute of Hygiene in September 1914. Women were to become a crucial part of the British war effort.

facilitate the sort of efficient total mobilization that was to prove so crucial to the Allies in the dark days of the war that were yet to come.

Prior to Lloyd George becoming prime minister, Britain had only slowly emerged from a period of 'business as usual'. During this time there had not been massive government interference in national life, because the politicians assumed there would be a swift and victorious conclusion to the war. Such was the confidence of the government in this outcome that the first budget of the war, presented by Lloyd George on 16 November 1914, did not make any provisions for new taxes, and raised existing taxes only a little in certain cases. The nation was lulled into a false sense of security, and a semblance of normality reigned while the war raged and support of the war continued to run high. 'Business as usual' ended with the Battle of Neuve Chapelle in March 1915, which revealed the undisputed need to fight a total war. The government responded and cautiously began to take up the slack in the nation's reigns.

'Governments have the entire responsibility for the home front. That front is always underrated by generals in the field. And yet that is where the Great War was won and lost. The Russian, Bulgarian, Austrian, and German home fronts fell to pieces before their armies collapsed.'
Lloyd George, *War Memoirs.*

Women at War

Women made some notable gains in Britain during the war years, hastening the introduction of universal suffrage after the war. In 1914 skilled male workers in munitions and ordnance factories began to leave work for the trenches, and non-skilled female 'dilutees' slowly replaced some of them. These women were largely working class, but also included some middle-class and upper-class women determined to 'do their bit'. By late summer 1915, women began to work in a wide variety of jobs; some women took over their husbands' jobs and became farriers and decorators, while others went into non-manual trades to become drivers and railway employees. Banks and offices also employed ever larger numbers of women in jobs traditionally reserved for men.

By 1916 women were in even greater demand than before due to the introduction of conscription, and were increasingly seen as a vital component in the war effort. This gave women both recognition and increased self-confidence and lent weight to the argument that they should be enfranchised. David Lloyd George said in July 1915, 'Without women victory will tarry, and the victory which tarries means a victory whose footprints are footprints of blood.' On 6 February 1918, an Act was passed enfranchising all women over the age of 30 who were married to registered voters.

A woman takes over her father's duties as Bill Poster and Town Crier in Thetford, Norfolk. The posters urge all men 'over military age or exempted' to join up as volunteers and 'help our boys abroad'.

During the spring of 1915, the government recognized the need not only to put men in uniform in order to fight, but also to put people in industry in order to produce. This delicate soldier–civilian balancing act required greater government control over British manpower resources as increasing numbers of men were required at the front, so replacements had to be found for them in the workplace. By the end of 1915, with some 2.5 million men having volunteered for military service, industry was having difficulty in finding suitable replacements – a situation that became no easier when universal conscription was introduced in May 1916.

The Munitions of War Act was passed in July 1915 in a desperate attempt to tackle these problems formally. The Defence of the Realm Act had been in place since August 1914 and enabled the state to assume wide powers, but the Munitions of War Act aimed to ensure that Britain had the quality of munitions required to fight the war successfully. The act ended the ability of trade unions to strike and engage in restrictive practices. Skilled jobs became open to the unskilled, semi-skilled, and to women – a situation that the unions did not like. Nevertheless, compensation in the form of higher pay, and even Labour Party representation in Lloyd George's five-man War Cabinet (in the form of Arthur Henderson), went some way towards appeasing them.

Others also gained benefit from the war. There were more opportunities for those looking for work and, thanks to longer hours and war bonuses, pay packets were fatter. The unintentional benefits that the war brought to some people certainly helped to sugar-coat the bitter pill of war. By 1917, however, a war-weary Britain was still suffering the trauma of the fighting-front casualties, still being subjected to **air raids**, and was also beginning to have to contend with price rises and the first real shortages of the war. Although there was no widespread privation, submarine warfare did lead to a shortage of some basic commodities, including sugar, coal, potatoes, and margarine, and this led to inevitable queues. On 8 April 1917, *The Observer* newspaper reported:

> 'The usual weekend potato and coal scenes took place in London yesterday. At Edmonton 131 vehicles were lined up at the gates of a coal depot at nine o'clock in the morning, while crowds numbered several hundreds. There were also bread and potato queues of such a length that the police had to regulate them, and newcomers had to inquire which was the particular queue that they wanted.'

Situations such as this led to increased government intervention during 1917 in order to minimize the suffering. The establishment of a food controller, a food ministry, rationing, and price controls were all a result of this difficult period and, as we shall see, so was increased propaganda. The fact that there was no major difficulty with civilian morale in Britain during the war is in no small part testament to the success of the government's mobilization programme.

Just like the British, the French also wanted to have civilian direction of their war effort. Although Joffre was the key figure in France during the first two years of the war, the civilians slowly reassumed their former primacy, and by December 1916 Briand (the French prime minister) had manipulated the Verdun crisis to replace Joffre with Gen Robert Nivelle. However, it was not until 1917 and the premiership of **Georges Clemenceau** that the right of the prime minister to have the final say over military policy was finally re-established.

Women coke workers help load a large bag of coal onto a carrier's back. Coal was vital for the pursuit of the war effort and, with all able-bodied men being sent to fight on various fronts, women were pressed into service in roles that had previously been only the preserve of men.

LONDON COUNTY COUNCIL.

AIR RAIDS

During danger from an air raid all children will remain inside the school buildings; all gates will be shut, and no one will be admitted. Crowding round the school premises only increases the danger.

No place is absolutely safe, but experience shows that children are safer in school buildings than if sent out into the streets.

The London County Council is doing all it can to secure the safety of the children, and it is hoped that parents will help by leaving their children entirely under the control of the teachers until all danger is over.

L.C.C. EDUCATION OFFICES.
June, 1917.

R. BLAIR,
EDUCATION OFFICER.

Watson & Son Limited Printers London Wall London

A London County Council air-raid notice issued in June 1917. The first Zeppelin airship raid on Britain took place on 19 January 1915, when two airships bombed Great Yarmouth and King's Lynn with the loss of four lives. Airship raids intensified during 1916, and in April East London was targeted five times.

Women operating cranes in a shell-filling factory in Chilwell, Nottingham. By April 1916, almost 200,000 women were being employed in war-related industries, and nor were they immune to death themselves – on the second of the month, 106 people were killed (many of them women) in an accidental explosion in a munitions factory at Faversham in Kent. And in Silvertown, East London, 69 women were killed and 72 injured when fire ignited 45 tonnes/50 tons of TNT high explosive, flattening a wide area of London's East End.

Strategic Bombing

The development of air power in World War I allowed for bombing raids to be carried out on factories, transportation, and even the homes of civilian workers. Although these fitful attacks failed to be of any strategic consequence, they did cause some panic, and valuable resources were diverted away from the fighting fronts for protection. The giant German Zeppelin airships (which had a range and bomb-carrying capacity far greater than aircraft of the day) first flew over British cities in night raids during 1915. By the end of 1916, however, the hydrogen-filled airships were made extremely vulnerable due to the development of incendiary bullets and effective night-fighting techniques. The introduction of twin-engined Gotha bombers in 1917 once again gave the advantage to the attackers, and they were used in several successful daylight raids. On 25 May 1917, for example, 21 Gothas flew over the English Channel from bases in occupied Belgium and dropped five tonnes of bombs on to Folkestone in Kent, killing 95 people and injuring another 260. These raids led to the deployment of defensive fighter squadrons in Southern England, and an elaborate London Air Defence Area. On 19 May 1918 the last Gotha raid on London took place, during which six bombers were shot down by fighters and a barrage of 30,000 anti-aircraft shells was fired. British attacks on Germany had begun in the autumn of 1916 with raids on industrial targets in the Saar basin. After six months the diversion of resources away from the Western Front brought the campaign to an end, but Gotha raids left the population wanting retaliation. The campaign that followed was not a success and was soon ended by the armistice.

Damage inflicted by the German Zeppelin raid on Great Yarmouth in early 1915 – the first airship raids of the war on Britain. These huge lighter-than-air craft were first used in anger by Germany on the city of Antwerp at the end of August 1914, and were perceived at the time to have no viable response. However, it was not long before their inherent vulnerability in terms of slow speed and flammability became obvious.

Although it took time for military control of the war to wane, the French ability to sustain it – although also slow to get going – soon gathered some momentum. The consortium system, created in 1916 by Etienne Clémentel, the minister of commerce, was an efficient and effective way of producing what France required to fight the war. The roots of this system were to be found in the French reliance on British economic support during the conflict. The situation meant that Britain controlled the majority of vital supplies that French industry required to fulfil production targets. As Britain virtually controlled French supply, so Clémentel justified his control of supply to individual firms. By doing this he diminished the power of companies and placed the government firmly in command of production, so that quality, quantity, and cost could be controlled. It was through this system that the French government ensured that prices did not spiral and the population's standard of living was not unduly diminished.

The contrast between how the Allies and Germany sustained their war efforts is telling. In Germany, the outbreak of war brought about a less dramatic change in the power structure, as the nation was already used to limits on parliamentary power and the dominance of the army. As the war progressed, however, the military grip on control of the war effort increased rather than declined, and the importance of the Reichstag (German parliament) diminished as a result. The influence of Hindenburg and Ludendorff, the 'Silent Dictatorship', from late 1916 onwards revealed the fast-developing emphasis upon the army in Germany. Indeed, the decision to begin unrestricted submarine warfare in February 1917 was taken against the wishes of Chancellor Bethmann-Hollweg, who resigned in July 1917 and was replaced by the pliable Dr Georg Michaelis.

Hindenburg and Ludendorff were not blinded to the fact that Germany needed to mobilize totally in this war of attrition, but the methods that they employed were not wholly appropriate. Building on the foundations for a centralized economy laid by the industrialist Walther Rathenau, the military partnership sought to overcome the shortages of key materials brought about by the Allied blockade by continuing to produce synthetic materials and by giving the army and industry full control over the economy. The 'Hindenburg Plan' demanded massive increases in industrial output, and by allowing industry to run it the aim was to ensure efficiency. However, the result was an imbalance between production and the well-being of a nation at war. Thus while the army continued to take men out of the workplace for the fighting front and firms grew fat on big military contracts, competition was crushed and costs spiralled. War production did increase, but at the expense of turmoil on the home front as the government lost control of inflation and shortages bit deep. The continuing Allied blockade, attrition on the Western Front, bureaucratic inefficiencies, and harvest failures only made a bad situation worse. For the average German citizen, official rations were insufficient and starvation was only kept at bay by the black market. The winter of 1916–17 was known as the 'Turnip Winter' due to the lack of food, and the morale of the nation began to suffer due to their many sacrifices and privations. By mid-1918 – and not dissociated from morale problems in the army – social disorder gripped the nation.

Clemenceau, Georges (1841–1929)

Georges Clemenceau was a very experienced politician by the time World War I broke out. Nicknamed 'the Tiger' on account of his ferocious attacks on politicians whom he disliked, he was one of the most powerful politicians in France before the war and was prime minister from 1906 to 1909. Although he was out of office for the first three years of the war, he became prime minister for the second time in 1917 at the age of 76, and struggled to regain civilian control over the war. He carried out his difficult role with great determination, and revealed many much-needed leadership qualities. After World War I, Clemenceau presided over the Paris Peace Conference but failed to secure for France the Rhine as a frontier, and was later criticized for being too lenient towards Germany. He served as prime minister until 1920.

A ruined shop in the French town of Abbeville near the English Channel coast.

To obtain meat for a meal, starving Germans set about the carcass of a horse that had been killed. As usual in wartime, civilians suffered heavily during the conflict – more than 250,000 German civilians died in 1917 as a result of starvation.

'The scene has changed fundamentally. The six weeks' march to Paris had grown into a world drama. Mass slaughter has become the tiresome and monotonous business of the day and the end is no closer... Gone is the euphoria.'

'Nowhere is the press so hobbled, public opinion so stifled, the economic and political class struggle of the working class so totally surrendered as in Germany.'

Rosa Luxemburg, 'The War and the Workers', *The Junius Pamphlet*, 1916.

Thus, Germany did manage to produce what the army required in most cases, but it was at the expense of the civilians left on the home front. During a protracted war when sacrifice was great, forgetting the needs of the 'producers' was neglect of an ultimately disastrous type. The Allies recognized the needs of their civilians, and while they too suffered as a result of the war, their morale was upheld as they were taken into partnership with the state for the duration. The German population, on the other hand, was cruelly exploited.

The Press at War

If civilians were crucial to the sustaining of the war, then it was a naïve nation that overlooked the information that they were fed about the conflict. Therefore the press was potentially a key tool in the government's propaganda war, but just as 'business as usual' dominated Britain in an

Men from the Hampshire Regiment attach leaflets to a propaganda balloon near Béthune, 4 September 1918. Even as late as April 1918, the Allied forces were in a serious situation on the Western Front, and it was at this point that Gen Haig issued his famous 'backs to the wall' statement with orders to fight to the last man.

Rationing

There were substantial variations in living standards in wartime Europe. In Germany, wartime wages dropped by an average of 10% each year during the conflict, while in France and Britain – although real wages were eroded early on – gains were made later. The amount of food available also varied considerably. In Germany the food that civilians could obtain was limited due to the army having priority, the Allied blockade, and poor harvests. Official German wartime rations did not provide anywhere near the calories required, and so the rest had to come from the black market. The Allied populations did not suffer nearly as much, because lines of supply were kept open, governments ensured that civilians did not starve, and agricultural production was at least maintained and often even increased.

Russian women and children receiving their bread ration. Even before the outbreak of World War I, poverty was widespread in Europe, accentuating class differences.

economic sense during the first two years of fighting, so the same could be said of the press. In fact the British government interfered very little with the press throughout the war. The self-regulation that dominated the relationship between newspapers and the war came about because the British press wished actively to help the government fight and win the war. The shelling of the northeast coast of England by a German cruiser in December 1914, for example, left over 100 people dead; while it could not be said that the story was sensitively handled, the report of the incident (accompanied by photographs of those who perished) coincided with a rush to the recruiting stations, the like of which had not been seen

FRIGHTFULNESS IN RUINS.

Ruins of the Zeppelin brought down near
Enfield on Sept. 3rd, 1916.

Skeleton of one of the Zeppelins brought down in Essex on Sept. 24th, 1916.

Wreckage of one of the Zeppelins brought down
in Essex on Sept. 24th, 1916.

The wrecked Zeppelin L.15, brought down at the mouth of
the Thames on March 31st, 1916.

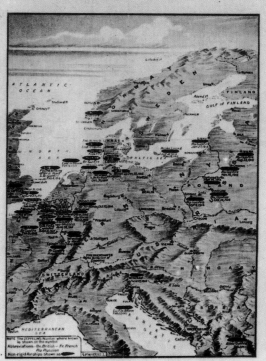

Where the Zeppelins have been brought down
(N.B.—This map does not include losses subsequent to Sept. 3rd, 1916).

Zeppelin L.20, wrecked off the coast of Norway
on May 3rd, 1916.

Wreckage of the Zeppelin brought down at Salonica
on May 5th, 1916.

Wreckage of the Zeppelin brought down at Salonica
on May 5th, 1916.

THE ALLIES' TOLL OF GERMANY'S ZEPPELIN FLEET.

German's war on children: funeral leaving the church.

After a German air-raid: funeral of some of the victims.

*British propaganda poster entitled 'Frightfulness in Ruins', issued in 1916 to try to convince the population
of the fallibility of the German airships. The poster gives a litany of Zeppelins 'brought down' over Europe.*

since August. However, while censorship of home news was remarkably lax, initial government censorship of war news was overly harsh and led to the creation of atrocity stories by copy-hungry journalists. Siegfried Sassoon wrote in his semi-autobiographical *Memoirs of a Fox-Hunting Man* (1928) that, 'The newspapers informed us that German soldiers crucified Belgian babies. Stories of that kind were taken for granted; to have disbelieved them would have been unpatriotic.' These atrocity stories (which were based in truth at this stage) might well have been the result of the government's clumsy handling of censorship, but at least the press created copy that sought to further British interests in the war. Indeed, the mass-circulation press also helpfully lashed out at pacifists, conscientious objectors, socialists, strikers, aliens, and 'shirkers' while continually praising the British military for their efforts.

The news department of the Foreign Office in London. Perhaps surprisingly, there was little government interference with the press during the war. However, censorship would have achieved little – particularly in relation to the high casualty figures among Allied forces – because by 1916 most families had already had to grieve for at least one relative lost to the conflict.

Was British popular support for the war therefore based upon a lack of real knowledge about the carnage that was taking place just across the English Channel? Although it might be expected that the population was shielded from the casualties – and to a certain extent this is true – the government soon realized that it was impossible to keep the nation ignorant about military losses (even if it might have been helpful). By the end of 1916 there were few families in Britain who had not grieved for a loved one. Major railway stations received trains of wounded soldiers and such men, dressed in distinctive blue uniforms, became a common sight on Britain's streets. Newspapers carried lists of about 4,000 casualties daily. It was also easy to read about casualties in the provincial press, which published not only casualty lists but also photographs of local men who

Soldiers wounded during the Battle of the Somme leave Charing Cross Station on 8 July 1916 after their arrival from France. Beginning on 1 July, the battle was an ill-judged attempt by Anglo-French forces to break through German lines with a massive infantry assault; it wasn't long before casualties were being taken in huge numbers.

RED CROSS OR IRON CROSS?

WOUNDED AND A PRISONER
OUR SOLDIER CRIES FOR WATER.

THE GERMAN "SISTER"
POURS IT ON THE GROUND BEFORE HIS EYES.

THERE IS NO WOMAN IN BRITAIN
WHO WOULD DO IT.

THERE IS NO WOMAN IN BRITAIN
WHO WILL FORGET IT.

THE DANGERFIELD PRINTING CO. LTD. LONDON

A British propaganda poster detailing German atrocities. Stories began to circulate in Britain of the most barbaric treatment of British prisoners by their German captors, and British newspapers even carried stories of Germans crucifying Belgian babies.

The government pass of an official British war photographer. Official photographers would have taken the majority of the photos reproduced in this book.

had been killed, together with a short obituary. These papers seem not to have been as rigorously censored as their national counterparts. Generally, local newspapers carried more truthful accounts than the nationals; during the battle of Loos in 1915, for example, the *Northampton Daily Chronicle* ran the headline, '7th Northampton's Cut Up'. Of course, civilians on the home front could never truly understand what it was like to serve in the front line, but the population did not lack information about the human cost of the war.

The relationship of the German state with the press was very different from that encountered in Britain. While a strategy of cooperation was made possible in London by prominent newspapermen and proprietors (such as Lord Northcliffe and Lord Beaverbrook) being well integrated into the social and political scene, in Germany newspaper proprietors were shunned. Consequently, although German newspapers were patriotic and generally supportive of the war at the outset, the fact remained that because newspapers reflected and did not shape political events, they began to reflect the increasingly desperate situation of the home front and even to question the validity of German war aims. In these circumstances, there was little that could be done in Berlin to stop them.

Throughout the war, the difficulty for Germany was that despite the increasingly strong grip of the military dictatorship upon the running of the war, they were increasingly impotent on the home front. The problems caused by the military regime in Germany were myriad but, crucially, by putting the needs of the fighting front before the needs of the home front, and by losing control of war production, they severely undermined the German war effort. Meanwhile, in both Britain and France the return to civilian control led to efficient production and policies designed to ensure a placid home front. The road to Allied victory in World War I was created on the home front.

CHAPTER 7
FRANCE AND RUSSIA STRETCHED

The year 1916 was to prove a crucial one in the war – it was a year in which the strategy of attrition began to bite deep and the ability to sustain total war was put through a series of tests. The long battles of 1916 on the Western Front resulted in massive casualties in return for relatively little ground, and although these protracted struggles had important long-term implications for the course of the war, the battles of Verdun and the Somme are widely considered to have been completely futile.

German Red Cross personnel carry a wounded British soldier away from the battlefield at La Boisselle during the Battle of the Somme, on 3 July 1916.

But perhaps these battles were an essential element of the war. Did they achieve anything concrete? Did Allied commanders learn anything from them? Was the Busilov Offensive on the Eastern Front also futile? And, crucially, can we say whether the 1916 offensives impacted on the rest of the war? If we could answer these questions, it is possible they would put the apparently reckless actions of some Allied commanders in a different light.

The damaged town of Verdun on 14 November 1916, seen from across the river Meuse. The Battle of Verdun was the longest and most costly of the whole of World War I; the countryside around the town became a sea of mud, and between them the Germans and French lost one million men.

1916 Strategy

The first meeting of representatives from the French, British, Russian, and Italian armies took place at Joffre's headquarters at Chantilly on 6 December 1915. Their aim was to discuss Allied strategy for the coming year – plans that were to have massive repercussions for millions of fighting troops and, ultimately, for the future direction of the war. Recognizing that the Central Powers were suffering greatly from having to fight on three separate fronts, the Allies decided at Chantilly to play on this weakness by coordinating their 1916 offensives. Thus a Franco-British attack on the Somme, an Italian push on the Isonzo, and a major Russian attack into East Prussia were planned.

In order to carry out these offensives, the Allies needed time to prepare themselves. The British, for example, needed time to train, equip, and deploy their 'New Army', the Russians needed time to recuperate after their 1915 setbacks, and all required time to stockpile munitions.

However, while the Allies were planning their offensive actions for the middle of the year, the Germans struck first.

The Battle of Verdun

The German decision to attack on the Western Front was influenced by the minimal threat posed by the Russians in the wake of 1915. The situation gave Falkenhayn the breathing space to strike a blow on the front that he considered the most important – the Western Front. He chose Verdun for his attack because he believed it was a city that the French would fight to protect to the bitter end – a necessity in view of the attritional battle that he intended to fight in order to 'bleed the French white'.

The means by which Falkenhayn hoped to achieve this was to advance towards Verdun, eliminate the salient in his line caused by earlier fighting, force the French to pour in vast numbers of reserves, and then destroy them with his artillery. However, what the plan assumed was that the German troops would be able to exert such a pressure on Joffre's troops that they would be unable to resist. It was a dangerous assumption to make, but was central to the way in which Germany fought the battle.

In an area studded with French forts and numerous lines of trenches, Falkenhayn endeavoured to break through to Verdun by concentrating his forces (the German Fifth Army under Crown Prince Wilhelm) to the east of

'Terrible in the desolation of the night, on fire, haunted by spectres of wounded men who crept along the narrow lanes by the city walls, Verdun was once more undergoing the destinies of war. The shells were falling along rue Mazel and on the citadel. A group of old houses by the Meuse had burnt to rafters of flickering flame, and as I passed them, one collapsed into the flooded river in a cloud of hissing steam.'
Henry Sheahan, 'A Volunteer Poilu'.

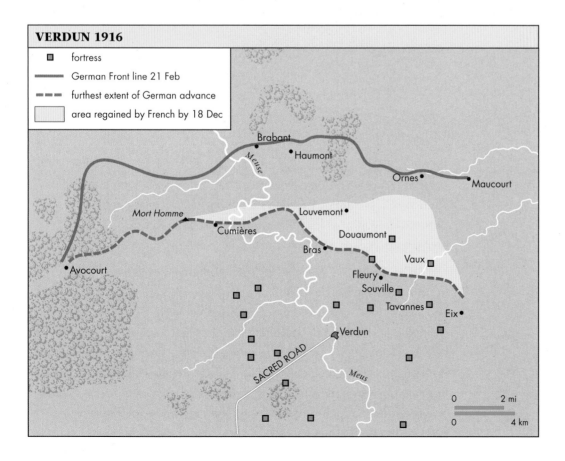

VERDUN 1916

- ◻ fortress
- ▬▬ German Front line 21 Feb
- ▬ ▬ furthest extent of German advance
- ◻ area regained by French by 18 Dec

Brabant
Meuse
Haumont
Ornes
Maucourt
Mort Homme
Louvemont
Cumières
Douaumont
Bras
Vaux
Avocourt
Fleury
Souville
Tavannes
Eix
Verdun
SACRED ROAD
Meus

0   2 mi
0   4 km

German officers survey the battlefield during the Battle of Verdun, February 1916. The German forces expected to take the town relatively easily, and indeed achieved some notable early advances. However, their commander, Gen Falkenhayn, had underestimated the resolve of the French forces in defending what to them was a symbolic city, and by July he was forced to call a halt to the offensive.

the River Meuse along a front of just 12.8 km/8 mi. As preparation for the assaulting infantry, 1 million shells were to fall on the defending Second Army in a 21-hour bombardment to be fired from 1,000 heavy guns.

The attack began on 21 February, and by the end of that day approximately 1 million German troops had managed to advance 5.6 km/3.5 mi after their artillery had crushed front-line resistance. The stunned French fought stubbornly in the days that followed, but the lightly-held Fort Douaumont fell on 25 February and the Germans were able to push on for another 2.4 km/1.5 mi. In Germany the church bells rang out in salute of victory, but such celebration proved premature as the French slowly began to regain some stability. The man behind this revival was **Gen Philippe Pétain**, the newly appointed commander of the sector, who had been advised to defend Verdun at all costs. The importance of the city was not lost on Joffre who, while understanding that militarily the city was of little consequence, knew that politically it had become an important symbol of French resilience. Indeed, Prime Minister Briand had told Joffre, 'If you surrender Verdun you will be cowards, cowards! And you needn't wait 'till then to hand in your resignation. If you abandon Verdun, I will sack you all on the spot.'

French soldiers loading a trench mortar at Limey, 5 March 1916. Trench mortars were introduced from 1915, and were valued for their ease of use and portability. French Dumézil mortars were the most widely used device of this type.

The first phase of the battle came to an end on 28 February as increasingly ferocious French artillery fire from the west of the Meuse began seriously to undermine the German ability to continue their attack. Already the frailties of the German plan were revealing themselves. The renewed German attack on 6 March was on an expanded front that included the area to the west of the Meuse, with a view to clearing it of artillery. This dilution of the German forces made it easier for Pétain to

Pétain, Gen Philippe (1856–1951)

Lacking combat experience, Pétain was a 58-year-old colonel when World War I broke out, and was given command of a brigade. He came to prominence during the Battle of Verdun when the defensive strategy that he espoused was severely tested. As commander of the sector, Pétain reorganized the artillery and, after ensuring that his lines of communication were secure, counterattacked. Having become a national hero as a result of the battle, he was appointed commander-in-chief in May 1917 and had the difficult job of restoring morale after the Nivelle offensives. His work was largely successful and helped the French withstand the pressure exerted by the Germans in the spring of 1918. However, during the final phase Foch was appointed commander of the Western Front and Pétain's role was diminished. After the war he was created a Marshal of France, and as a member of the Higher Council of National Defence he advocated a purely defensive military strategy. He became head of state during the German invasion in June 1940 and signed an armistice with Hitler. Having removed the seat of government to Vichy, a health resort in central France, Pétain's government collaborated with the Germans. Pétain was taken to Germany after the Allied invasion, but returned in 1945 and was sentenced to death for treason, the sentence later being commuted to life imprisonment.

King George V with Gen Julian Byng and Gen Pétain in the French town of Albert on the Somme, in July 1917.

Badly wounded Canadian soldiers on their way back to England for proper medical treatment. Like a number of other countries from Britain's then empire, Canada responded enthusiastically to calls for volunteers to help with the war effort, suffering an estimated 60,000 casualties during the conflict.

defend, and the French reinforcements were able to take advantage of this in a way that Falkenhayn had not predicted. The resistance the French put up was far in excess of that expected by the German high command, and was in no small measure a result of recent improvements that had been made to the defences in the area. These included new roads for efficient resupply and a reorganization of the trench system. They had given Joffre the confidence to say, just prior to the German assault, 'I ask only one thing, and this is that the Germans will attack me, and if they do attack me, that it will be at Verdun.' By early March the crucial supply artery leading up to Verdun (known as the 'Sacred Road') was carrying 3,000 trucks, 4,000 tonnes/3,920 tons of supplies, and 20,000 men a day.

British troops receiving dinner rations at a field kitchen in the Ancre river area on the Somme battlefield, October 1916. The following month, the British launched one final Somme offensive – against the three villages of Beaumont Hamel, Beaucourt, and St Pierre – and 5,000 German prisoners were taken on the first day.

During March the Germans advanced on the west bank of the Meuse, but failed to secure the vital high ground of Le Mort Homme and to clear the area of French artillery. These guns were devastating the attacking German formations and were turning the battlefield into a quagmire. By the time of the third German assault south of Douaumont on 9 April, German progress had slowed to a crawl over terrain that had been turned and re-turned by exploding shells, until the once-green vista had been replaced by a mud-brown sea littered with corpses. Many small villages simply vanished for ever. In such terrible conditions the troops fought on, often hand to hand, in freezing water-filled shell-holes, and to the incessant pounding of the guns. This was a cruel battle that played havoc with the fighting spirit of the troops involved. The decision taken by Pétain to rotate units frequently was crucial to his success in maintaining morale, and so Verdun (like Ypres for the British) saw the majority of Joffre's regiments pass through over the course of the year.

Meanwhile, the Germans were being sucked into 'the mincing machine' of Verdun in a way that Falkenhayn had not intended. By the end of May, Le Mort Homme fell, but the French artillery continued their work and, although no further significant progress was made in the western sector of the battlefield, the slogging match continued to the east. The Germans

Supplying Armies

Armies require great quantities of supplies to keep them in the field, and even more when they are fighting: food, water, and ammunition being critical. When coupled with the huge numbers of troops at the front (by 1918 the British army was 5.4 million men strong), the intensity of the fighting in World War I meant that not only was resupply crucial, but it also had to be timely. Ships, railways, motor-buses, trucks, horses, and men were all used to move stores and equipment from one place to another. During the war, 3.25 tonnes/3.2 million tons of foodstuffs, 5.48 tonnes/5.4 million tons of fodder and 5.28 tonnes/5.2 million tons of munitions were shipped from Britain to the BEF alone. Servicing the supply lines was not too difficult when the fighting was static, but in the advance, when extended lines of communication had to stretch over churned-up ground in order to resupply fighting troops quickly, it was very difficult. By the end of the war, the British advanced only short distances on relatively narrow fronts, in order to ameliorate these problems and to be in a position to consolidate their new ground prior to the launch of a fresh offensive.

Food rations stacked high in a storage warehouse. Keeping soldiers supplied was a precision exercise – particularly as the dramatic increase in mechanization during World War I made armies so much more mobile than they had been in previous conflicts.

Drinking water stored in sandbagged sunken water butts off the road between Albert and Pozières, in August 1916. Maintaining supplies to large numbers of men on the Western Front was a logistical challenge of the first order.

The wasteland of the Ancre valley in November 1916. The force of military bombardments used to 'soften up' enemy defences and provide cover to advancing infantry laid waste vast expanses of countryside on the Western Front – with quagmires and shattered tree-trunks proving a major hindrance to any form of transport.

German soldiers find a comrade lying on the Cambrai battlefield, but they are too late to save him.

German casualties in a front-line trench near Guillemont on the Somme, 3 September 1916.

achieved a measure of success on 7 June with the taking of Fort Vaux, but this was their last achievement of the battle. There was some sense in the German attack beginning on 21 June to capture the forts of Souville and Tavannes on the high ground directly in front of Verdun. Indeed Pétain had prepared a plan for withdrawal, but the exhausted German troops failed to break through and casualties were heavy – in early July, a single German regiment reportedly lost 80 officers and 3,200 men in less than four days' fighting. This was the problem for the Germans: in a battle designed to weaken the French irreparably, Falkenhayn's troops were receiving as much damage as Joffre's. This situation meant that the German offensives at Verdun had to be halted, especially when compounded by the opening of the Somme offensive to the north.

Sorting out the packs of the dead and wounded to retrieve letters and other personal effects for forwarding to relations, at Guillemont on the Somme in September 1916.

'Do you want to see something odd, mon vieux?' said one of the pompiers to me; and he led me through a labyrinth of cellars to a cold, deserted house. The snow had blown through the shell-splintered window-panes. In the dining-room stood a table, the cloth was laid and the silver spread; but a green feathery fungus had grown in a dish of food and broken straws of dust floated on the wine in the glasses. The territorial took my arm, his eyes showing the pleasure of my responding curiosity, and whispered, "There were officers quartered here who were called very suddenly. I saw the servant of one of them yesterday; they have all been killed."'
Henry Sheahan, 'A Volunteer Poilu'.

In the three months that followed, the French reorganized and reinforced themselves prior to their own offensive that began on 24 October to the east of the Meuse. Nivelle's attacks eliminated the bulge that had been made in the centre of the French line, and reclaimed Fort Douaumont on the first day and Fort Vaux on 2 November. A further attack on 15 December, on a wider front, saw the French advance up to 4 km/2.5 mi and take 11,000 prisoners. These assaults – the last of the battle – put the Germans under great pressure, and although not all the ground that they had lost since February was retaken, German losses were very heavy in terms of men and equipment.

The Battle of Verdun was the longest and most expensive of the war. In the unrecognizable countryside around the city, the Germans lost 434,000 men and the French 542,000. The troops that fought at Verdun were involved in a battle that had fast become a national myth, and the trauma of the event was etched on the face of every veteran. In the words of Pétain, 'In their unsteady look one sensed visions of horror, while their step and bearing revealed utter despondency. They were crushed by horrifying memories.' The battle was nothing short of a disaster for the Germans, because although French losses were enormous, by mid-1916 the British

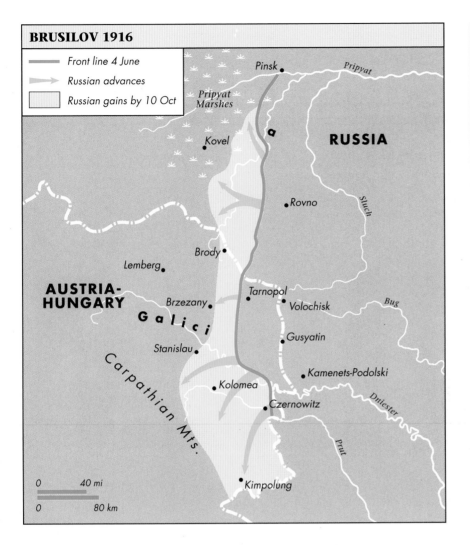

BRUSILOV 1916

— Front line 4 June

→ Russian advances

☐ Russian gains by 10 Oct

Pinsk

Pripyat

Pripyat Marshes

Kovel

RUSSIA

Rovno

Sluch

Brody

Lemberg

AUSTRIA-HUNGARY

Galici

Tarnopol

Brzezany

Volochisk

Bug

Gusyatin

Stanislau

Kamenets-Podolski

Kolomea

Czernowitz

Dniester

Carpathian Mts.

Prut

Kimpolung

0   40 mi

0   80 km

The Artillery

When World War I began, the fluidity of the battlefield meant that highly mobile field guns, such as the French 75mm, were the ideal weapons to provide fire support. However, with the establishment of a stalemate (and especially trench deadlock), heavier pieces firing high-explosive shells were required, especially howitzers such as the British 12-in siege howitzer which fired a 750-pound shell 13,870 m/14,300yd. This static warfare required huge numbers of heavy guns (the French had 300 heavy guns in 1914 but 7,000 by 1918), massive stockpiles of shells, and large numbers of 'gunners'. Prior to an infantry attack, the artillery would reduce the enemy's defences and then provide fire support during their assault. The British preliminary bombardment before the Third Battle of Ypres in 1917, for example, consisted of 4.3 million shells over a 19-day period. However, such bombardments during the first three years of the fighting were not always successful, and although the enemy trenches were often decimated, the wire was not always cut and the enemy's guns not always incapacitated – but they did churn up the ground and give away the element of surprise. The development of 'silent registration' by the British in 1917 – a means of registering targets without the need for surprise-depleting ranging fire – was therefore a great improvement. World War I was primarily an artillery war, and such weapons caused 58% of all casualties.

A huge 16-in German mortar weapon called Dicke Bertha. Mortars were characterized by a relatively short range and very high trajectory – even late in the war, they only had a range of around 1,800 m/2,000 yd, but such massive projectiles created vast craters on landing.

army was in a position to step forward and take the strain of the Allied fighting effort on the Western Front. Germany had no such ally and, as the Battle of the Somme raged, Falkenhayn was dismissed.

The Brusilov Offensive

1915 had not been a good year for the Russian High Command with a great deal of territory lost, heavy casualties taken, and an evident shortage of arms, munitions, and equipment that undermined their fighting capabilities. However, Gen Mikhail Alexeyev, the Russian chief of staff, was confident of what the tsar's forces could achieve in 1916. Having survived the many setbacks of the previous year, Russia was on the verge of overcoming its resource crisis, and new troops were taking their places to bolster the fighting front. While it was undoubtedly true that the Russian army was some way from being a first-class fighting outfit, it was certainly capable of offensive action – despite what Falkenhayn thought. As if to prove this to themselves, the high command decided to launch an offensive on 18 March either side of Lake Narotch, some 128 km/80 mi

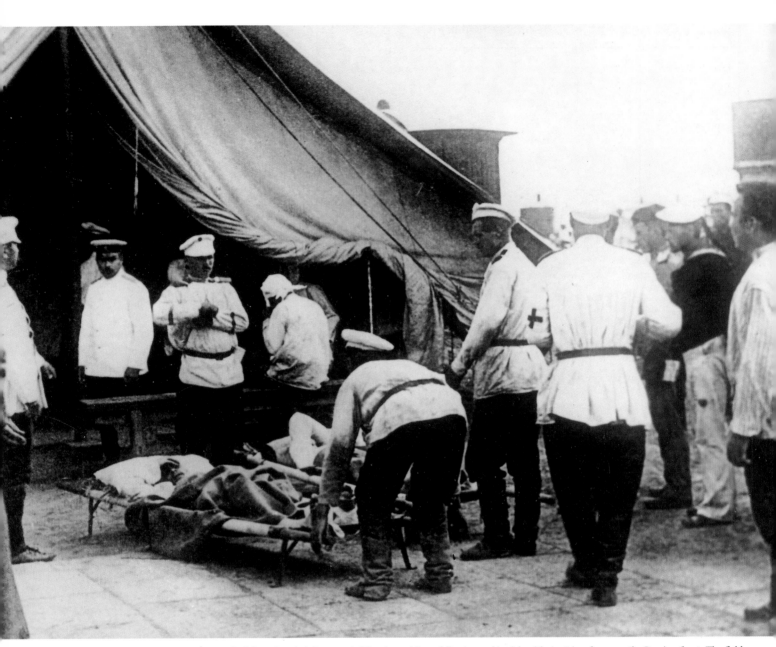

A temporary Red Cross hospital for wounded Russian soldiers, following a skirmish with Austrian forces on the Russian front. The field hospital shown was erected in an open courtyard, the flagstones outside enabling the medical staff to keep the tent relatively free from dirt.

to the northwest of Minsk. However, the results were not particularly gratifying. Despite matching the number of German guns, the Russians made little headway against their enemy and suffered over 100,000 casualties (the Germans lost just 20,000). Although hardly affecting the Eastern Front strategy in the short term, the failure depressed the commanders of the Northern Front, and this was to have important ramifications for the remainder of the fighting in 1916.

The Russian high command was well aware of its obligations to Allied strategy for 1916 (a major offensive in May) and, despite the setback incurred on the Northern Front, agreed to **Gen Brusilov's** request to push into Galicia on the Southwest Front without any great increase in his resources. His plan was to attack along the entire front in order to surprise and dilute the enemy, and he ensured that his preparations made it difficult for his enemy to concentrate their forces against him. The fact that there was to be no main effort concerned Alexeyev greatly and, right up to the last moment, he tried to convince Brusilov that a breakthrough could not be achieved by such wide dispersal of his forces. However, Brusilov stood firm, and on 4 June an artillery bombardment commenced that was designed to shatter the Austrian front line and break the wire in preparation for an attack on the following day.

The infantry assault began at dawn on 5 June. The initial advance was a great success, and the 37 divisions of the Central Powers were immediately put under pressure by the 38 Russian divisions attacking them. Indeed, the Austrian Fourth Army at the northern end of Brusilov's front quickly lost cohesion early in the battle, when one of its corps collapsed. By the second day of the offensive the Russians had taken 44,000 prisoners, with Gen Kaledin's Eighth Army and Gen Shcherbachev's Seventh Army making great strides forward. With the whole front beginning to crumble, the introduction of reserves was desperately required to maintain the tempo of the attack, but none was made available. Had Gen Evert made a big effort in the north at this stage (and he did have reserves) the Central Powers might have been placed under intolerable pressure, but his attack on 2 July was irresolute. The failure of the March attack had come back to haunt the Russian high command.

Brusilov managed to advance 96 km/60 mi in the first four weeks of his attack and took 350,000 prisoners, but this rate of advance could not be maintained. Suffering from over-extended lines of communication and exhaustion, Brusilov's momentum began to suffer badly. Coupled with the inadequacy of Evert's demonstration in the north, this gave the Central Powers the breathing space they so desperately required to reinforce and stabilize their line. The Carpathian mountains were once again at the limits of Russian offensive capabilities, and despite further attempts to push forward in July, they could not achieve any momentum and the fighting continued into September. However, the campaign was an undisputed Russian victory and had important consequences. The fact that 450,000 men of the Austro-Hungarian army were taken prisoner during this offensive was a mortal blow to their manpower resources. Unfortunately, by the end of the year the Russians had lost all the territory that they had so recently taken, and were counting the cost of 1 million casualties (with perhaps a similar number deserting). A weakening heart could not sustain such haemorrhages for much longer.

On the Eastern Front at least, the Central Powers seemed to be winning the war of attrition, and their future seemed even more assured by the

Brusilov, Gen Alexei (1853–1926)

Brusilov had seen a great deal of action by the time he took command of the Russian southwestern front in March 1916, having fought the Austrians in Galicia during the previous year. The offensive that bears his name relieved pressure on the Western and Italian fronts by drawing German units east to cover the losses sustained by Austro-Hungarian forces. The attack so decimated the Austro-Hungarians that they were never able to play an important role in the Central Powers alliance again. Nevertheless, it also cost the Russians nearly 1 million casualties, and this further exacerbated the dissatisfaction that was to lead to revolution during the following year. Brusilov was in favour of the tsar's abdication, and became commander-in-chief in the wake of the March revolution. After the war Brusilov was commander of the Red Army, which drove the Poles to within a few kilometres of Warsaw in 1920 before being repulsed by them.

Commander of the Russian forces, Gen Brusilov, contemplates the military situation on the Eastern Front.

capture of the oil and wheat resources of Romania. The Romanian declaration of war on the Central Powers was badly timed. Having been shaken out of neutrality by the hope of territory that might accompany an Austrian defeat, they found that the strategic situation had radically altered by the time they invaded Transylvania. Rather than providing crucial manpower resources in July when the Central Powers were being stretched at Verdun, the Somme, Isonzo, and Galicia, they waited until August to reveal their hand – by which time the Central Powers had drawn breath. In these circumstances Falkenhayn, recently dismissed as Chief of the Imperial General Staff and the newly appointed commander of the Ninth Army, coordinated a counterattack made up of German, Turkish, Austrian, and Bulgarian troops. Suffering 310,000 casualties, the unprepared Romanian forces were quickly despatched, and Bucharest was captured on 6 December.

The Year of Attrition

Looking at 1916 as a whole (including the Battle of the Somme), the huge casualties, negligible territorial gain, and massive expenditure of resources make it hard to see how its offensives could be regarded as anything but abject failures. The sacrifices that these attacks necessitated certainly took their toll on some key decision-makers that year, for by December Britain had changed its prime minister, Germany had introduced its 'silent dictatorship', and 'Papa' Joffre had been replaced as commander-in-chief in France. The strain of total war was undoubtedly beginning to show in all the major belligerent states, and two of them (Austria-Hungary and Russia) were on the verge of collapse. Such circumstances, however, did not make it any clearer as to which side would ultimately win the war. Although France had suffered heavily in the Battle of Verdun, Britain was emerging from the shadows as a force to be reckoned with. Meanwhile Germany, which was stretched by the fighting on two fronts, had crucially seized Romania's resources and looked forward to the collapse of Russia and an end to the fighting in the east. 1916 might not have been a year of outstanding military victories, but it set the scene for the war's darkest year and marked a period of great transition.

CHAPTER 8
THE BATTLE OF THE SOMME
1 JULY–19 NOVEMBER 1916

Introduction

When it started the Battle of the Somme looked to be one of the potentially decisive battles of the war. No-one could have predicted the appalling cost in human life that was to result. It was during this long battle, which saw the British Expeditionary Force (BEF) and Kitchener's Army lead a major offensive against the Germans, that Haig's troops became a potent fighting force.

A British soldier rests near Aveluy Wood, September 1916.

The origins of the battle can be traced to the desire of the French
Commander-in-Chief, Gen Joseph Joffre, for an Anglo-French offensive in
1916. The logical place for this attack was where the two armies met, just
north of the River Somme in Picardie. Haig would have preferred an
attack in Flanders but, under pressure from his superiors, a joint attack
was agreed. However, the plans for this offensive were thrown into
disarray by the German attack on the French at Verdun in February 1916
(see Chapter 7). This event made an offensive on the Somme all the more
important to Joffre as he sought to divert German resources away from
Verdun, but now the brunt of the fighting would have to be borne by
the British.

Planning and the Plan

Haig's plan for the Somme offensive was audacious – **Gen Sir Henry
Rawlinson's** Fourth Army was to advance 2.4 km/1.5 mi on a 22.4-
km/14-mi front, and thus enable **Lt-Gen Sir Hubert Gough's** Reserve
Army to advance through the gap and seize Bapaume before swinging
north towards Arras. However, while pandering to his commander-in-
chief's craving for a breakthrough, Rawlinson thought that this was unlikely
to occur quickly. The Fourth Army therefore planned a lengthy artillery
bombardment in order to weaken the German positions, followed by an
infantry advance towards shallow objectives, and then a period of
consolidation before the start of the next phase of operations.

*A still from the British propaganda film 'The Battle of the Somme'. A British
Royal Marine artilleryman cleans a 15-in shell near Acheux in July 1916.
The message painted on the shell casing indicates the shell's destination.*

A night-time bombardment on the Somme battlefield, the prelude to the attack on Thiepval, September 1916. The Germans had held Thiepval since the beginning of the Somme offensive in July, but just 11 days after their introduction to the battlefield, a British assault using 13 tanks broke the deadlock.

'*(The Somme) is capital country in which to undertake an offensive when we get sufficient artillery, for observation is excellent and with plenty of guns we ought to be able to avoid the heavy losses which the infantry have always suffered on previous occasions.*'
Rawlinson, to a colleague: February 1916

Rawlinson was confident of success, but Haig – despite being unable to offer any more guns – demanded greater depth to the artillery bombardment in order to facilitate a rapid breakthrough. Haig got his way, but with no more guns to prepare the ground, the result was a massive dilution in fire.

The weaknesses of the plan were not immediately apparent. When the preliminary bombardment commenced on 24 June, its ferocity initially engendered a spirit of optimism in many quarters on the British side – an optimism that upbeat intelligence did little to diminish. Others were, however, less sure of the plans. Rifleman Percy Jones of the Queen's Westminster Rifles, 56th (London) Division, noted in his diary on 26 June that his divisional commander and his staff were:

Gough, General Sir Hubert de la Poer, 1870–1963

Hubert Gough was both a divisional and corps commander on the Western Front before being given command of the Reserve (later Fifth) Army at the age of just 44. His arrogant demeanour made him unpopular within the BEF and although some of his successes on the Somme were impressive, Gough lacked attention to detail and had a rather cavalier attitude towards casualties. Nevertheless, Haig liked Gough's boldness and chose his army to lead the attack in the Third Battle of Ypres that opened on 31 July 1917. Less than a month later, however, the commander-in-chief replaced the Fifth Army with Plumer's Second Army due to Gough's lack of progress and heavy casualties. 1918 was hardly a better year for this once rising star of the BEF, for on 21 April 1918 the German 'Spring Offensive' opened and Gough's Fifth Army were broken and forced into rapid retreat. Gough was removed from command shortly afterwards.

February–June:	Planning of an Anglo-French Somme offensive.
24 June:	Somme preliminary bombardment commences.
1 July:	Somme offensive begins. Fourth Army attacks at 0730 hrs. Failure north of Albert–Bapaume road but considerable success to the south of it. 57,470 British casualties on this day.
2 July:	Somme offensive continues. Reserve Army mount operations north of Albert-Bapaume Road and Fourth Army endeavour to exploit their first day successes south of it.
2–13 July:	Fourth Army endeavours to secure Contalmaison and three woods in order to capture the German second line defences.
12 July:	Mametz Wood is finally captured.
14 July:	Successful dawn attack on the German second line.
15 July:	the Battle of Delville Wood begins
5 August:	Australians capture Pozieres.
15 September:	Battle of Flers-Courcelette begins. Flers and High Wood are captured. First use of tanks in battle.
7 October:	Le Sars taken in deteriorating weather.
5 November:	Butte de Warlencourt is captured.
13 November:	Final Somme offensive, the Battle of the Ancre, begins. Beaumont Hamel and Beaucourt are taken in this battle.
18 November:	Haig declares the Battle of the Somme at an end. British casualties 419,654. German casualties approximately 600,000.

`...busy telling us that we shall have practically no casualties because there will be no Germans left alive to oppose us. On paper the plans are A1 [perfect], but if the Germans obstinately refuse to die and make way for us, our scheme will become impractical.'

Although some officers were sceptical about what was actually being achieved during the final few days of the artillery onslaught, their voices were drowned out by the roar of the guns.

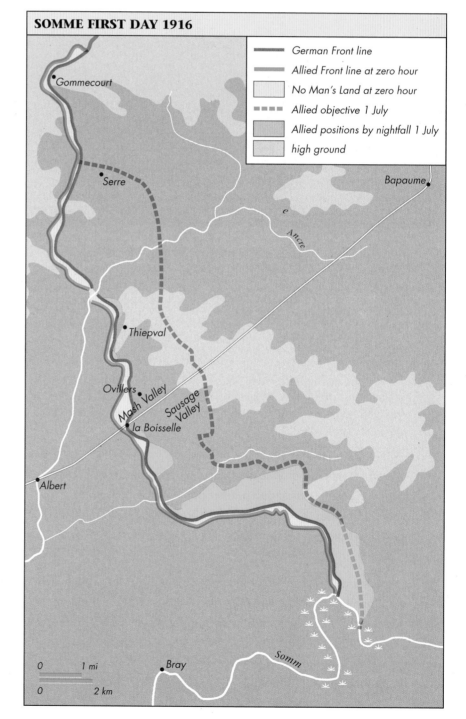

SOMME FIRST DAY 1916

German Front line
Allied Front line at zero hour
No Man's Land at zero hour
Allied objective 1 July
Allied positions by nightfall 1 July
high ground

SUNDAY PICTORIAL, July 2, 1916.

MR. WINSTON CHURCHILL WRITES IN NEXT ISSUE

SUNDAY·PICTORIAL

CIRCULATION MORE THAN ONE-MILLION-EIGHT-HUNDRED-THOUSAND COPIES.

No. 69. | Registered at the G.P.O. as a Newspaper. | SUNDAY, JULY 2, 1916. | The Paper with "The Daily Mirror" Behind It. | One Penny.

THE BIG ADVANCE: "ALL GOES WELL FOR ENGLAND AND FRANCE"

An advance by the British in France after preparing the way with smoke bombs.

Our boys after the advance at St. Eloi.

One of the great guns firing on the German trenches.

The "Fighting Fifth" after taking the German positions.

A British big gun in action during a big bombardment.

A heavy British howitzer in action in the West.

British troops hurrying up to the firing-line in motor-cars.

The nation was thrilled yesterday to hear that the Great British offensive on the western front had begun at last. Sixteen miles of German front trenches have been captured by our gallant soldiers to the north of the River Somme. Many prisoners have been taken. The French are also attacking with great success, while the terrible bombard- ment of the German trenches by the British artillery continues unabated. Thus it may be said that the great British offensive, for which we have waited so long, has started well. The photographs above illustrate incidents in previous British advances against the German lines in France and Flanders.

The Battle of the Somme 1 July–19 November 1916 **105**

The First Day: 1 July 1916

During the night of 30 June, the British infantry marched several miles up to the front, each man carrying at least 30 kg/66 lb of equipment. By the time that they arrived in the front line in the early hours of 1 July, most were exhausted by a journey through trenches made muddy by the rain that had fallen steadily during the previous few days. At 0730 hrs, zero hour, the artillery barrage that had latterly been concentrating on the German front line moved forward, and 66,000 men of the BEF's first wave left their trenches and started to move steadily towards the German trenches.

'You are about to attack the enemy with far greater numbers than he can oppose to you, supported by a large number of guns...You are about to fight in one of the greatest battles in the world, and in the most just cause...Keep your heads, do your duty, and you will utterly defeat the enemy.'
Commanding Officer for the 94th Brigade: 30 June 1916

In the few minutes that followed, as the infantry entered a shell-holed wasteland, Germans began to climb out of their deep **'dugouts'** and took up defensive positions in their almost unrecognizably damaged front line. At the same time, the German guns that had lain silent during the previous week began to open fire, and a wall of explosives rained down on the British trenches and No Man's Land. All along the front, the British infantry suffered such massive casualties that by noon few divisions north of the Albert–Bapaume road were still moving forward. Although the fighting continued throughout the rest of the day, by nightfall it became clear that very few divisions had reached their objectives, and many had failed even to reach the German trenches.

The Reasons for Failure

The failure of so many divisions to cross No Man's Land should not be attributed to any single factor, but the failure of schemes designed to reduce German defensive effectiveness did little to help matters. A diversionary attack at the extreme northern end of the line was conducted by two divisions of Gen Sir Edmund Allenby's Third Army in an attempt to take some German attention away from the Fourth Army. In practice, the attack provided little in the way of diversion and cost 6,700 British casualties.

A huge mine exploding at Hawthorne Ridge, heralding the start of the Battle of the Somme on 1 July 1916. The offensive was a joint British and French effort aimed at breaking through the German lines, so that the cavalry could advance rapidly. The Allies fired nearly 250,000 shells at the German trenches in little more than an hour.

Other largely unsuccessful attempts to overcome the German defences were also tried, and included the explosion of a number of mines underneath enemy strong points just before zero hour. The mine that was detonated at 0720 hrs under Hawthorne Ridge Redoubt did destroy an important German strong point but, by announcing the imminence of the infantry assault, it also diminished what little surprise the British attack had left after a week-long preliminary bombardment.

However, the most important factor in the British difficulties in No Man's Land on the morning of 1 July was that the preliminary bombardment failed to achieve what Rawlinson assumed it would, namely the virtual annihilation of the German defences. The preliminary bombardment was meant to meet three crucial objectives: the cutting of the barbed wire defending the German position; the destruction of the German trenches; and a drastic reduction of the German artillery. However, the wire was only successfully cut in front of XIII Corps at the southern end of the British line. Despite the firing of 455 heavy guns and 1.7 million shells in the preliminary bombardment, why did it fail on the majority of the front? There were numerous problems – not least the fact that there were too few guns, many of which had worn-out barrels that fired unreliable ammunition. As much as 60% of this was shrapnel which, fired from field guns, was useless at destroying trenches and ineffective at cutting barbed wire.

The difficulties that this caused the infantry approaching the German front line were tremendous. Banks of poorly-cut wire lost attackers valuable time, and in many cases stalled the attack altogether. Either way, the failure to cut the wire completely meant that the infantry lost crucial momentum across No Man's Land and, as a consequence, this made the job of the German machine gunners much easier. A good example of the sorts of losses sustained by the infantry who were confronted by uncut wire can be seen in the result of the attack put in by the 8th Division in front of the village of Ovillers, just north of the Albert–Bapaume road. With the Germans also overlooking No Man's Land on three sides in this area, British losses were devastating. One of the division's battalions, the 2nd Middlesex, suffered 540 casualties on 1 July out of a notional strength of about 800 men.

In addition to the problems caused by uncut wire, there were the difficulties caused by the failure of the preliminary bombardment to destroy German trenches and bunkers. All along the front, although some sections of trenches were destroyed, substantial portions of them (including deep dugouts) were not. Consequently, many Germans and their weapons survived the preliminary bombardment, and re-emerged into the sunlight as soon as the British bombardment moved off their front line at zero hour. German machine gunners on the high ground of Sausage Valley, south of the Albert–Bapaume road, survived the artillery

Dugouts

A dugout was a shelter made in the wall of a trench and varied in size from a shallow scrape large enough for one man to a large subterranean room (a bunker) for several men. Although trenches were normally deep enough to afford some protection from various deadly projectiles, most did not entirely eliminate the danger caused by shell fragments or snipers. Dugouts provided greater protection and the deeper and stronger they were, the more protection they afforded. The German trench system was very elaborate as the German army was on the defensive and required surroundings that would enable their men to survive massive bombardments and then resist enemy attacks. It was not uncommon for German dugouts to be 9–12 m/30–40 ft deep and house a dozen men.

British officers outside a former German dugout. The picture clearly demonstrates the strength of the German defensive positions. The depth and robustness of the dugouts afforded significant protection from the allied bombardments during the Battle of the Somme.

'When the English started advancing we were very worried; they looked as though they must overrun our trenches. We were very surprised to see them walking, we had never seen that before, I could see them everywhere; there were hundreds. The officers were in front. I noticed one of them walking calmly, carrying a walking stick. When we started firing, we just had to load and reload. They went down in their hundreds. You didn't have to aim, we just fired into them. If only they had run they would have overwhelmed us.'
Musketier Karl Blenker, 169th Regiment.

A patrol crawling up towards German trenches during the Battle of Albert, 1916.

The Pal's Battalions

Local communities often took the lead in recruiting volunteers for Kitchener's New Army and this led to numerous units being drawn exclusively from a particular place. With their unique esprit de corps these units quickly became known as 'Pal's Battalions'. Although there were a number of middle-class units, such as the Public Schools Battalions, most Pal's Battalions were drawn from the sports clubs, coal mines and factories of the great northern industrial towns. So strong was their identity with a specific place that although they were given battalion numbers according to the Regiment to which they were attached, the vast majority retained their nicknames – Hull Commercials, Sheffield City, Barnsley, Accrington, and Leeds Pals.

onslaught. They had plenty of time to ready themselves for defence as the 34th Division struggled over 457 m/500 yd of No Man's Land and then stopped in front of the enemy wire.

The 34th Division suffered 6,380 casualties, and the story was similar elsewhere along the line. At Serre to the north of the Fourth Army's attack, the German machine gunners cut down 31st (Pal's) Division until about midday when they had nothing left to shoot at. One of the division's battalions, the Accrington Pals, suffered over 85% casualties on 1 July.

The British troops were not only cut down by machine gun fire but also by German artillery. In all, 598 field and 246 heavier pieces survived the British counterbattery fire. The strength of German machine gun and artillery fire meant that the British troops who had made a lodgement in the German lines could neither be reinforced nor withdrawn, and most were eventually wiped out by counterattacks. This was a problem that the 8th Division had to contend with as they attacked Mash Valley when, having attained a foothold in the German front line, the enemy shells that fell behind them cut them off from any potential support. This predicament was exacerbated because any subsequent movement forward was impossible due to a barrage that was fired in support. A lack of guns meant that this not only provided an incomplete shrapnel curtain, but also lifted off the German front line too early and moved ahead of the infantry too quickly.

A German trench-gun crew in action during the Battle of the Somme in the summer and autumn of 1916. The range and calibre of armaments increased steadily throughout the war.

A Lewis gun in action in a front line trench during the Battle of the Somme. Note how exposed the gunner becomes when aiming over the top of the trench.

First Day Success

Despite these problems, some divisions north of the Albert–Bapaume road did manage to penetrate the German front line. However, such success was only ever on the front of a single division, and this in itself caused problems. The 36th (Ulster) Division managed to advance 1.2 km/0.75 mi into the German defences near Thiepval, but the failure of the divisions on either flank to make a similar advance meant that the Ulsters very quickly became isolated and highly vulnerable. With their lines of communication overstretched and their flanks wide open, the Ulster Division was gradually pushed back during the day, and by nightfall the troops were back in their own trenches again.

Many of the units that did manage some success on 1 July, the Ulsters included, employed innovative infantry tactics to aid their advance, rather than relying solely on the artillery. These tactics were used even though they had not been actively encouraged by Rawlinson, who had thought that crossing No Man's Land would not be difficult owing to sufficient artillery preparation. Some brigade and battalion commanders, perhaps worried about the reliance placed on the preliminary bombardment, ordered that their troops move into No Man's Land while the artillery concentrated on the German front line, so that they could then rush the enemy trenches when the barrage lifted. When the 97th Brigade of the 32nd Division used these tactics on 1 July, it succeeded in capturing the Leipzig Redoubt near Thiepval while, in comparison, its sister brigade, the 96th, used tactics outlined in the Fourth Army Tactical Notes and was cut down.

However, sustained success relied upon far more than just appropriate infantry tactics. The successes of XVIII Corps south of the Albert–Bapaume road, in which it captured all of its objectives on 1 July, and XV Corps, which penetrated well into the German defences and held onto its position, came about as a result of a mixture of ingredients. It was crucial that in this area the German defences were less deep than those further to the north. This meant that in order for the Germans to make use of the protection that the dugouts afforded during the preliminary bombardment, they had to come well forward. Thus, with the British infantry starting out from advanced positions in No Man's Land

Soldiers from the 13th Royal Fusiliers resting on the Albert–Bapaume Road near Albert on 7 July 1916, after the attack on La Boisselle the previous day.

British soldiers with two wounded German prisoners at La Boisselle on 3 July 1916 during the Battle of the Somme. By the following day, the French had taken 4,000 German prisoners and breached the German line along a 9.6-km/6-mi stretch.

with the wire well cut in front of them and some divisions experimenting with a 'creeping barrage', a high proportion of the German defenders were overrun in the first rush. Add to this the fact that there were fewer enemy guns on XV Corps' and XIII Corps' front, and the greater success achieved south of the Albert–Bapaume road – including the impressive French advances – becomes easier to understand.

Nevertheless, despite the successes in the southern sector of the front, the overall amount of ground taken was tiny. Costing the British 57,470 casualties including approximately 20,000 dead, it became the bloodiest day in the history of the British army. On the same day the Germans suffered approximately 2,200 casualties, although if one also adds in those casualties lost during the preliminary bombardment then the figure moves closer to 8,000.

A panoramic view of the battlefield at Thiepval in September 1916. The ultra-wide-angle shot clearly conveys the extent to which the surrounding countryside had been laid waste during the conflict.

Troops take coils of wire to forward positions near the village of Beaumont Hamel in September 1916. Before the arrival of the tank, wire was widely used as an almost insurmountable obstacle to infantry advance.

The Battle of the Somme is remembered for these enormous first-day casualties and as a disaster. However, it did not begin and end on 1 July 1916, and it was many long weeks before the guns rested again.

The Battle Continues: Fourth Army

Disappointed that the first day of the battle had not been the resounding success that he had hoped, Haig reassessed the situation as soon as information would allow. Thus, from 2 to 13 July 1916, Gough's Reserve Army began to assume responsibility for the battle north of the Albert–Bapaume Road, but the principal thrust of operations was where the greatest success had been on the first day, exploitation conducted by Rawlinson's Fourth Army on the right. During this period they strove to secure Mametz Wood, Contalmaison, Bernafay Wood, and Trones Wood as they pushed towards the German second line which ran just beyond Pozieres on the Albert–Bapaume road, but in front of Bazentin le Petit, Bazentin le Grand, Longueval, and Guillemont. If the second line were taken here, then it would render the German front line and second line vulnerable on Gough's front.

Although Bernafay Wood was captured with few difficulties on 3 July, Mametz Wood was a different proposition altogether. When the wood was attacked by the 38th (Welsh) Division on 7 July, the thick undergrowth and the trees felled by the barrage made their job a particularly difficult one and the attack stalled. A renewed attempt on 10 July was successful, but it took until 12 July to finally clear the wood. Meanwhile Contalmaison had been captured on 10 July, and plans were afoot to capture Trones Wood and push up to the German second line.

This push was much more successful than the slog that had immediately preceded it. The attack began at dawn on 14 July after the skilful assembly of infantry in No Man's Land in the dark. With the sudden intensification of a three-day preliminary bombardment five minutes before zero hour, the Germans cowered and were then fallen upon by the infantry advancing behind a creeping barrage. A 5,400-m/6,000-yd stretch of the German second position between Longueval and Bazentin le Petit was swiftly captured. However, despite this impressive attack, there were still difficulties in exploiting the success, and Delville Wood and High Wood loomed menacingly in front of Rawlinson's troops.

A British sentry makes his way forward to his post at Beaumont Hamel to the northwest of the Somme battlefield, July 1916. The British attack on the village of Beaumont Hamel was part of the final Somme offensive in November 1916, intended to take three villages that had held out since the beginning of the battle in July.

During this period of the battle, the fighting was grim. Far from fighting battles in order to attain a breakthrough, these were tortuous battles of attrition where territorial gains were made at the expense of very heavy casualties. Nevertheless Haig made the decision to continue his offensive while preparing for another big set-piece assault in mid-September. He hoped that this would be decisive.

The Battle of Delville Wood, from 15 July to 3 September, was one of the most gruelling and gruesome of the entire Somme fighting. Although the wood was captured and consolidated on 27–28 July, the fighting there continued sporadically for over another month as the Germans tried to

The devastated landscape that had been Trônes Wood in November 1916. The constant barrage of shells and the continuing taking/retaking of this territory by the Allies totally destroyed the wood.

recapture it. Meanwhile, attacks were launched between 20 and 30 July on High Wood, which was not finally to be captured until 15 September. Rawlinson also tried to ease the progress of the French Sixth Army on his right by seizing Guillemont and Ginchy. On 3 September fighting began to take Guillemont, and by 9 September both that village and Ginchy had fallen. The pattern everywhere was the same – heavy shelling, German counterattacks, and steady, remorseless (but deadly slow) advance. The Fourth Army advanced about 1,094 m/1,000 yd between 15 July and 14 September and took 82,000 casualties. But on Rawlinson's front the line had been straightened ready for the mid-September push.

The Battle Continues: The Reserve Army

The situation was not dissimilar on the northern side of the Albert–Bapaume road, where other gains were being made. Reserve Army operations were of growing importance, not only to gain important objectives for their own sake, but also to protect the left flank of the advancing Fourth Army. By 4 July La Boisselle had been taken, and on 17 July Ovillers was captured. Creeping up the Albert–Bapaume road, the battle for Pozieres came next, and between 23 July and 5 August the Australians of I Anzac Corps were involved in bitter fighting for the village and for the ruined mill on the crest of the ridge immediately beyond it. The Australian success here was at the expense of heavy casualties, but gave the BEF good observation over the surrounding terrain. However, the Reserve Army was still going to have to slog its way through various lines of enemy trenches northwest of the Albert–Bapaume road and threaten

The Birth of Tanks

Tanks were developed in response to the difficulties in overcoming trench deadlock and were the product of the British Landships Committee established by Winston Churchill at the Admiralty in February 1915. The first design, 'Little Willie', was an impractical metal box with tracks mounted at the sides, but the second design was a more successful rhomboid shape with caterpillar tracks encircling the body and the armament mounted on sponsons on each side. A prototype of this design, named 'Mother', passed its trials in February 1916 and an order for 100 tanks, produced as the Mark I, was placed. These machines were codenamed 'Tanks' during their development in order to give the impression that mobile water-tanks were being constructed rather than armoured fighting vehicles.

The main street of Flers, north of Guillemont, lies in ruins after the Battle of Flers–Courcelette 15–22 September 1915. This was the first British use of the tank in battle, although only 32 tanks made it to the front line out of the 49 originally available.

A prototype British tank undergoing testing at Burton Park, Lincoln, in January 1916. Known as 'Mother', design commenced at the end of August 1915, and the tank moved under its own power for the first time on 6 January 1916.

Thiepval from the rear. In the ensuing operations, the names of these trenches and strong-points – Fabeck Graben, Zollern Graben, Stuff Trench, Stuff Redoubt, Regina Ridge, and Mouquet Farm – would become depressingly familiar to the Reserve Army as it fought for them through to September and October and, in some cases, as late as mid-November.

Time passed and in mid-September Haig's set-piece battle, the Battle of Flers–Courcelette, had begun.

The First Tanks in Action

The Battle of Flers-Courcelette, involving both the Fourth and Reserve armies, was Haig's attempt to snatch a chance at a breakout after a period of wearing the Germans down, and was coordinated with a French Sixth Army attack to the south. Tanks were introduced into battle for the first time on 15 September, although only 49 tanks were available to Haig on the eve of battle, and only 32 actually made it to the front line ready to fight. It is a matter of conjecture as to whether the high command should have waited until more tanks were available in order to unleash them in overwhelming numbers rather than in the 'penny packets' that were actually used in mid-September.

Nonetheless, the tanks supported 12 divisions of infantry attacking on a 16-km/10-mi front with a creeping barrage rolling in front of them, and with objectives that included the German third line. The appearance of the tanks caused panic among some German units, but generally the Germans put up stout resistance and soon recognized the tanks' limitations. The

'It was a monstrous sacrifice ... The Australians never forgot Pozieres, nor the English staff which sent them there, nor the mates killed, nor the New Army Divisions which had failed so often on their flanks, nor the thousands of scenes of horror and heroism, nor, the most terrible of all, the ceaseless, merciless, murdering guns.'
The official Australian historian, CEW Bean, writing on the Battle of Pozieres.

British transport wagons in the mud, during the Battle of the Somme, November 1916. The atrocious weather conditions severely hampered the operations and fighting capability of both German and Allied troops.

Icicles hanging from the roof of a dugout in Bernafay Wood on the Somme near Montauban, November 1916. The wet weather of October 1916 was followed by a cold spell, and the first snow of the winter fell the day before the Somme offensive was ended, on 17 November.

British advanced 2,285 m/2,500 yd on a 4113-m/4,500-yd front on the first day, with Flers (famously) captured by 41st Division with the aid of four tanks and Martinpuich taken. During the Battle of Morval, 25–28 September, those places that had not yet been taken – including Morval, Lesboeufs, Combles, and Gueudecourt – were captured. The ground taken on 15 September was about twice the amount captured on 1 July for about half its cost in casualties. Even so, it was not the decisive blow that Haig and Rawlinson had sought, as the German line was not broken.

Gough Attacks

Meanwhile, the Battle of Thiepval Ridge was being fought by Gough's Reserve Army, which launched the biggest operation it had yet undertaken, and

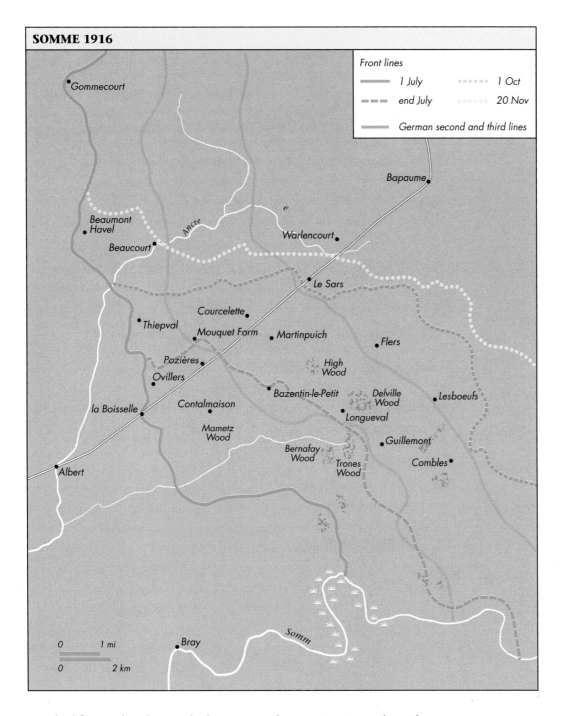

SOMME 1916

Front lines
—— 1 July   ·········· 1 Oct
- - - end July   ·········· 20 Nov
                    German second and third lines

Gommecourt

Bapaume

Beaumont
Havel
Beaucourt

Ancre

Warlencourt

Le Sars

Courcelette

Thiepval
Mouquet Farm   Martinpuich   Flers

Pozières
Ovillers   High
                      Wood

                      Bazentin-le-Petit   Delville   Lesboeufs
                                           Wood
la Boisselle   Contalmaison   Longueval

                      Mametz
                      Wood   Guillemont

                      Bernafay
                      Wood   Combles
Albert   Trones
                              Wood

0   1 mi
0   2 km   Bray   Somm

attacked from Schwaben Redoubt to Courcelette on 26 September. The
German garrison of Mouquet Farm surrendered on the first day of
Gough's attack, and Maj-Gen Maxse's 18th Division took much of
Thiepval itself, completing the clearance of the village on 27 September.

But, as often happened in 1916, the offensive lost momentum. It was not
until 14 October that the last German defenders were ejected from the
Schwaben Redoubt, while the Canadian Corps was still fighting for parts
of the Regina Trench as late as the second week of November.

The failure to achieve a breakthrough in these large-scale and coordinated
assaults of the second half of September from both Fourth and Reserve

Army fronts could, and probably should, have been reason enough for Haig to halt the offensive. But he continued, partly due to the over-optimism of his intelligence chief, Brig-Gen Charteris, who helped to persuade him that, if the BEF kept up the pressure, the Germans would eventually crack.

Between 1 and 20 October, therefore, as the weather deteriorated and the ground became a quagmire, the Fourth Army inched towards Le Transloy. Le Sars, 5.6 km/3.5 mi from Bapaume, was taken on 7 October. An attack on the Butte de Warlencourt was begun on the same day, and continued until the Butte was entered on 5 November.

The final push came with the Battle of the Ancre after a further month of attritional fighting. The bad weather caused the attack to be postponed repeatedly, and played havoc with morale. Eventually, on 13 November, Gough's Fifth Army (as it was now called) attacked at Beaumont Hamel and along the north bank of the Ancre – this time the British had one gun every 32 m/35 yd of line – and there was success. The 63rd (Royal Naval) Division took Beaucourt, and the 51st (Highland) Division entered the ruins of Beaumont Hamel itself. Haig pronounced himself satisfied. On 18 November the battle came to an end, and on 19 November the Battle of the Somme was closed down.

Conclusion

When one looks at the ground gained during the Battle of the Somme – a strip of land 9.6 km/6 mi deep at its deepest and 32 km/20 mi wide – at a cost of some 419,654 British and Dominion casualties (the French lost a further 204,253 on their sector), it seems as though the offensive can only be judged a futile waste. However, it is not always valid judge the success of a battle solely by the amount of ground taken and casualties lost. The Germans suffered in the region of 600,000 casualties and this affected them greatly – indeed, after the battle they were totally exhausted. One could even argue the scale of the German losses had an impact during the battle itself. By the end of July the Germans had lost 160,000 men, and were forced to go on the defensive at Verdun. That, if nothing else, was one achievement of the Battle of the Somme.

CHAPTER 9
THE IMPACT OT ATTRITION

The results of the 1916 fighting had important implications for the strategic decisions made by the Allies and the Central Powers during the following year. The decision taken by Britain, France, Russia, and Italy to continue with their great offensives into 1917 appears to reveal a lack of imagination, or even callousness. However, judged against a background of Allied expectations of a major military breakthrough, it makes a little more sense. Thus, Russia planned to attack at both ends of its line; the French sought to mount an offensive to seize the Chemin des Dames; the British were to push out of Arras; and once again the Italians would campaign on the Isonzo.

The crowded streets of Petrograd on 11 March 1917, just three days after the Russian Revolution had broken out. On the following day, 17,000 soldiers from the garrison in Petrograd joined the crowds in the streets protesting against the tsar.

The Hindenburg Line

The *Siegfriedstellung* (or 'Hindenburg Line', as it was called by the British) was a strong defensive line running from Arras to Laon, and reflected the German decision to remain on the defensive on the Western Front until after Russia had been despatched from the war. Consisting of a series of strongly fortified positions some 24–40 km/15-25 mi to their rear, protected by artillery and constructed during the autumn and winter of 1916, the Germans had to abandon the territory that they had so stoically defended during the Battle of the Somme in order to take up their new positions. By destroying everything in their wake as they pulled back to the Hindenburg Line during March and April 1917, the Germans denied the British many potentially useful supplies and caused many casualties through their meticulous booby-traps. Once established in their new defensive position, the Germans enjoyed a front that was 41.6 km/26 mi shorter than it had been, and this allowed ten divisions to be freed for other duties. Part of the Hindenburg Line was taken by the British in the Arras offensive in the spring of 1917, and the line was breached again during the Battle of Cambrai that November, but it generally resisted attack until the summer of 1918.

Meanwhile, the Germans looked to strengthen their positions in the east and the west following their exertions on both fronts during 1916. They had no plans to assault the Russians, and undertook a general withdrawal back to a strongly prepared defensive position in France – the **'Hindenburg Line'** – between March and April 1917. The Germans then entered a new phase of total war under Hindenburg and Ludendorff, and looked to a U-boat campaign to fulfil their objectives for that year (see Chapter 10).

The year 1917 was to prove the penultimate one of the war, and in many ways was a transitional year, but a glance at the outcome of the Allied attacks reveals little to intimate that victory was near. Indeed, by December the British, French, and Italians had all suffered military setbacks (with only Haig's army spared significant morale problems), and the Russians were on the verge of leaving the war.

Russia in Revolution

The Russian exit from the war was prompted by great turmoil on the home front. While political tensions had been running high in the country for a number of years, the war fanned the flames of discontent, and the threat to the tsar's rule grew with every military setback. In the capital, Petrograd, a wave of strikes broke out on 8 March and the army could not be relied on to quell the disturbances that accompanied them; indeed some troops were actively involved in the disorder. In the early months of 1917, the morale of the army was very low (there were 2 million desertions in March and April), and the desire for a fundamental change to the political system was increasingly evident among the troops. In such circumstances it was clear that there could be no Russian offensive in the spring, and so all plans were cancelled.

Gen Kornilov (centre), the provisional government's commander-in-chief, beside other officers of the Russian Army during the Russian Revolution in March 1917. The provisional government proved to be only a temporary measure and it was swept aside by the Bolshevik Revolution in November of the same year.

FINAL RUSSIAN EFFORT

Legend:
- Russian advances
- limit of Russian advance 16 July
- Central Powers advances
- limit of Russian retreat 4 Aug

Bug

Brody

Lemberg

Zloczow

Tarnopol

Brzezany

AUSTRIA-HUNGARY

Halicz

Kalusz

Dniester

Stanislau

RUSSIA

Kolomea

Khotin

Czernowitz

Prut

0   20 mi
0   40 km

Kerensky, Alexander (1881–1971)

A trained lawyer, Alexander Kerensky was first minister of justice, then minister of war, and eventually prime minister of the provisional government that came to power in Russia in March 1917. Convinced that the continuation of the war was in the best interests of Russia, Kerensky undertook a new offensive under Brusilov's command in July 1917, but its failure and subsequent enemy successes severely undermined his position, and the Bolshevik revolution took place in November. Forced to flee to France, Kerensky eventually went into exile in the USA in 1940.

Alexander Kerensky, prime minister of Russia following the March 1917 revolution, in his cabinet room during the provisional government that lasted until November of the same year.

By mid-March the tsar had recognized that there was no future for his regime, and three days after the appointment of a provisional government by the Petrograd Soviet (a revolutionary council of workers, soldiers, and Duma members) he abdicated. The leaders of the provisional government – briefly Prince Lvov and then **Alexander Kerensky** – believed in the continuation of the war, and sought a great military victory to unite the country and strengthen the position of the new administration. The offensive that resulted – known as the Kerensky offensive, but commanded by the new Commander-in-Chief, Brusilov – began on 1 July. Attacking on a 64-km/40-mi front, the 31 Russian divisions pushing forward near Brody failed to make much of an impression, but a second attack further south a few days later did surprise the enemy, and there was some initial success. Here, on a 96-km/60-mi front, Gen Kornilov's Eighth Army pushed the Austrian Third Army back some 32 km/20 mi, but the timely arrival of German reinforcements (together with some Russian disciplinary problems) meant that there was no exploitation phase. The German counter-offensive that began on 19 July in the north advanced 16 km/10 mi on the first day, and within two weeks had managed to push the Russians back beyond their starting

The Russian women's 'Battalion of Death' training in Petrograd in September 1917. The battalion was formed by the provisional government, and surrendered to the Bolsheviks on the night of 7–8 November. The soldiers are armed with a shorter cavalry version of the Nagant – the standard Russian service rifle.

line. These circumstances forced the Germans to re-evaluate their decision not to attack the Russians, and on 1 September von Hutier's Eighth Army struck at Riga on the Baltic and gained rapid success. While important in terms of the tactics that the Germans employed – the 'hurricane bombardment' and infantry infiltration – this attack was also important at the strategic level as it plundered the last reserves of Russian morale.

The replacement of Brusilov by Gen L G Kornilov failed to restore an irretrievable situation, and the Russian army soon disintegrated. Forced to retain strong links with the old order in order to continue the war, the provisional government was swept aside by revolutionary fervour and the Bolsheviks seized power on 7 November 1917, led by **Lenin**. Although wanting an end to the war, the Bolsheviks found that the revolution itself was not enough to achieve it and so Lenin and Trotsky, the new Commissar for Foreign Affairs, entered into negotiations with Germany. The result was the Treaty of Brest-Litovsk, signed on 3 March 1918 after a German invasion during the previous month had forced their hand. The

Soldiers and civilians in Petrograd read news sheets issued by the Duma during the Russian Revolution.

*On 16 November 1917 during the Russian Revolution in Petrograd, revolutionaries remove the
tsar's portrait from the façade of the Duma and destroy other relics of the imperial regime.*

*Baron Richard von Kühlmann, German foreign minister, signs the Treaty of Brest-Litovsk on
3 March 1918, accompanied by the Austrian foreign minister Count Czernin. The treaty required
Russia to give up all claims to the Baltic provinces, Finland, the Ukraine, and the Caucasus –
amounting to one third of its pre-war population and arable land, and 90% of its coalfields.*

Lenin (Vladimir Ilyich Ulyanov) (1870–1924)

Born in Simbirsk on the River Volga and trained as a lawyer, Vladimir Ilyich Lenin was a Marxist from 1889. His brother had been executed a few years before for attempting to assassinate Tsar Alexander III. Lenin was sent to Siberia for spreading revolutionary propaganda between 1895 and 1900. In *What is to be Done?* (1902), he advocated a professional core of social democratic party activists spearheading the revolution in Russia, a suggestion accepted by the majority (Bolsheviki) at the London party congress in 1903. Lenin was active during an attempt to seize power in Russia in 1905 but was forced into exile when it failed. The Germans were aware of the potentially disruptive effects of the Bolsheviks on the Russian war effort, and consequently helped to transport Lenin from Switzerland through German and Austrian lines back to Petrograd in April 1917. He led the Bolshevik revolution that November. Lenin became leader of the Soviet government, and concluded peace with Germany in the March 1918 Treaty of Brest-Litovsk. Between 1918 and 1920 he organized successful resistance to White Russian (pro-tsarist) uprisings and foreign intervention. Lenin effectively controlled the Soviet Union from the overthrow of the provisional government in November 1917 until his death, although he was injured in an assassination attempt in 1918. He died in 1924.

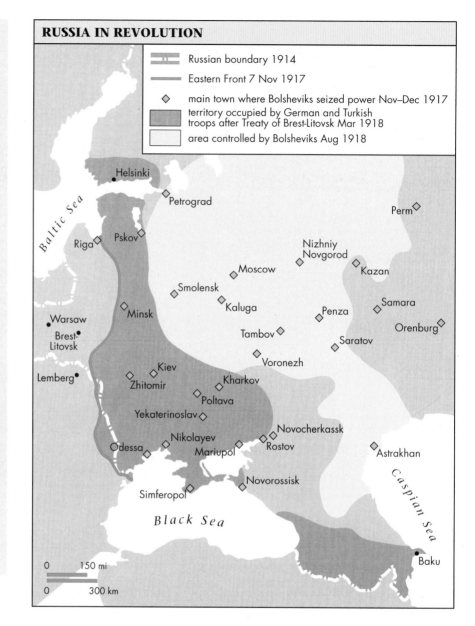

RUSSIA IN REVOLUTION

- Russian boundary 1914
- Eastern Front 7 Nov 1917
- ◇ main town where Bolsheviks seized power Nov–Dec 1917
- territory occupied by German and Turkish troops after Treaty of Brest-Litovsk Mar 1918
- area controlled by Bolsheviks Aug 1918

terms of this agreement might have been hard on Russia but, argued Lenin, they were preferable to a continuation of fighting and additions to the 9 million casualties that the nation had already taken.

Arras

As the Russian March revolution was in full swing, Britain and France were busy preparing for their contributions to 1917. The French 'Nivelle offensive' in the Chemin des Dames was to be supported by a British drive in the Arras sector, which went some way towards placating a British prime minister who was determined that Haig should not deliver another 'great futile offensive'. Indeed, to undermine the power of the BEF's commander-in-chief, Lloyd George went so far as to argue at the Calais Conference of 26 February 1917 that Haig should be subordinated to the French for the rest of the war. Although this request was diluted so that **Nivelle** took overall

The headline in the 11 February 1918 edition of the Berlin newspaper Berliner Lokal-Anzeige *proclaiming the end of the war against Russia. Lenin and the Bolsheviks had wanted to end the war, but found that more than simply a revolution was required to achieve this aim. As a result, they entered into negotiations that led to the Treaty of Brest-Litovsk in March 1918.*

command only for the forthcoming offensive, the relationship between Army headquarters and the government was irrevocably soured by the prime minister's machinations.

The British were the first to attack in the Allied offensives of spring 1917. Gen Horne's First Army was tasked with seizing Vimy Ridge in order to protect the flank of Gen Allenby's Third Army as it battled through the Hindenburg Line. The capture of Vimy Ridge by **Lt-Gen Byng's** Canadian Corps (accompanied by a British offensive at Arras) on 9 April was a success and included a five-day preliminary bombardment and aerial battle. However, the Vimy success revealed that there was a chronic difficulty in turning the hard-won Allied penetration and consolidation of German lines into an exploitation phase that would capture deeper objectives. In fact, this problem was replicated along the entire length of the Third Army's front, for although all of its divisions quickly achieved gains of at least 1,800 m/2,000 yd, the tempo of the attack was soon lost, and the fighting

Nivelle, Gen Robert (1856–1924)

Robert Nivelle was a regimental commander at the outbreak of war in 1914, but was rapidly promoted as a result of his leadership and boldness. By the end of 1915 he was in command of a corps, and within months took charge of the French Second Army. His success as commander of the French counterattacks at Verdun in the autumn of 1916 was a great boost to his career, and he took over from Joffre as commander-in-chief at the end of the year. However, the rapid rise of Nivelle was followed by an equally dramatic demise. The offensive on the Aisne that bears his name opened in April 1917, but failed to fulfil the high hopes that Nivelle had for it. Together with the widespread mutinies that the attack provoked, this led to his replacement by Gen Pétain. Nivelle ended the war commanding troops in North Africa.

The taking of Vimy Ridge in April 1917 – Canadian soldiers advance with a tank across No Man's Land. Note the lack of a trailing wheel on the tank; early versions were equipped with a wheel at the rear, but this was soon found to be superfluous.

At the Scarpe at Blangy on 22 April 1917, during the Battle of Arras, artillerymen row an ammunition pontoon up-river while men of the Highlanders walk along a specially constructed light railway line on the bank.

Naval gun firing over Vimy Ridge at night behind Canadian lines in the spring of 1917. After the war, France gave 100 hectares/250 acres of land on Vimy Ridge to the people of Canada, on which Canadian trees were planted and a large memorial constructed to commemorate the 11,000 or more Canadian soldiers who were killed on the battlefield but whose bodies were never found.

reverted to a far-less-profitable slogging match. The fighting around Arras continued until the middle of May – the last phase being highly attritional – by which time the BEF had lost 150,000 men and the Germans over 100,000. Clearly the British were going to have to pay closer attention to what was required in order to sustain infantry momentum – all-arms cooperation, logistics, and the movement of artillery – before mobility could return to their sector of the front.

The Nivelle Offensive

While not forcing decisive breaks in the Hindenburg Line, the Arras offensive did show signs of promise in its opening days. However, the same could not be said of the hapless French offensive that began on 16 April to seize Chemin des Dames (a road overlooking the Aisne river). Following a two-week bombardment by the French Fourth, Fifth, and Sixth Armies, the attack shared painfully common characteristics with many previous Allied pushes: failure to take territory, and heavy casualties.

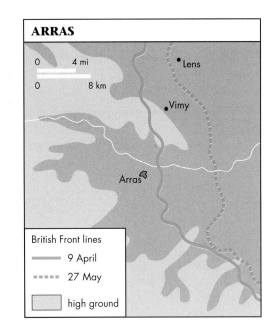

ARRAS

| 0 | 4 mi |
| 0 | 8 km |

• Lens
• Vimy
Arras

British Front lines
——— 9 April
······ 27 May
high ground

British soldiers leave the Arras front by train in May 1917, although unfortunately for them as 'guests' of the Germans. However, in some ways they were the lucky ones – at this point, twice as many British as German troops were being killed in the renewed attacks of the Arras offensive.

Byng, Lieutenant General Julian (1862–1935)

Julian Byng was a highly competent British commander who was given divisional command in 1914 and was sent to command IX Corps at Gallipoli a year later. Having recognized that there was little that could be done to revive the campaign, Byng advocated and planned what proved to be a highly successful evacuation of the peninsula. By May 1916 he was in command of the Canadian Corps that seized Vimy Ridge in April of the following year as part of the Arras offensive. His success saw him promoted to the command of the Third Army during the summer of 1917, and within months he had planned and launched an offensive at Cambrai, which managed to breach the Hindenburg Line through the use of new artillery tactics and close cooperation between the infantry and tanks. Although failing to achieve a breakthrough at Cambrai, the battle was crucial in the evolution of British fighting methods, and helped to restore surprise to British operational art. 1918 proved to be a successful year for Byng, as the Third Army held up very well to the German spring offensive and performed well in the British attacks that led to the armistice.

An official telegraph from the War Office notifying family of a loved one's injuries. It graphically illustrates the horrifying injuries sustained by men fighting at the front.

Lt-Gen Sir Julian Byng, commander of the Canadian Corps on the Western Front from May 1916. Byng led the Canadian forces during the successful assault on Vimy Ridge near Arras, in which they advanced a distance of 6.4 km/4 mi on a 16-km/10-mi wide front.

Despite employing a number of innovative fighting methods, the German defensive deployments (in depth and on reverse slopes) made their lines far more difficult to penetrate than in the Arras sector. Although the offensive managed to move forward on a front of 25.6 km/16 mi, there was no breakthrough, and the creation of a salient 6.4 km/4 mi deep cost the French nearly 190,000 casualties. The failure of Nivelle's plan to restore mobility to the front was followed on 29 April by the first **French army mutiny**. From this point on until well into the autumn, various units refused to obey orders and, as a consequence, fatally undermined the high command's ability to sustain offensive action. Having been mauled at Verdun during the previous year, and despite the presence of the enemy on French soil, the army refused to sacrifice themselves any more in another battle of attrition (few people realise that France lost nearly twice as many men as Britain during the war). In such circumstances Nivelle's position was no longer viable, and his replacement by Pétain – a general officer who was well known for his emphasis on defensive warfare – marked a watershed in French strategy as the offensive was halted.

During 1917, French morale problems were widespread (68 divisions out of a total of 112 were affected), but it did not lead to the collapse of the army. The changes that were made in the wake of the battle did a great deal to stave off much wider disobedience, as they directly addressed the grievances that had helped to popularize disobedience within the ranks – living conditions, leave, and food were all improved and generally welcomed. Under Pétain mass offensives were ruled out, and from late-1917 onwards the main responsibility of the French army was to hold the line. In that case, responsibility for Allied offensive action on the Western Front would then fall to the BEF. Both Haig and Lloyd George soon realized, therefore, that another great British attack was more likely as a

Securing scaling ladders in British trenches on 8 April 1917, the day before the Battle of Arras. The design and steepness of these ladders amply illustrate the difficulty soldiers had in even getting out of the trenches for an attack. It was hardly surprising that many were sitting targets as they struggled to go 'over the top'.

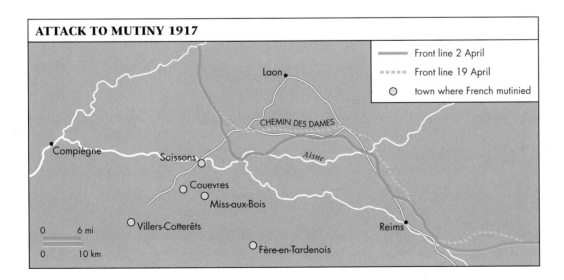

ATTACK TO MUTINY 1917

Front line 2 April

Front line 19 April

○ town where French mutinied

Laon

CHEMIN DES DAMES

Compiègne

Soissons

Aisne

Couevres

Miss-aux-Bois

Villers-Cotterêts

Reims

Fère-en-Tardenois

0   6 mi

0   10 km

Gen Otto von Bülow (centre) on the Italian front, where he commanded the Fourteenth Army of mixed Germans and Austrians at Caporetto in 1917. The Austro-Hungarians had been on the point of collapse, and appealed to the Germans for help. The combined force launched a strong counterattack on the Isonzo area, resulting in the near-destruction of the Italian Second Army.

Italian troops advance along a steep front-line trench in the mountains of Italy. The inhospitable terrain of the Italian Front made military operations very difficult and, as a result, strategic targets such as mountains were often taken and retaken several times by opposing forces.

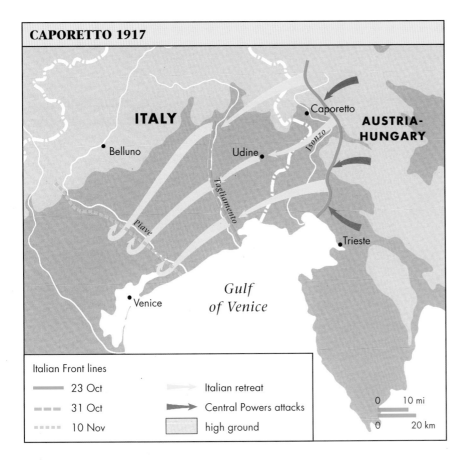

CAPORETTO 1917

ITALY

Belluno

Udine

Tagliamento

Piave

Isonzo

Caporetto

AUSTRIA-HUNGARY

Trieste

Venice

Gulf of Venice

Italian Front lines

——— 23 Oct

- - - - 31 Oct

····· 10 Nov

Italian retreat

Central Powers attacks

high ground

0   10 mi

0   20 km

result of these circumstances: the Third Battle of Ypres was born of French military ill-discipline.

Caporetto

If Allied strategy could be described by the words 'more of the same' for 1917, it was true for no other nation more than it was for Italy. In launching the tenth and eleventh battles of Isonzo during the spring and summer of 1917, Cadorna was following a well-trodden path, but war-weariness was beginning to creep into his army, and heavy casualties had a pronounced effect upon troop morale. Sensing their enemy's difficulties, the Central Powers began to prepare their own offensive and struck on the Isonzo in late October.

The Battle of Caporetto was a disaster for the Italians; in less than a month they were pushed back 128 km/80 mi and lost all of the territory that they had previously won at the cost of over 1 million casualties. The retreat of the 35 Italian divisions on the Isonzo beginning on 24 October was a victory for the fighting methods employed by the 41 assailant divisions of the Central Powers. German tactical developments in the form of a short, sharp 'hurricane' bombardment for maximum surprise and psychological impact, rapidly followed by fast-moving infantry infiltrating weak points in the Italian line, were both highly successful and led to some units advancing 19.2 km/12 mi on the first day alone. Although this

'Some men of the line regiment who had appeared on our right started running back. I shouted out to them to halt, but they took no notice, I pulled out my revolver and very nearly shot at them, but I thought it wouldn't do any good, as they all had their backs to me so would have thought that anyone hit was hit by a German bullet.'
'Why I didn't shoot my men', Lt William St Leger, taken from *People at War 1914–1918*, edited by Michael Moynihan.

'Everybody was afraid. If any man says he never felt fear, I don't care who he is, he's a liar. You all tried not to show it, but everybody felt the same. But when the whistle blew and you went over the top, your fears all went. You never thought about the danger once you were out there among it, but it was that waiting, waiting, waiting in the trenches to go over that got your wind up.'
Rifleman F C White, taken from *The Roses of No Man's Land*, Lynn Macdonald.

British officers anticipate a welcome period of home leave as they await the departure of the train taking them from the Italian Front. The rigours of fighting – particularly on the Western Front – meant that spells of leave were essential for preserving morale and fighting efficiency.

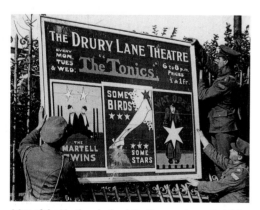

Men of the Northumberland Fusiliers erect an advertising board publicizing a concert party with The Tonics at Bapaume in France on 17 October 1917. Maintaining troop morale is crucial in any war, but was especially important in the deadlock that characterized the Western Front for much of World War I.

forced the virtual collapse of the Italian Second Army, the Third and Fourth Armies did manage to keep their shape as they withdrew, first to the Tagliamento and then to the Piave on 10 November. An inability to turn tactical success into something more sustained, however, led the Central Powers to bring their attack to an end without successful exploitation – a situation that was to haunt the Germans again on the Western Front during the spring of 1918.

In the aftermath of this shocking setback, the Italians reassessed their strategy. Having lost over 275,000 men through being taken prisoner during their retreat (although there were only 30,000 other casualties), and with Cadorna having been replaced by Gen Armando Diaz, the decision was taken to forgo large-scale offensives until the strength of their enemies had been severely undermined. It is true that Italy had been severely shaken by Caporetto, but with the enemy encamped on their soil the nations rallied and, just like the French, the army resolved to fight on.

The events of 1917 revealed that a state of war-weariness had certainly established itself within some of the major Allied states – if not all of them. The Russian Revolution, French mutinies, and the Italian retreat at Caporetto were all symptomatic of the massive sacrifices that nations had to make in order to fight the war. But if events on the fighting fronts pointed towards an advantage to Berlin, Vienna, and Constantinople in 1917, the entry of the USA into the war during that same year gave them great cause for concern.

CHAPTER 10
THE USA ENTERS THE WAR

World War I is not often thought of as a conflict in which naval power
had an important impact, but although the war at sea between 1914 and
1918 might have lacked the sort of great engagements that had been
seen in previous total wars, sea power was crucial to its final outcome.
Indeed, German naval strategy played an important part in the US
decision to enter the war on the Allied side in 1917 – an event that had
enormous consequences in this attritional war, and which required
Germany to re-evaluate its military objectives for 1918.

Part of the British Grand Fleet steam in line astern during a snowstorm. The Grand Fleet was a key element in the Battle of Jutland, and although it sustained
heavy losses, its commander Admiral Sir John Jellicoe had proved that the German High Seas Fleet could not operate at will in the North Sea.

'To illustrate how easily ships were sunk I'll give the following instance ... I casually looked across to the destroyers on the other side of the merchantmen and saw a cloud of water ascend in the air near a destroyer; shortly afterwards, only a few minutes, her bow went up in the air, and she slid, stern first, under the water ... Suddenly she began to settle down, and in about ten minutes she had gone.'
J Willey, 'War At Sea', taken from *True World War I Stories*, Robinson Publishing Ltd (1997).

Bringing coal up from the bunkers to the stokers on a British battleship. Such a job in the dark and confined environs of the ship's boiler-room was filthy work.

A German submarine puts to sea as its crew lines up on deck. The first British ship to be sunk by a U-boat was the cruiser HMS Pathfinder, on 3 September 1914. While Allied shipping perfected a number of defences against submarine warfare, German submarines continued to wreak havoc throughout the war.

The War at Sea – 1914

The war at sea did not turn out in the way that many people expected. With the naval arms race between Britain and Germany having started in the late 1890s, and the *Dreadnought* having had such an impact upon the public consciousness, it was not unreasonable for the British population to have expected a great showdown between the Grand Fleet and the German High Seas Fleet in the North Sea. However, in reality the war at sea was marked from the outset by attrition in which both sides, fearful of losing capital ships, endeavoured gradually to erode the enemy's ability to sustain their war effort.

The crew of a German submarine, or U-boat, in the conning tower of their vessel. Germany used U-boats to try to blockade Britain and starve it into submission, and although the plan ultimately failed, the effects were felt severely in Britain.

For the Germans this strategy was conceived as a result of their inferiority in terms of numbers of capital ships and a desire to ensure that this weakness could not be exploited by their enemy. For the British, even with superiority in numbers, the fleet was not something that they wished to imperil unless they had to, as not only did it safeguard the empire, but also the British Isles themselves. To this end, Churchill said that the commander-in-chief of the Grand Fleet, **Admiral Sir John Jellicoe**, was 'the only man on either side who could lose the war in an afternoon'.

Therefore, German naval strategy planned to nibble away at the Royal Navy while also blockading Britain. The whittling-down of British maritime assets was to be achieved by tempting Royal Navy squadrons into the

Jellicoe, Admiral Sir John Rushworth (1859–1935)

John Jellicoe was an experienced sailor by the time war broke out in 1914, having fought in Egypt in 1882 and having been wounded during the Boxer Rebellion. His knowledge of naval gunnery resulted in his appointment as the Director of Naval Ordnance in 1905, and on 4 August 1914 he was made Commander of the Grand Fleet. Although he was expecting a major naval engagement early in the war, it was not until the Battle of Jutland in May 1916 that he took on the German High Seas Fleet. Jellicoe has been criticized for his cautious nature, and this was on view during Jutland, when he decided not to risk his own vessels despite the possibility of being able to annihilate Admiral Scheer's force. Nevertheless, it has to be remembered that the preservation of the Grand Fleet was essential to Britain's ability to sustain its war effort, while the destruction of the High Seas Fleet was not. Despite the strategic success of Jutland, Jellicoe was removed from command and became First Sea Lord, before being dismissed by an unimpressed Lloyd George in December 1917. He was made a peer in 1918 and was appointed Admiral of the Fleet in 1919.

John Jellicoe, commander of the Grand Fleet from August 1914 to 1916. Jellicoe took on the German High Seas Fleet during the Battle of Jutland in May 1916.

A letter home containing sketches from a British seaman describing how the three Allied battleships Irresistible *and* Ocean *(British) and* Bouvet *(French) met their fate on 18 March 1915 at the entrance to the Dardanelles, which had been mined by a Turkish vessel.*

'A submarine had been spotted, and with the destroyer circling around at full speed, belching out the while a thick, black smoke screen, we raced as fast as the engines would turn over, to a place of comparative safety, that being a small river on the north coast of Africa. There we were literally bottled-up for three days together with another crowded transport, while our underwater foe patrolled the river's mouth waiting and watching for us to come out.'
Reginald C Huggins, 'Torpedoed In The Aegean Sea', taken from *True World War I Stories*, Robinson Publishing Ltd (1997).

North Sea, where they would then be destroyed piecemeal. This was the intention behind the shelling of English coastal towns such as Lowestoft and Hartlepool in November and December 1914, and the engagement that took place on 24 January 1915 on the Dogger Bank, in which the Royal Navy managed to sink one German vessel and damage another. Generally, however, the British were not lured out into the open sea, and as a consequence they unhinged their enemy's plan. Interestingly, it was the sinking of three British cruisers on 22 September 1914 by a German

U-boat that revealed more about the future of German naval strategy than the exploits at Dogger Bank.

U-boats were central to the other strand of German strategy: blockade. This strategy was also followed by the British. Attempts to cut off overseas supplies started soon after the outbreak of war and had a global impact due to the far-flung nature of the belligerents' colonial possessions. The Royal Navy, for example, was to be found chasing enemy vessels in the Mediterranean during early August, although two German cruisers, the *Goeben* and *Breslau*, managed to evade its clutches and ended up in Turkey (where they helped to push Turkey into the war on the side of the Central Powers). In another action it was Admiral von Spee's German 'China Squadron' that took the initiative and sunk two British cruisers off the west coast of South America on 1 November. Nevertheless, Spee's next move on 8 December, an attack on Port Stanley (the capital of the

Sinking of the *Lusitania*

On 7 May 1915, Commander Schweiger of the German navy was patrolling in submarine U-20 in the southern entrance to the Irish coast off the Old Head of Kinsale. Three months earlier the Germans had declared all waters around the British Isles a 'war zone'. At about 1340 hrs, Schweiger suddenly saw the Cunard liner *Lusitania* in the submarine's sight on the final leg of its passage from New York to Liverpool. Half an hour later the submarine fired two torpedoes. The first caused a great explosion: the liner keeled over and sank within 20 minutes. About 2,000 passengers had been on board; of these, 1,198 perished, including 291 women and 94 children. Among the dead were 128 US citizens. As their bodies drifted on to Kinsale, a great outcry of protest came from neutral USA. In Ireland, then a part of the UK, the coroner's court found the Kaiser guilty of wilful murder. The sinking brought home to the combatants and neutrals the ugly and deadly nature of modern warfare. At the same time, the USA grew closer to the Allied cause.

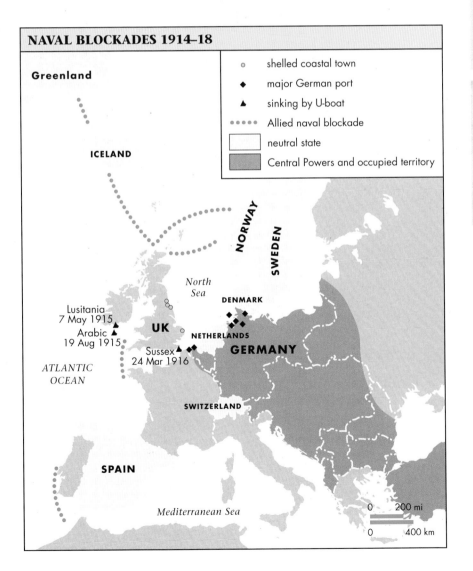

NAVAL BLOCKADES 1914–18

Greenland

○   shelled coastal town

◆   major German port

▲   sinking by U-boat

•••••   Allied naval blockade

☐   neutral state

▨   Central Powers and occupied territory

ICELAND

NORWAY

SWEDEN

North Sea

DENMARK

Lusitania 7 May 1915

Arabic 19 Aug 1915

UK

NETHERLANDS

Sussex 24 Mar 1916

GERMANY

ATLANTIC OCEAN

SWITZERLAND

SPAIN

Mediterranean Sea

0   200 mi

0   400 km

LONDON & NORTH WESTERN RY
Available for Three Months
Via Birkenhead or Runcorn & Chester Whitchurch & Shrewsbury or Manchester or direct Via Crewe, and with liberty to call at B'ham Coventry Kenilworth Warwick Leamington Stratford-on-Avon Via Blisworth & Oxford Via Bletchley
Issued on CUNARD Steamer LUSITANIA
LIVERPOOL (Riverside) To
LONDON (EUSTON)
First] 847(S) [Class
TURNOVER) EUSTON FARE 29/-

A facsimile of the last ticket (for a train journey from Liverpool to Euston) issued to a passenger on the SS Lusitania *before it was torpedoed by a German U-boat in May 1915, with the loss of nearly 1,200 lives.*

Beatty, Admiral Sir David (1871–1936)

David Beatty was a gifted sailor, and served in both Egypt and China before the outbreak of World War I. While serving as Churchill's naval secretary (1911–13) he cultured some impressive contacts before being appointed commander of the Grand Fleet's Battlecruiser Squadron in 1913. Beatty was an aggressive and daring commander, and was therefore well equipped to direct a force that sought to find the enemy quickly and hold them until the main force arrived. He was successful in this role at Heligoland Bight, Dogger Bank, and Jutland, although in the last of these his decision to engage the enemy and the tardiness of the information that he passed on to Jellicoe have been criticized. After Jutland, Beatty took over command of the Grand Fleet from Jellicoe, but he had precious little opportunity to reveal his talents again during the war.

Admiral Sir David Beatty – Commander of the Grand Fleet's battlecruiser squadron and later placed in command of the entire Grand Fleet upon Admiral Sir John Jellicoe's appointment as First Sea Lord – with a Brazilian admiral on board the British battleship Queen.

A German mine explodes in coastal waters. Usually laid by surface craft rather than submarines, mines claimed many more ships than did gunfire, although the British became proficient at minesweeping.

Scale

Lighthouse

"THETIS"

Destroyed by
Submarine

"IPHEGENIA"
"INTREPID"

ZEEBRUGGE

Church

Wharf
(now removed)

X shows position from which
photograph was taken, dotted
lines show area included in
photograph

Lock

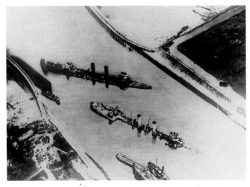

Two ageing British cruisers, Intrepid *and* Iphegenia, *lie
sunk at the entrance to the canal at Zeebrugge to deny
German submarines access to the North Sea (a third
vessel used in the raid,* Thetis, *is out of shot). The
deliberate sinkings on 23 April 1918 were the result of
an audacious plan to prevent U-boats from using the
canal at Zeebrugge as a base for launching attacks on
Allied shipping in the North Sea.*

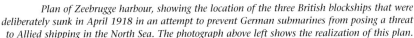

*Plan of Zeebrugge harbour, showing the location of the three British blockships that were
deliberately sunk in April 1918 in an attempt to prevent German submarines from posing a threat
to Allied shipping in the North Sea. The photograph above left shows the realization of this plan.*

British Falkland Islands) was met by the Royal Navy battlecruisers
Inflexible and *Invincible,* and only one German ship escaped their guns.

In this sort of war at sea, the British certainly had the advantage, not only
in their numerical superiority, but also in the size of their empire and the
access to friendly ports that it provided. Thus, by the end of 1914, many
German overseas squadrons were unable to return home because the
Royal Navy had them pinned down.

Meanwhile the blockade of Germany and Britain had begun in earnest.
For the British, this meant patrolling the North Sea and English Channel in
order to ensure that no vessels either reached or left the ports of the

NORTH SEA BATTLES 1914–16

0   150 mi

0   300 km

*North
Sea*

Jutland

Dogger Bank

DENMARK

Heligoland Bight

UK   NETHERLANDS

GERMANY

◆ site of major battle

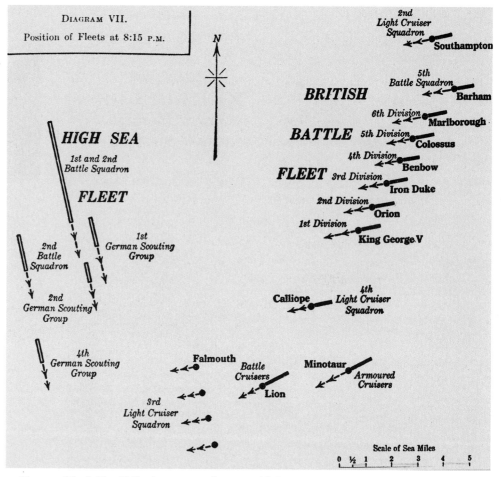

DIAGRAM VII.
Position of Fleets at 8:15 P.M.

N

2nd Light Cruiser Squadron
Southampton

BRITISH
5th Battle Squadron
Barham

6th Division
Marlborough

BATTLE
5th Division
Colossus

4th Division
Benbow

FLEET
3rd Division
Iron Duke

2nd Division
Orion

1st Division
King George V

HIGH SEA
1st and 2nd Battle Squadron

FLEET

1st German Scouting Group

2nd Battle Squadron

2nd German Scouting Group

4th German Scouting Group

Calliope
4th Light Cruiser Squadron

Falmouth
Battle Cruisers

Minotaur
Armoured Cruisers

Lion

3rd Light Cruiser Squadron

Scale of Sea Miles
0   ½   1   2   3   4   5

Diagram of the Battle of Jutland – an excerpt from an article by commander of the Grand Fleet Admiral Sir John Jellicoe in the book These Eventful Years. *The battlecruiser* Lion, *Admiral Sir David Beatty's flagship (shown at the bottom of the diagram) was damaged in a long-range duel with German battlecruisers at the start of the battle.*

Submarines

Submarines were a relatively new development in World War I with the first British boats completed in 1902 and the first German equivalent four years later. In 1914, Britain and France had about half of the total number of submarines in existence while Germany had just 24. Nevertheless, Germany took the lead in submarine design and sought to produce large 'cruisers' that could act as independent offensive weapons. The British, meanwhile, developed smaller vessels for reconnaissance, and these worked closely with the fleet. However, it is the work of the U-boats in their unrestricted role that is most readily associated with the employment of submarines in World War I. Although the largest number of U-boats that the Germans had in service at any one time was 140, they managed to sink 2,439 Allied and neutral ships in 1917, and 1,035 in 1918.

Central Powers. For the Germans, it meant laying mines along the English coast in an attempt to undermine the Royal Navy's freedom of movement, and conducting submarine warfare. The German use of U-boats against all shipping destined for Britain – including that coming from the USA – revealed to many neutral countries for the first time the increasingly total nature of the war. However, the sinking of the **Lusitania** on 7 May 1915 revealed that this was a high-risk policy, as the loss of US life inevitably raised the hackles of the USA. Indeed, when a further three US citizens were drowned following the sinking of another vessel on 19 August, the US reaction led the Germans to abandon their policy of sinking ships without warning – although it was to return just 18 months later.

The war at sea in 1915 was therefore dominated by the establishment of blockades, and a desire on the part of the rival fleets to keep a healthy distance between each other. The appointment of the aggressive Admiral Scheer to the command of the High Seas Fleet in January 1916, however, saw a change in tack.

The Battle of Jutland

The only great naval battle of the war, the Battle of Jutland, took place when Scheer took a chance and decided to put the German High Seas Fleet to sea. However, this bold move was anticipated by Admiral Sir John Jellicoe who, with the benefit of intercepted German signals, left Scapa Flow with his Grand Fleet while **Admiral Beatty's** faster battlecruisers left from the Firth of Forth. Beatty's scouts encountered the vanguard of the German battlecruisers on the afternoon of 31 May and gave chase as their enemy turned away. After a long-range duel, during which Beatty's flagship *Lion* was damaged and another two battlecruisers were sunk, the main body of the High Seas Fleet hoved into view. Knowing that the Grand Fleet was following behind, Beatty turned to join them and by the evening had brought his ships into line. When the two fleets began to engage soon after, both sides suffered casualties – including the British

'Being a non-swimmer at the time, I was unable to get clear of the ship, and her enormous bulk seemed likely to topple over on me at any moment, supposing I was not sucked down one of the huge funnels by the in rush of water. That actually did happen to our Chaplain. He was, subsequently, vomited out again like a rocket and suffered no ill effects, when the water charging up against the heated boilers caused an explosion.'
Reginald C Huggins, 'Torpedoed In The Aegean Sea', taken from *True World War I Stories*, Robinson Publishing Ltd (1997).

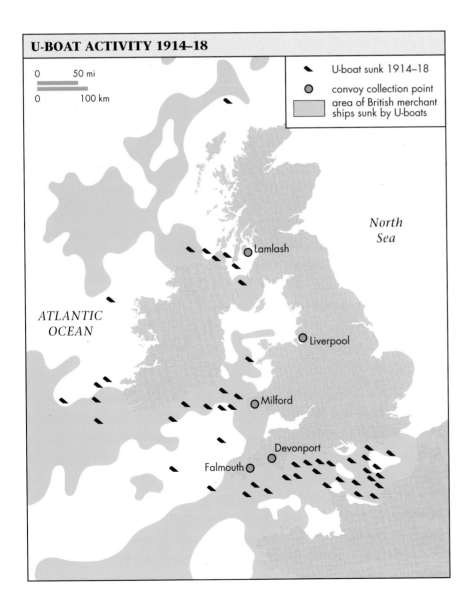

U-BOAT ACTIVITY 1914–18

| 0 | 50 mi |
| 0 | 100 km |

- U-boat sunk 1914–18
- convoy collection point
- area of British merchant ships sunk by U-boats

North Sea

ATLANTIC OCEAN

Lamlash

Liverpool

Milford

Devonport

Falmouth

A sea scout learns to identify passing vessels from the coastline of Britain. With the English Channel being such a crucial shipping route for access to northern European ports, it was vital that it remained open. Observation by non-fighting personnel helped to take the load off troops who were fit enough to fight.

battlecruiser *Invincible*, which was sunk – but Scheer became increasingly aware that the Royal Navy had the ability to completely destroy his fleet. As the Germans manoeuvred out of the range of the British guns, Jellicoe could have given chase, but instead he decided to reposition his own forces between his enemy and their route home. As Scheer moved into range once more, the Grand Fleet's guns opened up but the Germans, covered by a salvo of 32 torpedoes, repositioned themselves. Jellicoe could have run the gauntlet of the torpedoes and might have inflicted a decisive defeat on Scheer, but he was unwilling to suffer heavy losses and the chance passed quickly. During the night Scheer made a break for home and, pushing through the lighter elements of the Grand Fleet, managed to return to his base: the battle was over.

Unlike the great land battles of the war, the Battle of Jutland was fought over a very short period of time, but its importance was not confined to the evolution of naval tactics. Although the British took the heavier losses in the battle, they won a strategic victory as Jellicoe confirmed that the German High Seas Fleet could not operate in the North Sea without the threat of destruction. After the battle the German surface fleet never ventured out of port in large numbers again – but German submarines did roam freely, and it was to them that Berlin increasingly turned.

German submariners on the turret of their vessel as they head for the sea in April 1917. In February, the Kaiser had announced unrestricted submarine warfare against all shipping, regardless of the cargo being carried.

LUSITANIA TORPEDOED BY GERMAN PIRATE

The Daily Mirror

CERTIFIED CIRCULATION LARGER THAN ANY OTHER PICTURE PAPER IN THE WORLD

No. 3,600. | Registered at the G.P.O. as a Newspaper. | SATURDAY, MAY 8, 1915 | 16 PAGES | One Halfpenny.

GIANT CUNARDER CROWDED WITH PASSENGERS CALLOUSLY SUNK WITHOUT WARNING OFF THE IRISH COAST.

Without warning the famous Cunarder Lusitania was torpedoed off the Irish coast yesterday. She sank in eight minutes, but, it is believed, many of the passengers have been saved. The United States is seething with anger at this crime against neutral passengers, including women and children. The pirates' disregard of the lives of Americans will undoubtedly compel President Wilson to take immediate and drastic action. Amongst the passengers were many famous Britons and Americans.

Submarine Warfare

After the Battle of Jutland, submarines gave Germany the sort of presence at sea that was denied their surface fleet. In operations in the Mediterranean and the Atlantic, these small vessels had a strategic impact as they sank large and expensive shipping. U-boats had already revealed their potential before 1916 at Gallipoli and in the waters around Britain during 1915; indeed, their success had so angered the United States that it led to the Germans cancelling their policy of 'unrestricted' submarine warfare. One-and-a-half years later, however, it was reintroduced in the hope that if enough merchant shipping were sunk, it would starve Britain into submission even if it did entice the US to enter the war. The whole campaign, however, miscalculated the ability of Britain to survive the losses, and the huge impact that the United States would have on the Allied war effort.

Despite its ultimate failure, the German unrestricted submarine warfare campaign did hurt Britain. In 1917 over 1,000 ships were lost to submarines, and in April of that year – the height of German action – more than 450,000 tonnes/500,000 tons of British shipping was sunk (and losses of Allied and neutral shipping were also running extremely high). The Royal Navy searched in vain for adequate countermeasures, but none had any great impact until the convoy system was introduced at Lloyd George's insistence. Although the Admiralty was against the dilution of the Grand Fleet's lighter vessels for convoy duties, the system quickly achieved results and from September to December 1917, less than 900 tonnes/1,000 tons of British shipping was lost.

The convoy system was a disaster for the U-boat campaign and the German attempt to starve Britain out of the war. By 1918 the German navy was impotent and, as a consequence, although the Allied blockade of Germany was biting increasingly hard (see Chapter 13), they could do little about it. The scuttling of the German fleet by its own crews at the end of the war was a reflection of Allied naval supremacy by this stage. Between 1916 and 1918, although the Germans had managed to inflict great damage upon British shipping, Allied production of new vessels – together with the arrival of the US battlefleet in European waters – served only to undermine German morale even further. Consequently, the war at sea ended in 1918, not with the bang of a decisive battle, but with the whimper of total subjugation of the German High Seas Fleet by the Grand Fleet and its allies.

The USA at War

The resumption of unrestricted German submarine warfare in February 1917 was a direct cause of the USA's entry into World War I. **President Wilson** had made it clear to Berlin that the sinking of US merchant

Wilson, Thomas Woodrow (1856–1924)

Wilson was an academic by training, but in 1910 he was elected governor of New Jersey, and two years later was president of the United States. He was re-elected president in 1916, by which time he was finding it increasingly difficult to keep the USA out of the conflict. The USA entered the war in April 1917 after the publication of the 'Zimmerman Telegram' and the reintroduction of German unrestricted submarine warfare. In January 1918 he issued his 'Fourteen Points' as a basis for a just peace settlement, and after the armistice played a central part in the creation of the League of Nations, although the USA did not join the League itself. In 1919 he suffered a stroke from which he never fully recovered.

A jovial US president Woodrow Wilson is driven through Manchester, England in the company of the city's mayor on 30 December 1918, as part of his visit to Europe following the Armistice.

Signalling from a US torpedo-boat destroyer to another ship in the convoy. At the outbreak of war, the US Navy possessed 56 such vessels.

shipping would lead to the USA joining the Allies in the war against the Central Powers, but Germany thought that it was a risk worth taking. In fact, relations between Washington and Berlin had been fraught for some time. The sinking of the *Lusitania* and the loss of other US lives in German submarine actions during 1915 had outraged the USA, and the infamous January 1917 'Zimmerman Telegram' heightened tensions even further. The encoded cable sent by German foreign secretary Arthur Zimmerman to the German ambassador in Mexico – suggesting that if Germany and the USA went to war, that Germany should assist Mexico in recovering the lost territories of Texas, Arizona, and New Mexico – was picked up by British naval intelligence and soon found its way to the White House. Wilson and the population of the United States were understandably furious, and by the time Germany returned to unrestricted submarine warfare, the momentum towards war was undeniable.

When the USA did declare war against the Central Powers in April 1917, the parity of resources (financial, human, and technical), which had been central to the development of stalemate on the Western Front and the war of attrition more generally, suddenly looked vulnerable. Wilson's decision to fight immediately brought financial stability, massive resources of raw materials, a huge production capacity, and valuable naval assets to the Allied cause. What the US did not have, however, was a large army. Nevertheless, the nation did have great mobilization potential, and it was just a matter of time before hundreds of thousands of US troops took their places on the Western Front under **Gen John Pershing**, the commander of the American Expeditionary Force (AEF).

US mobilization was rapid. By July 1917, in addition to the regular force of 125,000 men, the entire National Guard had been mobilized and conscription was in force. By May 1918 there were more than half a million US troops in France, and by the time of the great Allied offensives that July, the figure had risen to over 1 million. Although the aim of providing 100 combat divisions for the Western Front was never achieved (as the war ended before such a figure could be reached), 7 regular, 17 National Guard, and 16 national army divisions were deployed – comprising approximately one-third of the total Allied force in November 1918. By the end of the war the US Army was 4 million men strong, of which over 2 million (including 1,250 US aircrew) were at the fighting front. Of these, some 264,000 became casualties, of whom 50,000 died.

The US Army did not really have much time to make its mark in the fighting on the Western Front, but the Germans undoubtedly felt its presence. Moreover, the importance of the contribution made by the AEF in France amounted to far more than the actions in which it took part. The arrival of so many fresh troops from across the Atlantic was an important fillip to Allied morale, and these forces would have had great potential if the war had dragged on into 1919. Such advantages had not escaped the attention of the German army either, and they were forced to reorientate their strategy in order to take account of US strengths if they were given time to mass and mature in the field (see Chapter 14). The USA tipped the balance in favour of the Allies, and although this did not make victory inevitable, without their presence on the Western Front, Allied victory would surely have been delayed.

Pershing, General John Joseph (1860–1948)

John Pershing had served in the Spanish War (1898), the Philippines (1899–1903), and Mexico (1916–17) before taking command of the American Expeditionary Force on 26 May 1917. During World War I, he fought hard to command in the way that he thought best and stuck to the principle of using US forces as a coherent formation by refusing to attach regiments or brigades to British or French divisions. Although he wished to build up his forces to the point where they could make their own mark on the fighting, the success of German spring offensives in 1918 forced him to allow some of his troops to be deployed in support of the French. The first major action of the US Army on the Western Front was in the St Mihiel offensive in September 1918, but the fighting in the Meuse-Argonne sector shortly afterwards was much more challenging. Pershing was successful in these offensives, although his progress was slow. He was made a full general of the US Army in 1919, a rank that had been previously held by only four people: Washington, Grant, Sherman, and Sheridan. In 1921 Pershing became army chief of staff, and he retired three years later.

Gen John J Pershing, commander of the American Expeditionary Force, on the quayside at Boulogne after landing in France on 13 June 1917. It was only a few weeks since the USA had declared war on Germany, and the US Army had a steep learning curve in prospect.

Recruiting poster for the US Navy in 1917. The USA declared war on Germany on 6 April 1917, when unrestricted submarine warfare had been in effect for two months. Both the US Senate and House of Representatives voted in favour of war by large majorities.

CHAPTER 11
FLANDERS

At the beginning of 1917, the strategic hope of David Lloyd George was for a series of Allied offensive operations that absolved the British of responsibility for massive Somme-like attacks – but he was to be disappointed. The failure of the French Nivelle offensive, the Russian Kerensky offensive and the Italian attacks on the Isonzo meant that by the early summer of 1917 the weight of Allied offensives had fallen squarely on to British shoulders. This was the last thing that Lloyd George had hoped for, but it presented Haig and the BEF with an opportunity to stamp their mark on the course of the war. The result was the Third Battle of Ypres and, as a curtain-raiser, the Battle of Messines.

Chateau Wood, Ypres, on 29 October 1917. A combination of heavy shelling and prolonged periods of rain had turned much of the area into liquid mud, making the battlefield extremely difficult to move across.

The Battles of Messines and the Third Battle of Ypres

The commander-in-chief of the BEF had long yearned for a major set-piece attack in Flanders. **Sir Douglas Haig** had attacked on the Somme in 1916 out of the need to service the entente, but his strategic thinking had always been focused on a push out of the Ypres salient and on the Belgian coast. The politicians eventually agreed to endorse a Flanders offensive, partly out of respect for the increased regard in which Haig was held after his early successes during the Battle of Arras but, more importantly, owing to a lack of alternatives. In many respects British politicians had been placed in a strategic straitjacket by the military failures of Russia, France, and Italy.

The action at Ypres began with a battle 4.8 km/3 mi to the south of the town to seize the Messines ridge. The attack began on 7 June and lasted for one week, and was deemed necessary because the position overlooked the British lines, and could have been used by the Germans to

The South entrance of the Cathedral at Ypres showing extensive bomb damage.

View across the Douve Valley, rear Messines, showing the bombardment of the town in progress.

Haig, Sir Douglas (1861–1928)

Douglas Haig was commander of I Corps at the outbreak of war, was promoted to command the First Army in 1915 and became commander-in-chief of the British Expeditionary Force in December of that year. Made a field marshal in 1917, Haig is more often remembered for the casualties that were lost in his massive set-piece battles such as the Somme (1916) and the Third Battle of Ypres (1917), rather than his victories of 1918, and his generalship remains highly controversial. Although always intending to launch offensives that would break the enemy line, many of Haig's offensives turned into attritional slogging matches leading to the massive expenditure of resources and men. Nevertheless, by early 1918, the development of British fighting methods, overseen and directed by Haig, was able to exploit weaknesses in the German army and led to the armistice and victory. Haig was a national hero at the time of his death, but his reputation began to fall after the publication of Lloyd George's memoirs – a situation from which it has struggled to recover ever since.

A formal portrait of Field Marshal Sir Douglas Haig on horseback, September 1917. As commander-in-chief of the Western Front 1915–18, Haig has often been saddled with the blame for pursuing reckless tactics that caused the huge Allied losses in areas such as the Somme, but it is questionable whether any other course of action was open to him.

observe preparations for the principal offensive. The position was so advantageous that the man in command of the Messines offensive, **Sir Herbert Plumer**, oversaw operations to place 23 enormous mines under the enemy front line on the forward slope of the ridge, in order to destroy key positions and create confusion when they were detonated simultaneously at zero hour. Plumer's meticulous preparation clearly sought to cancel out as many German advantages as possible – the mines were a part of that – but more important was the ferocity of the preliminary bombardment. In an attempt to obliterate the enemy's trenches, cut the wire and destroy the German guns, the BEF deployed 2,266 guns on a 19.2-km/12-mi front – a trebling of the density of the guns that had been used during the Battle of the Somme just 12 months before. The guns at Messines laid down 3.5 million shells in their 'softening up' operations and at 0310 hrs on 7 June, 19 mines were detonated and 90,000 Allied infantrymen attacked behind a creeping barrage. When coupled with the impact of the standing barrage that dropped in their rear areas, the surprise and confusion that Allied fighting methods engendered within the German defences reaped great reward for Plumer, and the ridge was taken for relatively few casualties in just a few hours. Difficulties in consolidating the position did lead to the fighting dragging on for a number of days, and losses did rise, but the break-in phase was a great success and certainly justified the time and resources that the British had spent on it.

Plumer, General Hubert Charles (1857–1932)

Hubert Plumer was one of the best British generals of the war – despite being the inspiration behind the cartoonist David Low's 'Colonel Blimp' (a caricature of an elderly, out of touch, and reactionary officer who placed more faith in horses than tanks). Having been commander of II Corps for the last months of 1914, he was promoted to command the Second Army, which then fought around Ypres for the next two years. His meticulous planning for the successful Battle of Messines in June 1917 was characteristic, and reflected his cautious nature. When he took over the Third Battle of Ypres from Gough later in the year, he restored momentum to the faltering offensive by pursuing achievable objectives that could be consolidated. He was sent to revive the Italian army in November 1917, but returned to command the Second Army against the German spring 1918 offensives. He was highly popular with his troops (who referred to him as 'Daddy'), and after the armistice he marched his army to the Rhine as part of the forces of occupation.

A German prisoner captured at the Battle of Messines Ridge, 8 June 1917. Ten thousand German soldiers are believed to have been killed instantly or buried alive by the huge mine blast a couple of days earlier.

Field Marshal Sir Douglas Haig (right) with his senior general Herbert Plumer (left), and Gen Lawrence. At the Third Battle of Ypres in October 1917, Plumer tried to persuade Haig to end the offensive against German forces because of the appalling casualty rate, but Haig remained unmoved.

Unfortunately for the British, however, although it successfully reintroduced an element of tactical surprise to the battlefield at Messines, the fighting here dealt a mortal blow to operational surprise for what was to follow at Ypres. It was understood that the Battle of Messines Ridge would give the Germans a warning that would give them time to brace themselves for the possibility of another British attack, but the decision not to launch the follow-up offensive until 31 July was disastrous. In giving the Germans time in which to strengthen their defences at Ypres, the British made an already difficult job all the more challenging. Even the month-long preliminary bombardment (which was supposed to severely undermine German defensive preparation) was something of a curse. By the time the British began their attack, the battlefield had been so torn up by the impact of 4 million shells that momentum would have been difficult to maintain, even if initial tempo had been gained (which it was not) and the weather had been dry (which it also was not). These difficulties taxed Gen Hubert Gough, Haig's inexperienced commander for the offensive, to the full and he was found wanting in many areas.

The initial objectives of the attack were a series of ridges (some so slight that they were barely recognizable as ridges on the ground) which, despite their lack of height, gave the Germans great defensive advantage. The aim was to take them rapidly, ease the pressure on the salient, and then use them soon after as launch-pads for thrusts towards deeper objectives. Like so many plans during the war, hope clouded reality, and four weeks into the attack so little ground had been taken that Haig replaced Gough with Plumer, and a whole new approach to the offensive was undertaken.

By the time Plumer took over the reins of command, the torrential rains of a Belgian summer had already turned the battlefield into a quagmire. In such circumstances, Plumer judged that it would be difficult to break the German line in the short term, and so decided on lengthy preparation before launching a series of 'bite and hold' attacks that better suited the situation he inherited. The results of his plan were the battles of Menin Road, Polygon Wood, and Broodseinde which, launched in fine weather, fulfilled his desire for limited advances that could be sustained and consolidated. Nevertheless, by the time that the British had restored an element of forward momentum to their offensive in September and October, the deteriorating weather severely hampered subsequent operations. To this end, the return of low cloud and rain meant not only that the battlefield was even more difficult to traverse, but also that aircraft were grounded and therefore unable to provide the artillery with the sort of information that made them much more effective. As a result (and with the original grandiose objectives for the battle already long forgotten), even the fight for limited objectives became a questionable exercise, but the struggle continued.

A soldier writes a letter home in Oostaverne Wood at the Battle of Messines Ridge, 11 June 1917. This battle was famous for the use of a massive detonation of 450 tonnes/500 tons of explosive in mine shafts dug under the German trenches – the resulting blast could be felt across the English Channel in Southern England.

'We left the trench and crossed the shell-torn hill by the railway cutting. The crater, which I expected to see as an immense jagged hole in the ground, was actually a large flat-bottomed depression like a frying pan, clear and clean from debris except at the further edge, where vestiges of one of the enemy's trenches showed through its side.
The poor devils caught in that terrible cataclysm had no chance. Yet what chance was there for anyone in that war of guns and mathematics?'
EN Gladden, 'At Messines Ridge In 1917', taken from *True World War I Stories*, Robinson Publishing Ltd (1997).

The decision to continue with the battle has become one of the weapons most frequently picked up by those wishing to attack Haig's reputation over the years. With the benefit of hindsight, he was clearly unwise to continue the push up on to Passchendaele Ridge, but it is possible that this decision was taken with future stark military considerations in mind. By denying the Germans Passchendaele Ridge (from which Ypres and much of the salient could be seen), Haig might have been not only thinking about the capture as a springboard from which a future Allied offensive could be launched, but also about thwarting any German ambitions of using it as an offensive springboard of their own, and about the removal of German artillery observation for the coming winter. If this were the case, Haig's decision to continue the offensive makes a little more sense.

MESSINES JUNE 1917

Front line 7 June
Front line 14 June
British mine
high ground

Ypres
Hill 60
Messines Ridge
Ypres-Comines Canal
Wytschaete
Messines
Warneton
Ploegsteert Wood

0   1 mi
0   2 km

Official Canadian photo of wounded Canadians and prisoners coming in from the battlefield during the Third Battle of Ypres. The Canadian Corps suffered particularly heavy casualties during the battle.

'I believe that this war, upon which I entered as a war of defence and liberation, has now become a war of aggression and conquest … I have seen and endured the suffering of the troops, and I can no longer be party to prolong these sufferings for ends which I believe to be evil and unjust.'
English soldier Siegfried Sassoon's Protest Statement. Read in Parliament 30 July, 1917. Sassoon, best known for his World War 1 poetry, also threw his Military Cross into the River Mersey as a further act of protest and defiance. Instead of being put on trial, Sasson was sent to Craiglockhart Military Hospital, a mental hospital. He returned to the front on November 26 1917.

A Passchendaele street in December 1917. Allied forces had taken the town on 6 November, but at the cost of many casualties.

Nevertheless, the continuance of the battle in horrific conditions up towards the brick dust that was the village of Passchendaele during October and November, although ultimately successful, cost the BEF some very heavy casualties (largely through the sacrifices of the Canadian Corps). The pictures and reports from this period in the battle have provided some of the most enduring images of the war.

The Third Battle of Ypres cost both sides an estimated 250,000 casualties, and created a vulnerable 8-km/5-mi salient (exposed flank) that was subsequently lost in just three days of fighting during the German spring offensives of 1918. It is true that the battle had inflicted more attritional losses on the Central Powers, but the outcome also meant that Lloyd George's nightmare had become reality, while Haig's dreams were left shattered and writhing in Flanders mud.

German assault troops occupying the rim of a recently exploded crater in the French sector of the Western Front, 1917.

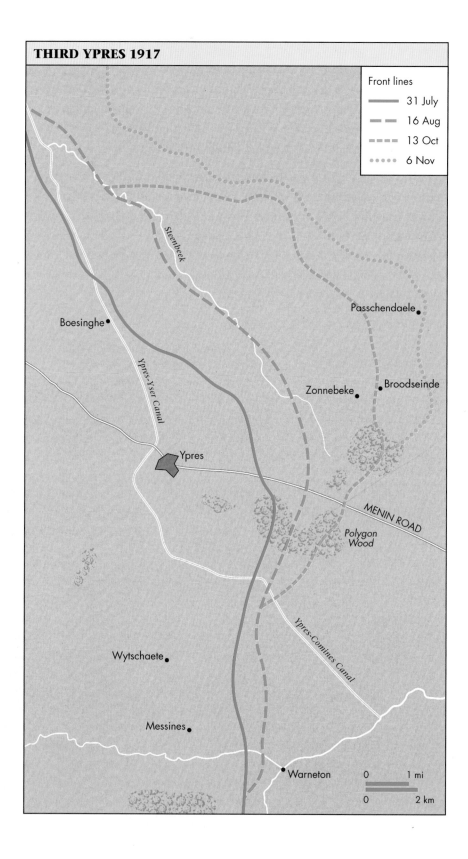

THIRD YPRES 1917

Front lines
— 31 July
— — 16 Aug
‑ ‑ ‑ 13 Oct
· · · 6 Nov

Steenbeek

Boesinghe

Ypres-Yser Canal

Passchendaele

Zonnebeke • Broodseinde

Ypres

Polygon Wood

MENIN ROAD

Ypres-Comines Canal

Wytschaete

Messines

0   1 mi
0   2 km

Warneton

'Far, far from Wipers I long to be.
Where German snipers can't get at me.
Dark is my dugout, cold are my feet.
Waiting for Whizzbangs to send me to sleep.'
Trench song from World War I.

The Trenches and Trench Routine on the Western Front

Like so many battles that came before it, the Third Battle of Ypres revealed the strength of the defence that dominated so much of the war in France and Belgium. The basis for that defence was a simple hole in the ground – the 'trench' – a word that is probably most commonly associated with the fighting on the Western Front. The first trenches of the war were rapidly dug in France on the Western Front in the autumn, and came about as a result of the need for troops to hold ground and at the same time protect themselves from enemy fire. These trenches, and the defensive systems of which individual trenches were a part, developed in sophistication over the years (especially on the German side) and remained a consistent feature of the fighting right up to the armistice in November 1918.

The stretch of ground that separated the opponents was known as 'No Man's Land' (varying in width between 27 m/30 yd and 0.8 km/0.5 mi), and it was here that dense belts of barbed wire were strung out in order

*'When Jerry shells your trench, never mind
And your face may lose its smile,
never mind
Though the sandbags burst and fly you have
only once to die,
If old Jerry shells the trench, never mind.'*
Trench song from World War I.

Men of the Border Regiment rest in a front-line trench in Thiepval Wood, August 1916. Rest was often hard to come by in the trenches. Even if the conditions did not militate against it, continual artillery bombardments were guaranteed to deprive soldiers of much-needed sleep.

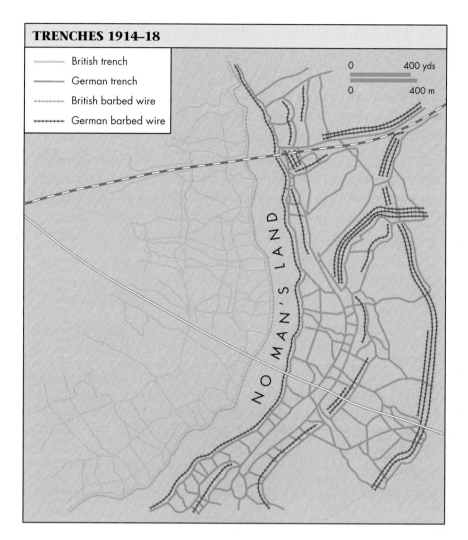

TRENCHES 1914–18

——— British trench
——— German trench
+++++++ British barbed wire
+++++++ German barbed wire

0   400 yds
0   400 m

N O   M A N ' S   L A N D

A German communication trench (Rupprecht-weg) in the Lievin sector of the Western Front near Arras, in the winter of 1915–16. Note the trench sign-boards, and the barbed wire ready for pulling down into the trench in case of attack.

to protect the approaches to the front-line trench or 'fire trench' as it was more properly known. The trenches, and those that came behind them, were not uniform in shape, construction, or use; these elements depended upon the sector in which they were located, their position on the battlefield and, most importantly, the nationality of the army that occupied them. For example, the trenches of the BEF were not straight but were made up of seemingly endless bays and traverses that formed a dogtooth shape, in order to minimize the destruction caused by shells and to prevent fire from the flanks raking long stretches of the line.

The men that dug such trenches did so at considerable risk to their safety, especially those closest to the enemy, and it was an enormously manpower-intensive, not to say exhausting, exercise. As a guide – and much depended on time of year and geology – it took 450 men six hours to dig 225 m/250 yd of trench. Once the line had been dug, it then had to be made habitable. One British infantryman, George Coppard, wrote in his memoirs, *With a Machine Gun to Cambrai*, that the fire trenches at Le Touquet in June 1915 were:

'... about six feet in depth from the top of the parapet, floored with duckboards, and were wide enough for two men to pass comfortably. A fire-step a foot or so high ran along each section of trench, enabling troops to adopt a good fire position in case of attack. The dugouts that there were afforded very little more protection than a shell-hole. Most of them were just excavations at the bottom of a trench sufficient to crawl into and stretch out for sleep ... In spite of the coffin-like dimensions, four men would squeeze in and be thankful for it.'

The trenches were dug to a depth that would, when heightened with sandbags, provide protection from shrapnel and shell fragments if not snipers, who, according to Coppard, were 'the loneliest and deadliest combatant in trench warfare ... lurking like a jackal ready to strike'. Men were most vulnerable to snipers when engaging in the constant maintenance that trenches required in the often-forlorn hope of stopping the walls from collapsing and the duckboards from flooding. Such maintenance duties occupied many troops in many hours of work every single day, because it was not just the front line that had to be kept in good order but the numerous defensive lines that made up the trench systems. All of these trenches served a specific purpose, and all had to be kept in the best condition if they were to perform their function properly. The fire trench

French and British troops digging trenches together during the Third Battle of Ypres 1917. This was often back-breaking work when the ground was hard or rocky, but was an absolute necessity for their protection.

'There was, under the hill on the British side, a wonderful system of saps and dugouts, a veritable underground settlement. The concreted and sandbagged posts above were joined by wooden stairways to the narrow bunk-lined sleeping quarters of the forward troops. Further down, passages lined with wooden planks led to larger barracks, and here were the headquarters offices and the dressing station, so far below the level of the ground that the heaviest shell bursting above caused but a distant tremor through the galleries.'
EN Gladden, 'At Messines Ridge In 1917', taken from *True World War I Stories*, Robinson Publishing Ltd (1997).

At the Battle of Karmakshalan-Florina, Serbian soldiers shelter in a trench at the front. The rocky hills made it difficult to dig deep trenches, hence the shallowness of this trench compared with those on the Western Front.

Portuguese troops in the trenches near Neuve Chapelle, 25 June 1917. Portugal did not officially join the war until 1916, but by the middle of 1917 40,000 Portuguese soldiers were serving on the Western Front, with 20,000 more in Portugal itself as reserves.

Officers of the 12th Irish Rifles wade through the porridge-like mud of a collapsed communication trench in February 1918, the result of a thaw following weeks of snow and frost. They had recently taken over from the French Sixth Division.

was connected to another, the support trench, by a communication trench some 63–90 m/70–100 yd long. This line contained troops who were used to support those in front of them if needed, and was also protected by barbed wire. About 360–540 m/400–600 yd behind the support trench was the reserve trench which contained troops ready to reinforce those in the front two lines. Behind this subterranean complex of passages and headquarters, dugouts, and stores came the field artillery and only beyond them, a little safety from the hell fire that so often brought death and destruction to those in the trenches.

French and German trenches were similar to those of the British, but with some important differences. The French system consisted of two lines: a front line that had some sectors that were fully manned, while others contained just sentries; and a support line that was fully manned and contained some deep dugouts. The French dismissed the need for a reserve line like that favoured by the BEF, and replaced it with their rapid-firing guns.

German trenches on the Western Front were far grander affairs than either the British or French equivalents, due to their more defensive posture in France and Belgium. Their trenches were often far deeper, with concrete bunkers, and extremely well equipped – many of them had electric lighting and running water. The German emphasis on defence meant that from the earliest days of the war they had greater depth to their position. In 1915 at Neuve-Chapelle, for example, the distance from the fully manned German front line through their support trenches to their reserve line was 4,500 m/5,000 yd, about five times the minimum depth of the British and French systems.

The intensity of the work that had to be done while garrisoning the front line was great, especially in those sectors where the two sides were consistently putting each other under pressure with trench raids, artillery bombardments, and the like. For the British it was common for troops to spend between four and eight days in the front line followed by a similar stretch in support and reserve, before a few days behind the lines for rest and recuperation (but often consisting of exhausting fatigue duties). This rotation of troops was crucial if the fighting efficiency of the troops was to be maintained. Nevertheless, there were what were known as 'cushy' sectors and in some of these there was even a 'live and let live' system in operation, an informal agreement between the troops to keep the fighting to a bare minimum which meant, for example, that at meal times both sides could eat in peace. To many troops, quiet sectors were the norm rather than the exception. The 7th Royal Sussex, for example, served in 21 sectors between June 1915 and January 1918, of which 16 were quiet. Moreover, not every day was spent under fire, as a year in the life of one British officer, Charles Carrington, reveals. Carrington noted that in 1916 he spent: 101 days under fire; 120 in reserve; 73 in rest; 10 in hospital; 17 on leave; 23 travelling; and 21 days on courses. It is also interesting to note that this infantry officer was only in action four times that year, and in No Man's Land with patrols or working parties just six times.

When in the front line, there was a routine to be followed that was dull but crucial both for the efficiency and safety of the troops. For British soldiers, the day began with morning 'stand to' at dawn, when the fire-step was mounted and the men were prepared to defend against an attack. Although dawn was a popular time for enemy action, invariably nothing happened and at 'stand down' sentries were posted and breakfast was taken. After breakfast weapons were cleaned and inspected while, for the remaining daylight hours, troops took their turn as sentries, or as members of fatigue parties or trench maintenance teams. It was also common for the men to catch up on their sleep during the day because it was during the night that a great deal of activity took place. After the dusk 'stand to' and dinner, the repairing of trenches in more exposed areas

Troops of the Winnipeg Battalion, the Canadian Corps, receive bombing instruction in June 1916. While Canada provided a large number of troops for the war effort – and also suffered a heavy list of casualties – significant anti-war feeling had manifested itself in Canada by the end of 1917.

Conditions in the Front Line

Life in the front line was not without its lighter moments, but it was undoubtedly dangerous and had few comforts apart from one's colleagues. Thus, when going up the line, a soldier's haversack and pockets would have been stuffed full of all sorts of things to help make his stay a little more bearable, including things like cigarettes and chocolate. Over and above the personal effects that a soldier would have to take into the line, there was also the military equipment that was required for the man to carry out his job successfully, which included not only his personal weapon and ammunition, but also trench stores such as bombs, ladders, wire, wire cutters, sandbags, and the like. In the line, no man would take off his clothing for at least a week and it was not uncommon for a soldier to go weeks without changing if he had been in intense fighting.

Life at the fighting front was a stressful experience, although few soldiers would have dwelt upon this. Trench conditions depended much upon the climate, but even in the dry and warm, ever present lice and rats exacerbated fear, homesickness, and the many other physical and mental strains upon a soldier's body. Every soldier had his breaking point; some veterans never reached it, others reached it after a number of months or even years, but some succumbed in their first action. 'Shell shock' was a physical manifestation of psychological problems caused by the strains of life in a dangerous environment. The reduction of stresses on the front-line soldier was, therefore, a function that commanders at all levels had to take seriously if the fighting efficiency of the unit was not to be diminished.

'And there in that nightmare of mud and wire, by the deathly light of occasional star-shells from over the way, we learned the landmarks to guide us: "Left by the coil of wire, right by French legs." "French legs?" "Yes, we took over from the French; the legs of one they buried in the side of the trench stick out a bit, you can't miss it." It was rather startling, but didn't seem to merit a second thought.'
A A Gladden, 'Varieties of Trench Life', taken from *True World War I Stories*, Robinson Publishing Ltd (1997).

Casualties and Medicine

World War I was supposed to be all over by Christmas 1914. The fact that it was not, and that there were so many casualties, took the military's medical organizations by surprise. The casualties that were presented to doctors for treatment sometimes had horrific wounds, mostly caused by artillery and landmines. Medical advances before the war meant that doctors had anaesthetics, and disease was less prevalent than it had been in previous conflicts. However, antibiotics did not yet exist and many soldiers died of infected wounds and other infections. Casualties were given first aid and assessed in the front line, and were then sent back to increasingly well-equipped medical posts. The British developed the Casualty Clearing Station. This was a mobile field hospital situated 1.6 km/ 1 mi behind the front line, and here surgeons worked on emergencies in theatres where up to four operations were being conducted simultaneously. From here the casualties would be moved back to base hospitals and then, in many cases, back home.

took place and patrols were sent into No Man's Land to check on the state of the wire and to gain intelligence. Sentry duty was also an important night-time duty, and the penalties for being caught asleep while at one's post were harsh, because it put the lives of many at risk.

The trenches of the Western Front were notoriously dangerous places, where troops lived on their nerves and recognized that one mistake could end their lives or put the lives of their comrades at risk. Homes to millions of soldiers at any one time, these vital defensive positions were hives of activity that helped to develop the sort of small-unit camaraderie that engendered a selflessness and 'professionalism' that kept troops going even in the most trying of circumstances.

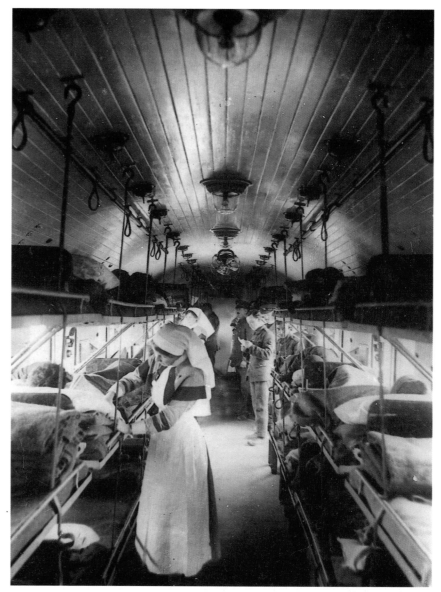

An Australian medical officer attends a wounded soldier at an advanced dressing station near Ypres, 20 September 1917. Significant progress in medical care during the war resulted in dramatic improvements in the survivability of those with serious wounds.

A ward on a British ambulance train near Doullens, 27 April 1918.

CHAPTER 12
NEW DEPARTURES

Despite the common perception that little changed in France and Flanders during 1917 – which was partly the result of the continuity in Allied strategy on the Western Front – the year was significant in terms of the application of new technology and fighting methods, and foundations were laid for the sustained advances that were to take place during the late summer and autumn of 1918.

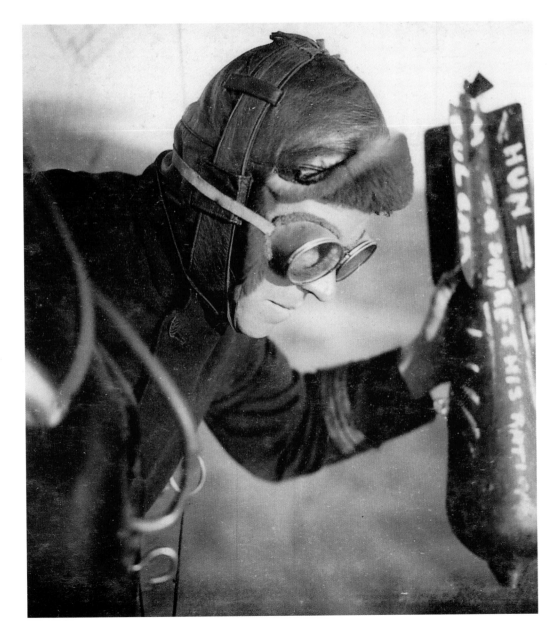

With aviation at an embryonic stage at the outbreak of World War I, bombing techniques were equally primitive – and dangerous. Here a British pilot drops a bomb over the side of his aeroplane cockpit.

The aerodrome at Dunkirk, with Nieuport fighter aircraft on the right. The Nieuport was one of several foreign aircraft types that the Royal Flying Corps used alongside home-produced models.

The Air War

The air war was not a new phenomenon in 1917, but aircraft did become far more integrated operationally as the year progressed. At the outbreak of the war – just 11 years after the first successful manned flight by the Wright brothers in the USA – aircraft had not been well tested by the military, and so the belligerent powers had precious few machines to deploy at the fighting fronts. In fact, the machines that they did have were capable of little, as early aircraft were not designed for the rigours of military operations, and were unreliable and delicate. Peacetime development with few resources and many onlooking detractors meant that the military potential of aircraft was fully examined only after the establishment of trench deadlock. However, by the end of the war, air power had been used in strategic, operational, and tactical roles.

Strategic bombing was not particularly successful during World War I, because early aircraft were lightly armed and did not have the capability of affecting the course of a battle or campaign (see p. 78, Chapter 6). The majority of aircraft were therefore used in a support role, and mostly above land. Initially the army used aircraft as 'eyes in the sky' for battlefield reconnaissance, watching the fall of shell for the artillery, and in intelligence gathering. The BEF, for example, was benefiting from accurate trench maps of enemy positions from as early as March 1915. Such was the importance of the work aircraft were doing that other aircraft were produced in order to stop that work being carried out: the fighter aircraft was born.

German aerial photograph taken the morning after the historic Zeebrugge raid of 24 April 1918, in which three obsolete Allied ships were deliberately sunk in the entrance to the Zeebrugge Canal. German submarines were a continuing menace to Allied shipping from 1915 onwards and the raid was an attempt to stop U-boats from gaining easy access to the North Sea.

The ability of fighter aircraft to engage enemy machines accurately and destroy them was crucial to their development. A major step towards achieving this came in 1915 with the invention by a Frenchman, Raymond Saulnier, of a system that allowed a pilot to fire through a turning propeller if plates were fitted to the blades to deflect the bullets. The shooting-down of a German aircraft by Roland Garros in a Morane-Saulnier Type L monoplane fitted with this device on 1 April was a boost to the Allies, but by July the new Fokker E1 boasted a machine gun that could fire through the propeller without the need for deflector plates. This technology was not only safer than Saulnier's invention, but also meant that more rounds were likely to hit their intended target – an important consideration. The Fokker went on to dominate the skies until 1916, for

'I know that I shall meet my fate
Somewhere among the clouds above;
Those that I fight I do not hate,
Those that I guard I do not love;'
'An Irish Airman Foresees His Death',
W B Yeats.

Photographic plates being handed to the pilot of a De Havilland day bomber at Serny Aerodrome on 17 February 1918. He was about to embark on a reconnaisance mission to photograph the results of recent bombing raids.

when it was flown using new tactics – such as striking in pairs and attacking the blind-spot on the tail of an aircraft by diving out of the sun – it was an awesome weapon. Indeed, by late 1915 British Royal Flying Corps (RFC) pilots grimly referred to themselves as 'Fokker Fodder'.

When the French massed aircraft together to form larger units during the Battle of Verdun, the Germans found it more difficult to achieve and maintain air superiority, and the balance tipped once more towards the Allies. During this period the Sopwith 1½ Strutter was put through its paces, but it was in a Spad VII that the French ace Georges Guynemer scored many of his 54 victories, and a **Nieuport 17** was the favourite mount of the most successful British ace of the war, **Capt Albert Ball**, VC, DSO, MC. These aircraft gave the Allies the edge that summer, but by the autumn of 1916 the pendulum of air superiority had once again swung towards the Germans who, having massed their Albatros DIIs and DIIIs into elite fighter units, swept the skies with great success. It was in a blood-red Albatros DIII that the most successful ace of the war overall, **Manfred von Richthofen** (the 'Red Baron'), achieved many of his 80 victories.

'Mills went off one day alone, on a photographic expedition, returned with a dud engine, and was well cursed by the C.O. for not getting the job done. He went off again, and never came back. Whether he was killed or spent the rest of the war roaming a prison camp in pyjamas, I never knew. It was not the C.O.'s fault. He was being hurried by the wing commander, who in turn, no doubt, was responsible for the photos to someone higher up. One machine and its occupant was a small price to pay for them.'
H F Taylor, 'August to November 1918', taken from *True World War I Stories*, Robinson Publishing Ltd (1997).

Capt Eddie V Rickenbacker of the US Flying Corps. Air combat developed remarkably quickly during World War I, considering the first manned powered flight had been made less than 15 years previously. Rickenbacker managed 26 'kills' in only a four-month period.

Four Bristol Fighters of 22 Squadron take off in formation from Serny Aerodrome on 17 June 1918.

King George V and Prince Albert visiting an aeroplane factory. With aviation still in its early stages, aircraft were constructed from wood and fabric, and carpentry skills were highly valued.

German dominance of the air continued into 1917; indeed, during the Battle of Arras the British lost 151 aircraft and 316 crew. 'Bloody April' saw losses that just could not be sustained by the British for very long and led to a dearth of experienced pilots. New airmen were rushed to the front, but their inexperience meant that most became casualties within a few weeks. The fighting was relentless, and despite the work of individuals such as Capitaine Rene Fonck – the most successful Allied pilot of the war with 75 successes to his name – large German formations (such as 'Richthofen's Flying Circus', which went where required to attain local air superiority in specific areas) continued to be successful. Nevertheless, with the help of new aircraft such as the Sopwith Triplane, Bristol Fighter F2A, SE5, and Sopwith Camel, the RFC slowly regained its poise. German aircraft development kept pace with that of the Allies – indeed the **Fokker DVII** introduced in April 1918 was probably the best German fighter of the war – but gradually the sheer number of Allied aircraft made it difficult for them to repeat the sort of superiority that they had enjoyed during 1917. The entry of the United States into the war was important in this regard, for by the summer of 1918 it had some 740 aircraft on the Western Front; indeed, Capt Edward V Rickenbacker achieved 26 'kills' in just four months of fighting.

By the time Rickenbacker was fighting over German lines, the role of aircraft had increased to include close air support. During the autumn of 1917 at Ypres, for example, the RFC flew low-level sorties over the battlefield in order to disrupt enemy ground units, fragment counterattacking, and bomb lines of communication. The Germans had gained some success with their own close-air-support missions at Cambrai in December 1917, and also during their spring-1918 offensives, but by this stage all that they could achieve was brief periods of air superiority in local areas. Meanwhile, the British turned the Royal Flying Corps into an independent organization – the Royal Air Force (RAF) – on 1 April 1918

Army Form W. 3348.

Combats in the Air.

Squadron: No. 10 Naval	Date: 15th Sept., 1917.
Type and No. of Aeroplane: Sopwith Camels B.3833, B.3912, N.6354.	Time: 4.30 p.m.
Armament: V.S. Maxims	Duty: Outer Offensive Patrol
Pilot: Flt.Sub-Lts. Macgregor, Johnston & Carroll.	Height: 10,000 feet.
Observer: -	
Locality: Moorslede.	

Remarks on Hostile machine:—Type, armament, speed, etc.

Albatross scouts and triplanes.

——— Narrative. ———

Flight Sub-Lieut. Macgregor.

1.   We were attacked from above by about 5 Albatross scouts and 4 triplanes. I got into good position very close on one triplane - within 25 yards - and fired a good burst. I saw my tracers entering his machine. I then had to turn and zoom to avoid hitting him with my machine. I next saw him going down in a vertical dive, apparently out of control.

2
&   I then engaged two of the Albatross scouts but without apparent result
3

N M Macgregor
F.S.L.

Flight Sub-Lieut. Johnston.

    I fired 140 rounds at one of these E.A. which appeared to go into a vertical bank, but I lost sight of him almost immediately.

Flight Sub-Lieut. Carroll.

    I saw one E.A. attacking one of our machines from the rear and turned on it, firing about 100 rounds, when the enemy machine made off. I observed no decisive result.

+ Decisive

A.C.Bell

Commanding Officer.

An air combat report from Second Lt A P F Rhys Davids, MC, on a mission he flew on 23 September 1917. The description reveals the extremely close quarters at which dogfights were fought – a function of the relatively slow speed of the aircraft involved.

Nieuport 17

The Nieuport 17 was a very popular aircraft with many Allied aces, including Albert Ball and Georges Guynemer. First seen on the Western Front in May 1916, this single seat biplane was fast (163 km/102 mph), manoeuvrable, had good pilot visibility, and, had an endurance of two hours. Armament was a Lewis machine gun on the top wing, but later variants employed a Vickers gun that was synchronized to fire through the air screw. The Nieuport saw service with the British, French, Italians, Belgians, and Russians during the war, and proved to be not only one of the most successful fighters of the conflict, but also one of the longest lived – indeed, the French were still using them in large numbers as late as August 1917.

with the intention of fully integrating air power into their offensives soon after. By the time of the Battle of Amiens in August this had been achieved, and during the last months of the war the RAF carried out a wide range of tasks – operational and tactical, defensive and offensive – to ensure that ground forces could sustain their advance.

Ball, Captain Albert (1896–1917)

Albert Ball was born in Nottingham, England and enlisted as an infantryman at the outbreak of war. He transferred to the Royal Flying Corps in 1915 and qualified as a pilot early the following year. Ball became an outstanding fighter pilot, and scored at least 44 victories in 12 months of combat flying. His favoured aircraft was the Nieuport 17, and he became a popular hero at home and on the Western Front. He was awarded the Military Cross in July 1916, the Distinguished Service Order a few months later, and a posthumous Victoria Cross. Ball met his death in a dogfight with von Richthofen's *Jagdgeschwader 1* in May 1917 aged just 20 years.

A Sopwith Pup makes the first successful take-off from a ship, from the aft turret of HMS Repulse on 14 October 1917. Considering that the Wright Brothers had only made their first powered flight 14 years before, the wartime progress in aviation was astonishing.

Capt Albert Ball, VC, DSO, MC, the British pilot ace who was credited with at least 44 'kills' in the air war. He was only 20 years old when he was killed in action on 7 May 1917.

An armaments officer about to attach a bomb to its underwing mounting position on a De Havilland day bomber at Serny Aerodrome on 17 February 1918. The advent of remote release mechanisms had made the bombing process more accurate and certainly much safer.

Aircraft were not decisive during World War I, but they did prove a useful adjunct to ground forces, and as their flexibility grew with the progress of technology, they became more fully integrated into military thinking. In total about 10,000 machines were used in the front line, and approximately 50,000 airmen lost their lives in the fight for the skies over France and Flanders. These figures alone reveal the importance attached to the attainment of command of the skies, and to stopping the enemy from doing the same.

A German poster warning of the danger to transport columns from enemy aircraft. 'Enemy airmen can see you here – transport must not stop here,' is the message.

Instrument panel of a DH9A biplane equipped with the Liberty engine. The sparseness of the instruments is striking compared with today's aircraft, and the notice at the bottom left of the panel – stating that the aircraft must be flown at an indicated airspeed of 128 kmh/80 mph at 13,000 m/40,000 ft when making a bombing run – emphasizes the vulnerability of these aircraft to enemy fire.

The Battle of Cambrai

Aircraft had an important role to play during the Battle of Cambrai; however, this Allied offensive is not best known for the employment of flying machines, but for the massed use of tanks. On 21 December 1917, church bells were rung in England for the first time since the beginning of the war to celebrate the British success at Cambrai, one of the first tests of recent tactical and technological innovations designed to achieve surprise. Although the battle ended in the first week of December with few of the initial British gains remaining, the first day of the offensive showed the Allies what could be achieved when emphasis was placed upon surprise and all-arms cooperation.

The origins of the Battle of Cambrai lay in the situation in which the British found themselves after the failure of the Third Battle of Ypres in early November 1917. Although it was late in the campaigning year, the commander-in-chief of the BEF, Field Marshal Sir Douglas Haig, was in need of a morale-boosting victory to encourage the increasingly war-

The interior of a British tank factory. The success of the home front in producing superior numbers of munitions in 1918 was one of the key factors that won the war for the allies.

weary civilians at home, and improve the spirits of the troops at the front. This is not to say that the battle was devised merely in order to protect Haig at a difficult time for him. Although a victory anywhere would have helped, a year that had started so brightly in April at Arras had faded in the autumnal gloom of Passchendaele, and a breakthrough at Cambrai was a distinct possibility in late 1917.

The Cambrai sector of the front was chosen for the attack as it was well suited to British offensive requirements, especially those that were to put so much emphasis upon surprise and the use of a large number of tanks.

British tanks going into action between Amiens and Bouchoir, during the Battle of the Somme. It was during this battle that tanks were deployed for the first time against the Germans.

Richthofen, Baron Manfred von (1892–1918)

Originally a cavalryman, Richthofen transferred to the air service in May 1915 and served as an observer on the Eastern Front before qualifying as a pilot. Although flying at Verdun, his transfer in August 1916 to *Jagdstaffel* 2 under the command of the ace Oswald Boelcke saw his tally of victories increase extremely quickly. A phenomenal shot, he relied more upon that than upon any tactical skill, and by February 1917 had over 20 Allied aircraft to his credit. He shot down many more British aircraft during 'Bloody April' and by its end had 52 'kills' to his name. Known as the 'Red Baron' on account of his blood-red aircraft, Richthofen became a national hero in Germany and was promoted to command *Jagdgeschwader 1* ('Richthofen's Flying Circus') in June 1917. The 'ace of aces' had scored 80 victories when he was killed during a dogfight over the Somme on 21 April 1918. He was buried by the Allies with full military honours.

Baron Manfred von Richthofen – the German flying ace known as the Red Baron, on account of the red Fokker Triplane he flew – with his pet dog Moritz. Richthofen achieved the first of his 80 'kills' on the Western Front in September 1916, but was himself shot down and killed on 21 April 1918.

Little Willie, the prototype British tank in September 1915. The original intention was to mount a rotating gun turret on top of the armoured box, but it was realized that the resulting silhouette would be too obvious to the enemy from a distance. A revised design incorporated outboard sponsons equipped with pivoting guns on either side of the tank.

A tank from H Battalion fails to negotiate a German trench near Ribécourt, southwest of St Quentin in northern France on 20 November 1917.

An observer officer descends by parachute from his kite balloon near Metz-en-Couture, 26 January 1918. Parachuting was in its infancy at this time, and the first successful parachute jump in action was not made until later the same year, when a German pilot baled out of his crippled aircraft over the Somme.

Despite its name, the battle was fought in the open fields and villages south of the town of Cambrai itself, which was a major communications centre just 9.6 km/6 mi behind the German front line. The countryside consisted of rolling fields and gentle valleys; the ground was hard chalk that had not been pitted by constant shelling, and there were plenty of woods and ruined villages in the vicinity, which would prove useful for concealing tanks, infantry, and guns prior to the assault. Add to this the major advantage that the Cambrai sector was being treated as a rest area for exhausted German troops (which meant that the 9.6-km/6-mi front to be attacked by the British contained only two German divisions and 34 guns), and this part of the front looked the ideal place to conduct a British attack.

Clearly Cambrai offered many offensive temptations, but the British never forgot that the strength of the German defensive positions in the area negated many of their advantages. The Germans had built a series of strong defensive positions along their front that they regarded as impregnable, and which the British called the Hindenburg Line. The German positions in front of Cambrai were 8.8 km/5.5 mi deep, made excellent use of the terrain, and incorporated thick belts of barbed wire, machine gun nests, and trenches designed to stop the progress of tanks. As a result, British success at Cambrai was far from guaranteed.

The British plan, devised by Gen Sir Julian Byng's Third Army, sought not only to break into the German front line, but also to achieve full-scale penetration and exploitation. The first objective of the Third Army was the main Hindenburg Line between the position known to the British as Bleak House and the Canal du Nord, the second objective was the Hindenburg Support Line, and the third objective was exploitation in the direction of Cambrai. This plan was passed by Haig who, despite a preference for more limited objectives and fears about the lack of troops available for the attack, decided not to alter the scheme. However, the commander-in-chief did reserve the right to curb the offensive after 48 hours if it showed no signs of success.

Fokker DVII

The first DVIIs entered service on the Western Front in April 1918 in von Richthofen's *Jagdgeschwader 1*, and were very successful right through to the end of the war. This single-seat biplane was probably the best German fighter of World War I, and quickly won the respect of Allied pilots. Its performance at high altitude was impressive, it was easy to fly, and visibility for the pilot was excellent. Eventually produced with a powerful 185 hp BMW engine in the summer of 1918, this aircraft could climb to 4873 m/16,000 ft in just 16 minutes. It was armed with two 7.92-mm Spandau machine guns, and managed to be both sturdy and highly manoeuvrable.

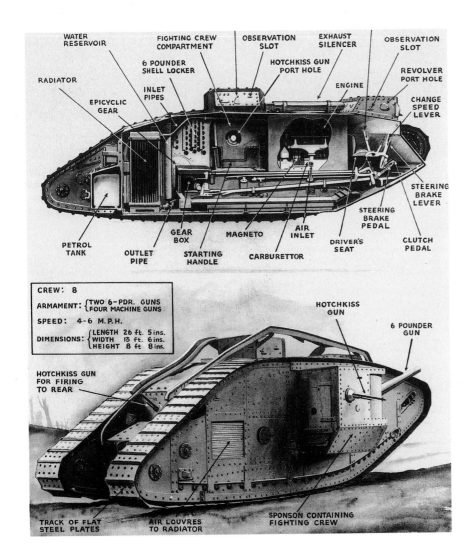

'So far, we had the sky to ourselves, but as we turned for home, I became aware of a number of black spots on our left, rapidly growing into a flight of enemy scouts. They did not dive on us, but hung behind, peppering away at the end machines of the "V" formation. Every one of us opened up with his two Lewis guns, and I had my first sight of a machine sent down in flames. Who hit him it was impossible to say, since he was the foremost in the attack, and the target of at least six guns. He suddenly dived. Petrol vapour streamed out like smoke behind him, then burst into flames. I watched as he rushed downwards, to fall to pieces 1,000 feet below.'
H F Taylor, 'August to November 1918', taken from *True World War I Stories*, Robinson Publishing Ltd (1997).

Annotated drawing of a tank. It shows the cramped and difficult conditions that the tank crews were expected to work in.

A tank held up at a German second line trench, November 1917. The photo clearly illustrates the limitations of the early tank design for crossing obstacles such as trenches.

'The roar of the engine, the nerve-wracking rat-tat-tat of our machine guns blazing at the Boche infantry, and the thunderous boom of the 6-pounders, all bottled up in that narrow space, filled our ears with tumult. Added to this we were half stifled by the fumes of petrol and cordite.'
F Mitchell, 'When Tank Fought Tank', taken from *True World War I Stories*, Robinson Publishing Ltd (1997).

To achieve Byng's objectives, the Cambrai plan had to be bold and highly innovative. One of the boldest moves was the way in which tanks were to be used; indeed, the use of the tank and the Battle of Cambrai have become synonymous in the minds of many who think about the use of armour in World War I. Not only were tanks used in the battle in numbers that had never been seen before, but the plan was based around what these machines could achieve. The Battle of Cambrai plan shows that the tank was no longer viewed as an appendage that might be of use in some way; it reveals that by November 1917 many, including Haig, regarded the tank as a key offensive weapon. Such thinking did not disregard the weaknesses that the early tanks had in abundance – such as a proneness to breakdown, slowness, and a lack of mobility. But during the previous year the introduction of an improved engine, extended range, more effective firepower, and strong frontal armour had at least ameliorated some of the most obvious weaknesses. Thus, by the end of 1917 it was thought that if hundreds of machines were to be used in an attack on level ground that had not been cratered by artillery fire or soaked by rain, armour was capable of creating its first major impact upon the battlefield.

A civilian boy with an anti-tank gun at Bohain following the Battle of Cambrai, October 1918. Even with peace in the offing, German forces continued to fight fiercely to retain the French cities they controlled, and the Allies opened up new offensives in Belgium to maintain pressure on their enemy.

However, the British planners of the Battle of Cambrai did not only rely upon tanks for success. As important as the use of massed armour were the new tactics that had been devised for a much older weapon of war: the artillery. Over the course of 1917, the artillery had developed tactics that managed to engage enemy trenches and the enemy's guns without having to use 'ranging fire', which had been necessary in the past in order to discover exactly where the shells from the guns would land. The importance of 'silent registration' was enormous, as it once again allowed operational surprise to be achieved. This development had come about as the result of lessons learned from previous battles: the application of technology that led to more accurate maps, survey techniques, and meteorological data; better aerial photographs (which provided more detailed knowledge about the layout of enemy defences); and the ability to fix enemy gun positions by sound ranging and flash spotting.

What these new artillery tactics meant in terms of the British plan was that, rather than there being days of preliminary bombardment, the guns would not open up until zero hour (the hour of attack) on the first day of the offensive. The roles previously carried out by the preliminary

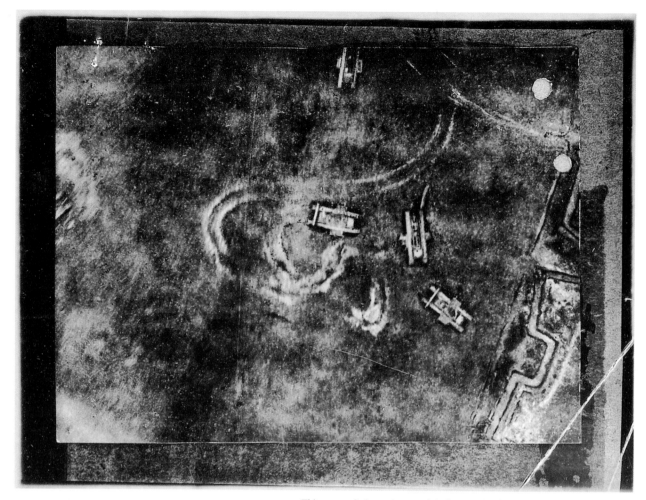

This unusual picture is an aerial photograph of tank manoeuvres on the ground during the Battle of Cambrai. Aeroplanes at this time were being increasingly used for observation and reconnaissance purposes during major battles.

'Looking down on one occasion I saw to my horror that we were going straight down into a trench full of men who, huddled together, were yelling at the tops of their voices to attract our attention. A quick signal to the gears-man seated in the rear of the tank and we turned swiftly, avoiding catastrophe by a second.'
F Mitchell, 'When Tank Fought Tank', taken from *True World War I Stories*, Robinson Publishing Ltd (1997).

bombardment still had to be accomplished, but in order to gain surprise they were conducted in a different manner. Instead of days of bombardment destroying the enemy barbed wire, the tanks would crush it. The German trenches would be destroyed by a 'jumping' barrage, which would move in a series of fairly big 'lifts' – each of a few hundred yards – on to the next German position. The counterbattery work against enemy artillery would only begin once tanks and infantry had started to move forward.

Although the replacement of a preliminary bombardment with new artillery techniques at Cambrai meant that fewer shells would be fired at the enemy, it was hoped that when greater precision was combined with the achievement of surprise, the artillery would actually become far more effective. The achievement of such precision and surprise was eventually central to the British success on the first day of the Battle of Cambrai.

The British offensive at Cambrai began at 0620 hrs on 20 November, when over 300 fighting tanks led six infantry divisions of the Third Army's III Corps and IV Corps into the attack. As the infantry and tanks moved off towards their objectives, the all-important artillery barrage began from 1,000 guns that had thus far lain silent. A mixture of smoke, high explosives, and shrapnel rained down upon German positions with an accuracy that not only destroyed large parts of their defences, but also moved forward in a manner that forced the enemy to stay in their deep dugout.

The surprise of the attack that morning, together with successful cooperation between the infantry, armour, artillery, and the 14 squadrons of the RFC that flew overhead to observe as well as to harass the German ground forces, meant that early success was achieved. The tanks rolled forward followed by columns of infantry through what the Germans had thought was impregnable barbed wire. When the tanks reached the German trenches, designed to be too deep and broad for armour to cross, the machines were able to drop fascines and move over them. Each fascine was 0.9–1.2 m/3–4 ft in diameter and consisted of 60 bundles of brushwood bound together by a chain and weighing about 1½ tons.

This technology worked well, and enabled the British to maintain their forward momentum. One tank commander later recalled that:

> 'Just before half-past six the barrage commenced … and we started off. Our first bump came fairly soon. We climbed a bank, crashed through the hedge on top and came down heavily on the other side. Our tank weighed some 28 tons. When it lurched it threw its crew about like so many peanuts … We clattered across No-Man's Land, crushing a path for the infantry through 50 yards of dense barbed wire. Then we crossed the main and reserve trenches of the Hindenburg Line – according to plan. The fascines were a great success.'

As the tanks carved their way into the German positions, the infantry moved in and mopped up. One platoon commander, Lt John F Lucy, tasked with filling in both German and British trenches so that the artillery could get forward and continue their support, remembered that the first few hours of the battle were 'astounding' as he watched 'whole sections, even platoons, of infantry strolling up the opposite enemy slopes behind [the tanks]'. This was a far cry from previous offensives, when the infantry often found the German wire uncut and machine gunners ready to cut them down.

By 0800 hrs the British had overrun the main Hindenburg Line along the 9.6 km/6 mi between the St Quentin Canal and the Canal Du Nord. However, while most of the German support line had been taken by 1130 hrs, there were problems in the centre, in front of the 51st (Highland) Division's objective of Flesquiéres Ridge. Some of the problems encountered by the infantry here came about as a direct consequence of a number of important alterations made by the divisional commander to the tank–infantry cooperation tactics that were being used by all other divisions. With the infantry struggling to move forward, the tanks continued their advance unsupported. Thus, when the slow-moving tanks

Illustration of the Battle of Cantigny, reproduced in the London Illustrated News. *The picture clearly shows the mixture of old and new tactics, with the cavalry in the foreground following a tank in the top right of the picture.*

came in range of a number of German guns behind the ridge that had not been destroyed by the British artillery, they suffered heavy losses.

The difficulties at Flesquiéres reflected a far greater problem. Although by early afternoon of 20 November the British had achieved massive surprise, and had managed to advance to a depth of 8,100 m/9,000 yd (a penetration not accomplished in four months of fighting during the Third Battle of Ypres), the attack had failed to achieve the all-important breakthrough. Although the failure to attain this on the first day was not devastating in itself, the British high command understood that with manpower resources for the offensive so severely restricted, a breakthrough would have to be achieved very quickly. The 4,000 British casualties and the 179 tanks lost on the first day did little to lessen the resource problem. Although reinforcements were found to help bolster numbers after 20 November, there was no possibility of so many tanks being replaced quickly and, to add to operational problems, the cost was bound to increase now that the element of surprise had been lost.

Nonetheless, despite these problems, a decision was taken to continue the offensive in the hope that, having weakened the Germans significantly on the first day, they would collapse after just one more push. Thus, although in late November 1917 new offensive ideas took an important step forward, more traditional assumptions and reactions took hold when innovative methods failed to realize decisive results early enough. This desire to keep plugging away at the Germans (while guarding against over-commitment of troops) led Haig to order the end of the attack on his right, whilst continuing the push towards Bourlon Ridge on his lift. Meanwhile, however, the Germans flooded the Cambrai area with reinforcements of such numbers that any further British attack would be rendered impotent.

Having survived the initial British assault, the Germans were well placed to defend against subsequent British offensive efforts during the final week of November. Although the Germans abandoned Flesquiéres during the night of 20–21 November, British progress towards Bourlon Ridge was disappointing and resulted in heavy casualties. After the innovation of the first day of the battle, many of the old Western Front problems began to seep back to haunt commanders as the days passed. The exploitation of success, for example, remained a difficulty, as the artillery still lacked the sort of mobility that would allow it to be moved forward quickly to support subsequent attacks. Poor communication remained a problem, and

An artillery observation officer on top of a ruined wall, during the Battle of Cambrai, November 1917.

A British dressing station during the Battle of Cambrai. In stations such as these the wounded would await transport to military hospitals behind the lines.

keeping troops supplied with all that they needed when they left their own front line was nearly impossible. Gradually, as the early coordination between guns, tanks, and infantry steadily waned, a less sophisticated slogging match ensued.

On 27 November, with the British having been fought to a virtual standstill and casualties mounting, Haig decided to call a halt to the offensive, which came to an end two days later. The problem was, however, that the attack had created a large salient in which troops and artillery were vulnerable to enfilade (or flanking) fire from either side, and constantly under threat of being cut off.

The obvious thing for the British to do was to withdraw from the salient. But as they were preparing to do this, the enemy counterattacked on 30 November, opening with an unregistered 'hurricane' bombardment of great intensity. Although the Germans attacked the northern part of the salient with little success owing to British concentrations there, their main blow was aimed at the southern end of the British line around Banteaux, where the British were at their weakest. This time it was the British who were to be surprised. German infantry tactics sought to exploit any fragility in the British line, and after an intense bombardment for over an hour, the infantry vanguard infiltrated through areas weakened by the

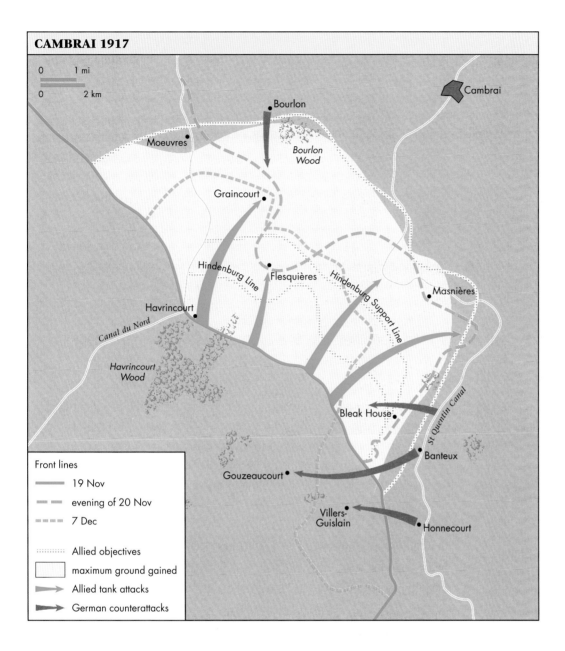

CAMBRAI 1917

0   1 mi

0   2 km

Cambrai

Bourlon

Moeuvres

Bourlon Wood

Graincourt

Hindenburg Line   Flesquières   *Hindenburg Support Line*

Masnières

Havrincourt

Canal du Nord

Havrincourt Wood

Bleak House

St Quentin Canal

Banteux

Gouzeaucourt

Villers-Guislain

Honnecourt

Front lines

— 19 Nov

-- evening of 20 Nov

-·- 7 Dec

···· Allied objectives

☐ maximum ground gained

➤ Allied tank attacks

➤ German counterattacks

artillery, bypassed strong-points, and then dealt with the British guns to the rear. By 1030 hrs, the Germans had managed to advance 12.8 km/8 mi into the southern British sector, which placed them well beyond what had been the original British line before the 20 November offensive.

Complete disaster for the British was averted by the timely arrival of reinforcements, and the increasing problems that the Germans also had in sustaining their push. As German momentum petered out, the British began to stabilize their line and fight back. With no chance remaining of severing the base of the salient, the exhausted Germans brought their counterattack to an end on 3 December. The battle itself finally came to an end four days later after one final British withdrawal to a more suitable defensive position. By the time it ended, the battle had involved almost 20 British divisions, a quarter of their forces on the Western Front.

Balloon Busting

A task that many fighter pilots found highly unsavoury was 'balloon busting'. Although it was important for the enemy's sausage-shaped observation balloons to be shot down, they proved extremely difficult targets, as they were situated just behind the front line and were heavily protected by anti-aircraft fire. Some daredevil pilots made their reputations by attacking them; the German Gontermann, for example, destroyed 18 balloons and 21 aircraft in just one seven-month period on the Western Front in 1917. Other great balloon busters included the US pilot Frank Luke, and the Belgian Willy Coppens.

Air mechanics manoeuvre a 'nurse' balloon – the equivalent of today's refuelling bowser – to fill up a Caquot kite observation balloon with gas near Meaulte on the Bray–Albert Road, 7 August 1916.

A British kite balloon falling in flames following an attack by enemy aircraft at Boyelles on 3 February 1918. Kite balloons were used to observe enemy activity, but became increasingly vulnerable as airborne weaponry improved throughout the war.

The Battle of Cambrai saw startling British success quickly followed by setback, and was consequently a draw. The gains achieved on 20 November were quickly wiped out by the German counterattack, which managed to inflict heavy loses upon the British and severely undermined their newly bolstered morale. For the British, the battle was most certainly not the success that they had wished. They had retained a little more ground of tactical importance in the northern part of the sector than they had relinquished in the southern part, but this was not the sort of achievement for which they had hoped. The battle cost the British 45,000 casualties – at least as many as those sustained by the enemy – and two-thirds of their tanks.

Nevertheless, the Battle of Cambrai did reveal that fighting on the Western Front had entered a period of transition. Many of the new fighting methods that were to be on show in the final year of the war were previewed in November 1917. The German hurricane bombardment and the use of infantry-infiltration tactics were seen in their spring-1918 offensives, while an unprecedented bombardment and coordination of the artillery, infantry, and tanks were to play key roles in the British offensives that ended in the armistice of 1918. However, as clearly visible as the new techniques on show by both sides during the Battle of Cambrai was the chronic problem of how to turn tactical success into operational victory. It was to be another eight months before the conditions were right for the British to find a solution to this problem.

Conclusion to 1917

The impact of the events of 1917 was complex, but crucial to the final outcome of the war. In a year in which the Germans were to undertake the defensive and the Allies were to continue their offensives, the Central Powers eventually revelled in the collapse of Russia, and Britain, France, and Italy all took painful body blows. However, although the Central Powers no longer had to worry about fighting on two fronts, and might have taken some solace from the fact that they had managed to withstand numerous Allied offensives, they still faced massive resource problems as the impact of attritional warfare bit hard on both the home and fighting fronts. Moreover, the defence conducted by the Germans during 1917 had been at the expense of huge numbers of casualties, and their attempt to knock Britain out of the war by a U-boat campaign had not only failed, but significantly backfired. The US entry into the war provided the Allies with a stable resource base from which they could launch offensives using keenly developed fighting methods that sought to exploit German weaknesses. However, before the Allies could launch these offensives, Germany would conduct one last great offensive of its own.

CHAPTER 13
PEACE OVERTURES

The sacrifices that were necessary for a nation to prosecute World War I were immense, and as the conflict entered its fourth year, an element of war-weariness had established itself within all of the major belligerent states. There were a number of attempts to secure a compromise peace in this atmosphere, and even the first ideas of what might constitute a suitable peace settlement. However, the reasons why these peace initiatives failed until further military manoeuvres forced political hands were indicative of the principled stance taken by war leaders, and even of a desire on the part of some populations to see the war through to victory.

A weary British soldier after weeks on active duty. The opportunity for a proper shave and a bath was eagerly anticipated by troops going on home leave or when billeted away from the front during rest periods.

War Weariness and the Home Fronts

It was clear from the disciplinary problems affecting a number of armies in 1917 that the sacrifices many fighting men were being ordered to make were beginning to overburden them. Even the British army – which did not suffer from the mutinies that affected the French – had good reason to feel demoralized as the result of an accumulation of offensives (the Somme, Arras, Third Ypres, and Cambrai) which, although begun with high hopes, ended up as bloody slogging matches. Nevertheless, although any sign of front-line war-weariness was undoubtedly a concern for any high command, war-weariness on the home front could have far greater repercussions, for it was the civilian who produced what the soldier needed to carry out his job, and it was also at home that political dissatisfaction could lead to swift, yet dramatic political change. A contemporary Jean-Louis Forain cartoon depicting two front-line soldiers reflects this situation simply, but accurately: 'Let's hope they hold out,' says one, 'Who?' asks the other. 'The civilians,' comes the reply.

Writing home from the front. Maintaining links with those left behind at home was an essential component in keeping up the spirits of front-line soldiers during the attritional conflict of World War I.

Although one might expect that troops at the fighting front had little idea of what life was like for civilians back at home, their knowledge was actually good as a result of going home on leave, and receiving letters and newspapers. It is true that many troops found it difficult to swallow the jingoism, war talk, profiteering, and 'shirking' that they found when on home leave, but they were keenly aware that the whole nation was making sacrifices in order to fight the war. Indeed, many German soldiers were appalled at the meagre civilian rations when they got back to their old towns and villages. The British blockade began to starve Germany successfully from 1916 onwards, and the policy of putting the army before the civilian population only exacerbated an already-difficult situation – many were on subsistence living, and some were even below it. Thus during the spring of 1917, news that the bread ration was to be cut led to a wave of strikes, with 300,000 Berlin workers downing tools in April. A crisis was averted only when these workers received assurances that rations would be increased. However, such 'solutions' were only short-term. By the winter of 1917–18, Germany was in crisis again as rations were cut and about 1 million workers from all over Germany went on strike; this was one of the few courses of action that civilians could take that would succeed in making politicians listen,

NOTHING is to be written on this side except the date and signature of the sender. Sentences not required may be erased. If anything else is added the post card will be destroyed.

I am quite well.

I have been admitted into hospital
  { *sick* } *and am going on well.*
  { *wounded* } *and hope to be discharged soon.*

I am being sent down to the base.

I have received your { *letter dated* _____
                         telegram ,, _____
                         parcel ,, _____ }

Letter follows at first opportunity.

I have received no letter from you
  { *lately.*
    for a long time. }

Signature only. }

Date _____

[Postage must be prepaid on any letter or post card addressed to the sender of this card.]

(25480) Wt.W3497-293 1,130m. 5/15 M.R.Co.,Ltd.

Field services postcard issued to British forces to enable them to write to friends and family using approved wording. Although the sending and receiving of letters was vital for maintaining troop morale, British commanders were conscious of the risk of military strategy and tactics being inadvertently communicated to the enemy.

Serving soup to civilians in Berlin from a 'Goulash Gun', the mobile soup kitchens seen in the poorer districts of the German capital. While German soldiers experienced undoubted hardship at the front, many were appalled when they discovered how meagre the rations were for their relatives back home.

thanks to the need to maintain war production at the appropriate level. But the people of Berlin, Leipzig, Hamburg, and Frankfurt were also well aware of the calamity facing Germany, and of what could be done while the war was still being fought. The population had been forced to make great sacrifices for the war from its earliest days, and by 1918 they had simply had enough. More than this, however, Germany was on the verge of revolution.

Years of shortages, price rises, and the government's policy of raising taxes by adding them to the price of goods all hit the poor far more than

A German propaganda poster, from 1914, calling for all countries to join together against the idea of war. Such ideas gained further support and credence in Germany during the years of hardship that followed for ordinary civilians, whose needs were sacrificed to those of the men at the front.

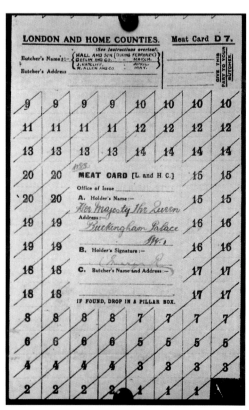

Even the British Royal Family was subject to the Rationing Order, as this 1918 meat card for Queen Mary shows. Note the precise terms under which meat could be obtained – the butcher's name, and the month during which they were authorized to supply – are clearly stipulated.

the rich. Add to this the fact that some of the rich got richer as a result of lucrative war contracts and that many maintained their pre-war standard of living, and one can understand why the less well-off believed that the wealthy were not as affected by the war as they were. By early 1918, the result was a divided Germany, and there was a constant threat of rebellion within the working classes at a time when national unity was not merely an advantage, but a necessity. The severe nature of Germany's deep social problems was commented on by an army report on the city of Magdeburg:

'The previous large gulf between rich and poor, which had largely been closed by the early days of war, now continues to widen, the more the longer. Among the poorer sections of the population a pernicious hatred against the rich and so-called war profiteers has built up, which one can only hope will not lead to a terrible explosion.'

DEFENCE OF THE REALM. E.P. 6.

MINISTRY OF FOOD.

BREACHES OF THE RATIONING ORDER

The undermentioned convictions have been recently obtained:—

Court	Date	Nature of Offence	Result
HENDON - -	29th Aug., 1918	Unlawfully obtaining and using ration books	3 Months' Imprisonment
WEST HAM -	29th Aug., 1918	Being a retailer & failing to detach proper number of coupons	Fined £20
SMETHWICK -	22nd July, 1918	Obtaining meat in excess quantities - - -	Fined £50 & £5 5s. costs
OLD STREET -	4th Sept., 1918	Being a retailer selling to unregistered customer	Fined £72 & £5 5s. costs
OLD STREET -	4th Sept., 1918	Not detaching sufficient coupons for meat sold ·	Fined £25 & £2 2s. costs
CHESTER-LE-STREET	4th Sept., 1918	Being a retailer returning number of registered customers in excess of counterfoils deposited - - - -	Fined £50 & £3 3s. costs
HIGH WYCOMBE	7th Sept., 1918	Making false statement on application for and using Ration Books unlawfully - - - - - - - - -	Fined £40 & £6 4s. costs

Enforcement Branch, Local Authorities Division,
MINISTRY OF FOOD. September, 1918

A September 1918 poster issued by the British Ministry of Food to deter retailers from breaking the Rationing Order. Britain's food supply had been severely jeopardized by the success of German submarines in sinking Allied shipping, and as a result the government had implemented strict food-rationing regulations for civilians.

Although the 'terrible explosion' in Germany did not take place until the end of 1918, combustion took place in Russia somewhat earlier. The war highlighted the disparity between the haves and have-nots in an already politically unstable Russia in ways that were similar to those in Germany. For example, while the wealthy were still eating well in the good restaurants of St Petersburg in early 1917, the workers were left wanting for basic foodstuffs. Therefore it was not without good reason that one of Lenin's revolutionary slogans on his return to Russia was, 'Bread, peace, and land'. As a consequence, the privations of the Russian people during World War I were not incidental to the political turmoil seen in that country during 1917, but a great motivational factor within it.

France was not without its morale difficulties on the home front either. Demonstrations in Paris during the spring of 1917 reflected the growing discontent that many felt at soaring prices, and ended in a mass protest on May Day and then strikes. In common with similar discontent in other nations, the call for higher wages was met and war production continued. By 1918, however, the strikes were back and this time they were politically motivated. Undoubtedly influenced by the issues resulting from the entry of the USA into the war and the political changes in Russia, the workers of provincial France forcefully raised the question of French war aims – although these workers were not revolutionary in their intent. This development shows that by 1918 the home front needed the reassurance that there were clear, just, and achievable political objectives – and the desire for such solace was not limited to France.

Rationing in Britain

As an island, Britain relied heavily on food and other essential materials being imported by sea, but from the beginning of the war German U-boats targeted British trade routes. By the winter of 1917–18 there were food shortages in London, and long queues quickly developed each morning outside shops selling food. Although most foodstuffs were occasionally in short supply, there was a chronic shortage of margarine, tea, sugar, and meat. The government endeavoured to get the population to buy alternatives to meat, such as eggs or fish, but the shortages continued unabated.

The government hoped that it would not be necessary to introduce rationing, but at the same time they were aware that people would soon become demoralized by constant shortages – as they were in Germany – and were prepared to introduce tough measures to avoid this. Propaganda posters encouraging people to cut back did not work on their own, and so there was little choice but to bring rationing to London and the surrounding areas in February 1918. By the end of April, the system covered the whole country. From that point on people had to produce ration cards in order to buy meat and fats such as butter, margarine, and lard. Each person was allowed only 425 g/15 oz of meat, 142 g/5 oz of bacon, and 113 g/4 oz of fat per week. This measure soon had the desired effect, and by May the queues had dwindled and the threat of civilian discontent had passed.

Queuing for food in the cobbled streets of a British town. Food rationing was implemented during World War I to try to ensure an equitable distribution of essential commodities. The slogan in the window of the shop on the right of the photograph, 'England Expects Economy', exhorts people to exercise restraint.

The shortages of some basic commodities in Britain led to the government's increased intervention during 1917 to minimize the suffering. The establishment of a bureaucracy to administer the flow of food and its price, when coupled with the introduction of rationing in 1918, certainly helped at a time when the civilian population was being asked to make more sacrifices than at any other time since the outbreak of hostilities. In this atmosphere, domestic propaganda was to play a vital role in boosting morale on the home front.

It was the task of the Department of Information, which was established in February 1917, to coordinate the propaganda effort. Propaganda offensives were launched across the land, with special treatment being given to areas where morale was believed to be suspect. Incidentally, such central coordination of propaganda was entirely missing in Germany, and this was to have important implications for that country in 1918. In Britain, the idea was to restate as often as possible the reasons why the war was being fought, to show workers who were contributing to the war effort that their input was appreciated, and to shame those who were not making sacrifices into doing so.

In the spring of 1917, the most famous propaganda achievement of the war was launched with the story that the Germans were converting the bodies of dead soldiers into lubricating oils, pig food, and manure. The story originated from a 'mistranslation' of a German newspaper article, and the Department of Information cleverly used it to remind the population that the struggle had to continue, as it was fighting a 'barbaric' nation. The first formal declaration of British war aims by Lloyd George in January 1918 was also intended to replenish depleted civilian fighting spirit. The prime minister began his war aims speech by saying:

> 'When men by the millions are being called upon to suffer and die, and vast populations are being subjected to the sufferings and privations of war on a scale unprecedented in the history of the world, they are entitled to know for what cause or causes they are making the sacrifices. It is only the clearest, greatest, and justest of causes that can justify the continuance even for one day of this unspeakable agony on the nations. And we ought to be able to state clearly and definitely not only the principles for which we are fighting but also their definite and concrete application to the war map of the world.'

This speech was certainly timely, for the first six months of 1918 saw morale severely tested on the home front. Not only did Britain stare defeat in the face as a result of the initial success of the German spring offensives, but the government was also forced to abolish all remaining exemptions on military service due to a manpower shortage caused by the massive losses of 1917. Yet the nation continued to support the war – they were war-weary, but not disillusioned.

Talks of Peace

War weariness was therefore an increasing problem on the home fronts from 1917 onwards, while the stoicism of the troops on the fighting front was being tested to the full. When such worrying signs for the belligerent governments are considered in the light of the unending casualties and the social, economic, and political changes that war brought in its wake, it might seem ridiculous that politicians did not reach a compromise peace before November 1918.

One of the most important reasons for the lack of a compromise peace before the end of the war was the way in which the nations had been mentally prepared for war over a protracted period (see Chapter 2). As the war was meant to be a crusade of good against evil for all

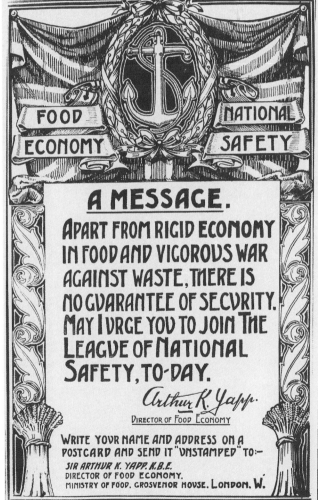

FOOD ECONOMY — NATIONAL SAFETY

A MESSAGE.
APART FROM RIGID ECONOMY IN FOOD AND VIGOROUS WAR AGAINST WASTE, THERE IS NO GUARANTEE OF SECURITY. MAY I URGE YOU TO JOIN THE LEAGUE OF NATIONAL SAFETY, TO-DAY.

Arthur K. Yapp.
DIRECTOR OF FOOD ECONOMY

WRITE YOUR NAME AND ADDRESS ON A POSTCARD AND SEND IT "UNSTAMPED" TO:—
SIR ARTHUR K. YAPP. K.B.E.
DIRECTOR OF FOOD ECONOMY.
MINISTRY OF FOOD. GROSVENOR HOUSE. LONDON. W.

Poster from 1917 displaying the message to the nation from Sir Arthur Yapp, Director of Food Economy in the British government. Propaganda became a crucial element in the war effort from the beginning of 1917, specifically targeting areas where the government believed that civilian morale was weak.

participants, having sent thousands if not millions to fight and suffered many casualties, how could there be peace unless the enemy had been vanquished?

By 1917, there were those who wanted to see a negotiated peace and, as we have seen, the question of war aims was brought to the fore, but generally most people thought that anything short of the defeat of the

Poster advertising the launch of a 'national standard dress' as a contribution to the war effort. Rationing during World War I was not limited only to food – any initiative that would conserve vital resources was welcomed.

Poster issued by the British government under the auspices of the Imperial Maritime League, cataloguing a list of German atrocities against women and children. The instances cited have apparently been verified by the Belgian, British, and French governments or the physician to the king of the Belgians, and are aimed at counteracting a perceived weakening in British fighting spirit.

US War Aims: The Fourteen Points

1. Open diplomacy; no secret treaty-making.
2. Freedom of the seas in war as well as in peace.
3. The removal of all economic barriers.
4. National armaments to be reduced.
5. Colonial disputes to be judged impartially, with equal weight being given to the interests of the subject populations and the claims of the colonial governments.
6. The evacuation by the Germans and the Austrians of all Russian territory.
7. The restoration of Belgian sovereignty.
8. All occupied French territory to be restored, and Alsace and Lorraine to be returned.
9. Italian frontiers to be readjusted along clearly recognized lines of nationality.
10. The peoples of Austria-Hungary to be given the opportunity for autonomous development.
11. Romania, Serbia, and Montenegro to be restored and Serbia given access to the sea. Balkan interstate relations to be settled on lines of allegiance and nationality.
12. The non-Turkish peoples within the Ottoman Empire to be given the opportunity for autonomous development.
13. The establishment of a Polish state with access to the sea.
14. A general association of nations to be formed to guarantee political and territorial integrity to great and small alike.

British government propaganda poster waging war on excess and waste, particularly targeting those who insisted on continuing to lead an affluent lifestyle while less fortunate elements of the population were enduring hardship and shortages.

enemy would be an insult to the war dead. This feeling was encapsulated in a poem written in 1915 by the Canadian medical officer, Col John McCrae:

> 'Take up your quarrel with the foe:
> To you from failing hands we throw
> The torch; be yours to hold it high.
> If ye break faith with us who die
> We shall not sleep, though poppies grow
> In Flanders Fields.'

In Germany, however, support for a negotiated peace certainly grew during 1918, and reached its height in the summer months after it became clear that defeat was close. However, up until this point, the German war leaders – just like those of Britain, France, Italy, and Russia – did not fully consider the option of a cessation of hostilities while they still had a chance of victory. Indeed, the USA had endeavoured to act as an honest broker between the warring nations while they were neutral. For example, Col House, who was President Wilson's unofficial envoy, came over to Europe in 1916 with a number of proposals that he hoped might form the basis for peace talks. These proposals centred on the German evacuation of Belgium and France, and the return of Alsace and Lorraine to the French, in return for German colonial compensation. House's overtures were rejected, however, mainly because the Allies were not interested in a compromise when they thought that they could still win the war. The removal of German forces from France and Flanders was not enough for the Allies: they wanted to guarantee peace for decades to come and, to them, this necessitated the destruction of their enemy's military power. Moreover, the Germans were also uninterested in peace, for in 1916 they too believed that their political aims could also be satisfied by military victory. The same attitude was also demonstrated by the Russians when, in mid-1915, peace terms offered by Falkenhayn were given short shrift by the tsar, who looked to the resurgence of his army to deliver the defeat of the Central Powers.

There were various other attempts by various bodies to try to get the two sides talking, but all failed. The Reichstag even passed a Peace Resolution based on no annexations in 1917 – a move that might be said to have reflected the growing mood of the population at the time. However, the vagueness of this declaration, and its insistence that all ground held by the German army had to be evacuated, was unacceptable to the German decision-makers and it was not acted upon. Such failed attempts at attaining peace reveal that it was far more difficult to bring a war to an end than it was to start one.

Wilson's Fourteen Points

In the USA, the subject of viable peace initiatives had been an on-going debate for a number of years by 1918. Nevertheless, it was not until some nine months after the USA had entered the war that the nation's war aims were formally declared. On 8 January, Woodrow Wilson addressed a joint session of Congress and outlined the USA's objectives in the Fourteen Points. The pressure on Wilson to outline US war aims had been growing for some time for, as in Europe, the population needed reassurance that they were fighting for good, moral reasons. More than this, however, the president also wanted to provide the solid foundations for peace against which proposals from other nations could be judged.

During the autumn of 1917, Wilson had asked a group of experts (known as 'The Inquiry') to produce a report on the war aims of all the belligerent nations, and to outline what they thought the USA's own goals should be.

Attitudes to the War and Daily Life in the USA

The popular mood in the USA in 1918 was intensely patriotic. Former president Theodore Roosevelt summed it up when he said, 'He who is not with us, absolutely and without reservation of any kind, is against us, and should be treated as an alien enemy.' President Wilson's Fourteen Points had given focus to US war aims, and people threw themselves into the war effort. Government propagandists in the Committee of Public Information ran campaigns to keep support for the war solid, and to make sure that US citizens were 'doing their bit'. To this end many people joined voluntary organizations such as the Red Cross, although many more helped to finance the war by buying war bonds. With the majority making sacrifices, anybody who seemed not to be joining in was treated with contempt. In Arizona more than 1,000 strikers were rounded up and transported into the New Mexico desert and abandoned – without food and water. The enthusiasm for the war lay partly in a government-sponsored hate campaign against the enemy, but this also resulted in a backlash against German-Americans that the authorities did little to stop.

The 1918 Flu Pandemic

As the war was coming to an end in the autumn of 1918, another catastrophe hit the world when millions of people died from a deadly influenza virus. It was impossible to tell where the pandemic sprang from, but the French believed that it came from Spain, and so the disease became known as 'Spanish flu'. As one doctor noted, 'It came like a thief in the night and stole treasure.' With little warning, it struck down the young and the old, the rich and the poor, and emptied classrooms and factory floors in a matter of days. The influenza was particularly dangerous to children and young adults. About a quarter of all those who died were aged 15 years or younger, and nearly half were under the age of 35. In the USA, 555,000 died; in Britain, 228,900; in Germany, 225,330; in France, 166,000; and in India a phenomenal 16 million people perished. Once someone became infected, the chances of recovery were slim. Fine gauze masks and antiseptic sprays were used to try to stop the spread of the infection, but they were of little use and there was no vaccine. In all, Spanish flu killed at least 20 million people – double the number who died in the war itself.

Prince Max of Baden, new chancellor of the German Empire, 3 October 1918. By the end of September that year, Germany was clearly going to lose the war, and Prince Max requested an armistice according to the terms of the Fourteen Points, which US president Woodrow Wilson had announced in January. Wilson rejected this overture because the German government was effectively a dictatorship by this time.

The Inquiry's report formed the basis of the Fourteen Points. The president's January 1918 speech was initially well received around the world (even Lenin applauded its vision), as the points seemed to reflect a desire shared by many people – not just for peace, but for a new beginning. They offered a future in which countries worked together to avoid war, and in which different peoples would have a say in how they were governed. However, it soon became clear that there would be problems implementing some of Wilson's proposals, and criticism of the president began to grow. Some Europeans argued that he did not understand the complexity of European relations, and that the points were therefore unrealistic. Others, including some of the USA's allies, thought that Wilson was trying to dictate what he wanted without wide consultation, and that his proposals were motivated by a desire to further US economic interests. Clemenceau said to this end, 'The Good lord only gave us Ten Commandments; the US president has given us fourteen.'

It was perhaps inevitable that each of the major Allied nations eventually found fault with one or more of the Fourteen Points. Nevertheless, although they were never formally agreed as general Allied policy, and in spite of what Europe's leaders might have thought, Wilson and his points became hugely popular in every war-weary Allied country. Indeed, by 4 October 1918, at a time when the Germans were being pushed back on the Western Front and were staring defeat in the face, the new German chancellor (Prince Max of Baden) sent a note to Wilson saying that he was prepared to make peace along the lines of his proposals. Although it was still not easy to turn Wilson's idealistic vision into a formal peace treaty, the Fourteen Points did help to end the war in November 1918, and later formed the basis of the Paris Peace Conference.

As we have seen, the last two years of the war did not see either the civilian populations or the troops in the trenches just blindly continuing to serve the war effort. War-weariness began to cut into the morale reserves of all those concerned during 1917, and in Germany in particular – a nation that suffered enormous privations as a result of the Allied blockade – there was even a desire for a compromise peace. An end to the fighting, however, was not on the agenda of any high command or government until either defeat was inevitable or military success had been achieved. In such circumstances World War I – a total war that had gained a momentum all of its own – was almost impossible to stop.

CHAPTER 14
THE SPRING OFFENSIVES

The Germans took a strategic gamble in 1917; they launched unrestricted submarine warfare in the face of threatening noises from across the Atlantic – and lost. The USA's resulting entry into the war was to have massive strategic implications in 1918, for the prospect of large numbers of US troops in France figured not only in the calculations made by the Allied staff as they made their plans for that year, but also those made by their German equivalents. Having decided that it would take several months for the BEF to recover from the punishment that they had received

Bullet-riddled corrugated iron shelter on Loos Crassier, 31 January 1918 – the result of intensive German shelling on the Western Front. Note the trio of wire-operated rifles (centre-bottom of the photograph) that could be fired without the sniper having to be exposed to the enemy.

Treaty of Brest-Litovsk

The Treaty of Brest-Litovsk was signed on 3 March 1918. Its main provisions consisted of the severing of Russia from Finland, the Ukraine, Lithuania, Courland, Livonia, and Poland (with these states coming under German control) and the loss of 90% of Russian coal reserves, 50% of its industry, and 30% of its population. Fifty German divisions remained in the East to enforce the treaty and they were called into action after the Ukrainian regime fell. Ukraine was entered quickly by the Germans, and within days they had reached Kiev and Kharkov, and in April they moved into Rostov. This dilution of German resources had important implications for the fighting on the Western Front.

The Paris Gun

On the morning of 23 March 1918, a German shell smashed into Paris and caused widespread panic. This projectile had not been dropped from an aircraft – against which there was some defence – but from a huge gun that was over 120 km/75 mi away. Developed by Krupps, this gun was known as 'Wilhelm's Gun' and had to be mounted on railway cars to be moved. The barrel was 34 m/112 ft long and, when fired, the shells reached an altitude of 38.4 km/24 mi. However, the bore increased with every shot, so each shell was of a slightly different calibre. The shelling continued for five months and the gun (or probably guns) fired 367 shells, the last of them falling on 9 August. The people of Paris suffered 256 deaths and 620 casualties as a result.

The so-called Paris Gun, the long-range weapon named after its use in the bombardment of Paris from March to August 1918. The gun had a range of approximately 128 km/80 mi, but its accuracy was not all it might have been, and the effect on civilian morale in the French capital was limited once the initial shock and surprise had worn off.

at Ypres and Cambrai in the second half of 1917, the Germans further calculated that the US presence in France would not really begin to make a difference until the early summer. Therefore the decision was taken to launch an offensive on the Western Front before the Allies were in a position to launch attacks of their own. The result was a *Kaiserschlacht*, or imperial battle.

Preparations

The decision of the Bolsheviks to withdraw from the war was central to Ludendorff's decision to attack. It was quite clear to the German high command that success in the west was dependent upon having as many divisions as possible available for the spring offensives in order to give them numerical superiority. However, although Ludendorff released as many troops as possible from the Eastern Front, another 1 million men were required to stay in order to ensure that the territorial ambitions of the German state in the region were fulfilled. Although Germany managed to secure 23 more divisions in the west than the Allies, they did so by scraping the bottom of the human-resource barrel in Germany. By 1918, attrition and continued obligations in the east saw the Germans struggling to find the resources required to continue the fight. This did not bode well for the army, and time was not on Ludendorff's side.

However, the Germans could boast some tactical innovations that were expected to restore mobility to the Western Front. In order to make units more flexible and capable of being more self-sufficient in their firepower the army reduced the number of men in each division but increased the firepower at their disposal to include 50 trench mortars and 350 machine guns (in a British division there were 36 and 64, respectively). Moreover, elite formations were attached to the divisions in an attempt to carry out specialist roles. For example, storm troopers were trained to lead attacks and infiltrate the enemy's front line. Advancing at speed in small units, the storm troopers would bypass strong points in order to destroy objectives that would impede the enemy's ability to react to the attack. This advance would then be exploited by attack troops and follow-up units who would 'mop up'. The emphasis that the infantry placed upon the paralysis of the enemy was also to be found in German artillery tactics. These tactics consisted of a hurricane bombardment – short in duration, but great in intensity – which sought to keep the battlefield itself solid, create surprise, and dislocate the enemy. This was to be achieved by targeting the opposition's rear areas, headquarters, and guns, before turning a neutralizing bombardment on to the forward zones shortly before the attack. By employing such tactics – most of which had been tried and tested on the Eastern Front – the Germans sought to crack open the Allied front.

Ludendorff's decision to focus the attentions of the German army on the British was based upon his opinion that they were the strongest opponent.

Indeed, his plan to attack between Arras and St Quentin aimed at amputating the BEF from the French army and then rolling the British back up to the English Channel. Haig's army was stronger than the French army at this stage – certainly in morale if not in numbers – but while Pétain had rallied his troops in the second half of 1917, the British had incurred heavy casualties and were suffering from manpower

Lewis gun post on the bank of the Lys canal at St Venant, 15 April 1918. The 0.303-calibre Lewis weighed 11.25 kg/25 lb, and could fire up to 600 rounds per minute, although with 47-round magazines it was really intended for short bursts of fire.

shortages (not helped by the 3.5 million men deployed in peripheral theatres), which necessitated the dilution and redistribution of units in an attempt to keep up to strength. It was in these circumstances that Ludendorff hoped to make his numerical superiority count, and so he deployed over three-quarters of a million men and 6,600 guns against the 300,000 defenders and 2,000 guns. His aim was to use his new tactics to break through the British lines and into open country, but just like the battles of 1914, much depended on the flexibility and mobility of his logistics and guns, for without these his desire to capture distant objectives would be doomed to failure, and this last great push would fail.

Rifles and Machine Guns

Western Front stalemate grew out of the strength of the defence, and three essential weapons for this purpose were the shovel, the machine gun, and the artillery. The shovel-dug trenches that protected troops from the effects of snipers or shrapnel (which showered metal balls towards the ground) and the machine gun made the direct assault of an entrenched position very difficult due to its rapid rate of fire, accuracy, and range. Although infantrymen were equipped with high-velocity rifles that were capable of 15 shots per minute in trained hands, the medium machine gun was equal to the fire of 60 riflemen. The British army soon became aware of the importance of the machine gun to trench warfare, and in 1915 formed the Machine Gun Corps (MGC) to coordinate its defensive deployment along whole sectors of the front. By 1918 the strength of the MGC was 120,000 men. The Vickers machine gun was a first-rate weapon, but it was too heavy and ungainly to move quickly in an attack, and so the lighter Lewis gun was developed. By 1918, however, both German and Italian troops were equipped with 'machine pistols', the first sub-machine guns.

Emerging from shell holes, German storm troops practise an attack at Sedan on the River Meuse in May 1917. Sedan was the location of a great success for American troops shortly before the Armistice in November 1918.

The Krupps works at Essen, Germany. As a key steel producer in the heart of Germany's industrial area, Krupp's was ideally positioned to divert its output to the production of the weapons of war once hostilities had broken out.

The German Spring Offensives

The first of what was to be a series of German offensives was launched against the stretched and poorly coordinated defences of the British Fifth Army on the Somme on 21 March 1918. The British commander, Gough, was attacked by 43 divisions, while he had just 12 exhausted divisions covering 42 miles of incomplete positions. Moreover, these BEF troops had just moved over to the system of 'defence in depth' which, with one third of the infantry crammed into the forward zone, was clearly misunderstood. Such a situation was caused at least in part by Haig's insistence that the sector was not the most important part of his front, and that it could be kept relatively weak as a consequence. A further 19 German divisions were also to launch a little further to the north against the better defences manned by 14 divisions of Byng's third army.

The opening hurricane bombardment was violent in the extreme and lasted for five hours. A British artillery officer, Capt Arthur Behrend, was asleep in his dugout when it began:

Men from the Punt Battery pose for the camera on one of their 38-cm/15-in guns on the Western Front in May 1918. Large-calibre weapons such as this were capable of firing significant distances, around 24–32-km/15–20 mi.

'I awoke in a start to find that everything was vibrating; the ground, the dugout, my bed. There was a crash and my door was blown off its hinges and the room was filled with the smell of high explosives. I sat in bed powerless to move – in any case one might just as well be killed decently in bed instead of half naked while struggling to get into one's shirt.'

At 0935 hrs the bombardment intensified on the British forward positions, and five minutes later the infantry assault began. The front line fell very fast as the storm troopers (many of whom had concealed themselves in the shell holes on No Man's Land during the bombardment) fell quickly on the fire trench in the fog and moved swiftly forward. Isolated parties of British defenders fought on, but in others their comrades were forced back. By the evening some 20,000 British prisoners had been taken, and Gough had been forced to retire back around 27.2 km/17 mi to the Crozat Canal – to ensure the security of the line, the Third Army followed suit. The British did not panic, but this was obviously a crisis of the highest order. Nevertheless, Haig took solace from the fact that the line had held in an orderly withdrawal while the Germans were seriously close to over-extending themselves.

A German machine gun section takes up a new position on the Montdidier–Noyon sector during the Battle of the Aisne, June 1918. Thanks to the efforts of a French codebreaker who decrypted a German radio message, French forces had prior warning of a major attack planned for 7 June between Montdidier and Compiègne.

British prisoners-of-war at a prison camp in Bruges. The huge numbers of prisoners taken by both sides during the conflict created a logistical headache – on 27 September 1918 alone, for example, the Allies took 33,000 German prisoners.

Foch, General Ferdinand 1851–1929

Ferdinand Foch joined the army in 1870 and gained a reputation as a theorist rather than as a fighting man. He was offensively minded and was closely associated with the cult of the offensive. However, his ability was tested as a commander when commanding the Ninth Army in the Battle of the Marne, but he successfully led the counterattack that repulsed the Germans. Foch was made assistant commander of the French forces of the north, taking full command in January 1915. He commanded the French right wing during the battle of the Somme in 1916, but later that year was sidelined into various administrative and consultative posts. His retirement was due more to political infighting than his age, and he was recalled by Pétain in 1917 to serve as Chief of the General Staff to coordinate Allied support for Italy following the defeat at Caporetto. Foch went on to coordinate Anglo-French forces in France, and became the Allied commander-in-chief in April 1918. He worked with Haig on the Allied 1918 offensives, and headed armistice negotiations in November of that year.

Gen Foch of France (left) with Gen Pershing at the Château du Val des Ecoliers, near Chaumont in the Haute Marne, on 17 June 1918. Foch pleaded with Pershing for several divisions to bolster up the 20 French divisions trying to keep German forces at bay on the Western Front. However, Pershing continued to insist that US forces would be more effective if they remained under US command.

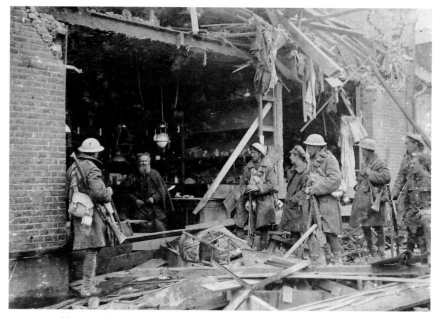

An old man is determined to carry on as usual amid the ruins of his shop in Amiens, 3 April 1918. Foch was determined to hold on to Amiens rather than yield to the Germans, but the town sustained a fierce bombardment. In the event, the German commander Ludendorff called off the offensive two days later as a result of the strong resistance his forces encountered.

In the days that followed, the Germans continued to take ground; by 4 April they were just 16 km/10 mi from the important rail centre of Amiens, but the defensive line still held. This was due at least in part to tenacious defence – indeed the decision taken at Doullens on 26 March to make **Ferdinand Foch** supreme commander over both Haig and Pétain immediately bore fruit as French reserves poured in to help support the British in their hour of need – but it was also due to Ludendorff's decision to dilute his forces over a wide front rather than concentrating them for a breakthrough to Amiens. This was an ultimately fatal choice; lacking manpower, artillery support, and essential supplies, the exhausted German troops simply ran out of steam after an advance of 64 km/40 mi on a 80 km/50 mi front in less than two weeks. The Germans suffered over 240,000 casualties, the British approximately 163,000, and the French 77,000.

Tactically, Operation Michael had been an outstanding success, but the taking of ground of no great strategic importance to the enemy did not turn the tide in favour of the Germans. Thus with fewer troops and resources, and stung by his failure on the Somme, Ludendorff looked to attack elsewhere. Operation Georgette took place in Flanders, and began on 9 April. This narrow-fronted thrust from Armentières to the La Bassée Canal sought to capture the railway junction at Hazebrouck but, most probably, also aimed at pushing through to the Channel coast. Similar fighting methods were used in this attack by the Sixth Army as had been used in Michael just a few weeks earlier. On the first day, the Germans decimated a Portuguese division that was serving with the British; and if it

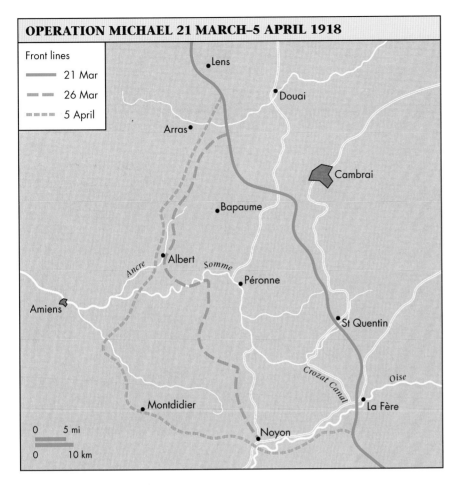

OPERATION MICHAEL 21 MARCH–5 APRIL 1918

Front lines
— 21 Mar
--- 26 Mar
···· 5 April

Lens
Douai
Arras
Cambrai
Bapaume
Ancre Albert Somme
Péronne
Amiens
St Quentin
Crozat Canal Oise
Montdidier
La Fère
Noyon

0 — 5 mi
0 — 10 km

'In some ways the attackers probably had a worse time than we. To a certain extent we could and did chose our own places and times for halting and showing fight. Our artillery, too, frequently continued to fire over our heads almost until we reached the guns.'
R G Bultitude, 'Retreat', taken from *True World War I Stories*, Robinson Ltd (1997).

had not been for the stoicism of the divisions on its flanks and the rapid move by other troops to plug the gap that had been created, far more damage could have been done. As it was, the Germans managed to advance 5.6 km/3 mi on the first day, but on 10 April the attack was widened, and two corps were forced to withdraw with few reserves *in situ* to lend support. With the situation deteriorating, Haig's Order of the Day of the following day ended:

'Every position must be held to the last man. There must be no retirement. With our backs to the wall and believing in the justice of our cause, each one must fight on to the end. The safety of our homes and the freedom of mankind alike depend upon the conduct of each one of us at this critical moment.'

By 12 April the Germans had managed to advance to within 8 km/5 mi of Hazebrouck, but again their push was running into the ground as the British lines of communication shortened and the attackers struggled to sustain their initial offensive momentum. Meanwhile, Ludendorff restarted his attack on the Somme, but with no success (although, interestingly, on 24 April the first tank battle took place at Villers-Bretonneux when four British tanks attacked three German machines). Nevertheless, by 25 April

An official German cinematographer films German infantry marching along a road near Albert in April 1918, during the German offensive in Picardy. Film techniques were still in their infancy at this time.

The Spring Offensives **201**

A 6-in howitzer in action by a farm pond during the Battle of Hazebrouck near Strazeele, on 13 April 1918. The situation for the Allies was looking increasingly grave at this point, and two days previously Haig had issued his infamous 'fight to the last' Order of the Day.

A gunner from the Machine Gun Corps fires at a German aircraft while his companion looks for signs of damage being inflicted, during the Battle of Lys in Belgium, 1 May 1918. The battle proved a turning point in the war, with German morale on the battlefield subsequently taking a significant dip.

the British were forced to withdraw from their hard-won position atop the Passchendaele Ridge to stronger defensive positions while, just a few miles to the south, Mount Kemmel was lost. Even so, the resilience of the BEF during this period was outstanding, despite these setbacks, and realizing that his exhausted troops were running into an ever-strengthening wall, Ludendorff brought the offensive to a halt on 30 April.

The ability of the BEF to take the body blows dealt by the first two spring attacks was demoralizing for the German army to say the least, and frustrating for Ludendorff. However, as time slipped away and US troops took their places in the line in increasing numbers, the German high command was forced to review its limited options for further offensive action, eventually settling on the Chemin des Dames. Here, Ludendorff assaulted French positions on 27 May, with 40 divisions supported by 3,500 guns and, for the third time that spring, took ground. The 16-km/10-mi

Supply tanks destroyed in the battle for Villers Bretonneux east of Amiens, April 1918. On the 24th of the month, German forces took Villers Bretonneux in the first-ever battle involving tanks from opposing forces. On the following day, a joint British-Australian force recaptured the village, taking 600 German prisoners.

'I informed the crew, and a great thrill ran through us all. Opening the loophole, I looked out. There some 300 yards away, a round, squat-looking monster was advancing. Behind it came waves of infantry and further away to the left and the right crawled two more of these armed tortoises.
So we had met our rivals at last! For the first time in history tank was encountering tank!'
F Mitchell, 'When Tank Fought Tank', taken from *True World War I Stories*, Robinson Ltd (1997).

advance on the first day had much to do with the decision taken by the French army commander, Gen Denis Duchêne, to fill his front line with troops; unsurprisingly, they were devastated by the German guns and were quickly overrun. By the end of the third day of the offensive, Ludendorff's men had penetrated to a depth of 64 km/40 mi and, to the high command's delight, Paris lay before them. The Germans had not been in such a position since 1914, but just like those hot August days four years earlier, the attackers found it difficult to sustain their forward momentum with such extended lines of communication. Thus, although the Marne was reached with the taking of Château Thierry (just 90 km/56 mi from Paris), the Germans had fought their way into a vulnerable position. In the van of the counterattacks that followed were the US troups.

Weary soldiers of the 17th Division rest at Henencourt, 26 March 1918, during the German offensive. On the previous day, German forces broke through between the British and French armies to capture Bapaume to the south of Arras, but the Germans became disheartened by the willingness of the Allies to counterattack – despite clear numerical superiority.

The first US action had been on 28 May when the US 1st Division engaged the Germans at **Cantigny**, and this was followed four days later by the defence of Château Thierry by elements of the US 3rd Division. On 6 June it was the turn of the 2nd Division to get to grips with the enemy in an attack at Bellau Wood which lasted for nearly three weeks. These were difficult times for the inexperienced American Expeditionary Force (AEF) and many mistakes were made and casualties taken, but Pershing's forces did not shirk from their responsibilities – far from it – and emerged much wiser from their baptism of fire. But it was not only the US troups who went on the offensive during this period; Gen Mangin's French Tenth Army penetrated the Soissons salient on 28 June, while the Forest of Nieppe was taken by two divisions of the British First Army. The Germans had certainly not destroyed the Allies' ability to react to their advances but, despite this, Ludendorff ventured forward once more.

'On the evening of the third day, as we shook our limbs and set guards and patrols moving, a whispered word went round that at 'Stand to' at dusk the Germans might attack in force. We lined up along the trench, and gulped our rum ration and literally ached for something to happen. But the sun went down and the gloom came on, and not a sound broke the solitude.'
Thomas A Owen, '"Stand to" on Givenchy Road', taken from *True World War I Stories*, Robinson Ltd (1997).

The First US Action – Cantigny

As the Germans threatened Paris in May 1918, a US attack west of the Aisne at Cantigny clearly revealed US potential. In late April, Gen Robert Bullard's US 1st Division occupied a sector of the front to the west of Montdidier as part of the French army, and in front of their position, on a hilltop, was the village of Cantigny. Held by the experienced German Eighteenth Army, Cantigny gave the enemy excellent observation and blocked the Allies' view of their rear area. As the village was of such great tactical importance, the 28th Infantry Regiment of Bullard's division was ordered to take Cantigny in mid-May. The regiment rehearsed thoroughly, and attacked on 28 May with support from US and French artillery, machine guns, mortars, tanks, flamethrowers, and engineers. The weight of the US attack soon led to success, and in a few hours Bullard's men took the village and 200 prisoners. During the consolidation of their newly-won prize, the unit came under an intense German barrage that lasted for 72 hours, and came with numerous counterattacks – but they were repulsed. The US had fought their first action and it had been a success. This was a boost not only to the morale of the US forces themselves, but to the morale of all the Allied armies at a time of numerous setbacks.

A US bombing party begins a raid at Badonvillers on 17 March 1918. With the arrival of US troops on the Western Front, the Germans embarked on a major offensive to try to break through Allied lines before US troops became available in large enough numbers to create an impact.

Fumigating soldiers' clothing at Bonvillers on 13 May 1918. With troops from both sides spending extended periods at the front in confined and insanitary conditions – and without the opportunity to wash or bathe – there was a real risk of major outbreaks of disease.

Having drawn reserves from Flanders, the Germans attacked one last time on 15 July. A lack of adequate planning time and resources meant that Ludendorff struggled to ensure that this attack had the same sort of impact as previous attempts. By this stage the defenders were prepared for the fighting methods of the tired Germans; indeed the French had even

US troops leaving a trench while under attack from a German tank at Breteuil, 11 May 1918. Less than two weeks previously, the British prime minister Lloyd George and French president Clemençeau had been involved in angry exchanges at the Abbeville meeting, where the US commander Gen Pershing resolutely refused to put US troops into the front line to shore up Allied defences.

received information that allowed them to let loose their own bombardment half an hour before the German hurricane bombardment began, and this had catastrophic consequences for the assembling infantry. Thus, although the Marne was crossed after the collapse of two Italian divisions, the Germans could not attain any momentum against the Allied defences, and the attack failed. French counterattacks began soon afterwards and were immediately successful; indeed, by the evening of 18 July, 400 guns and 15,000 prisoners had been taken. By the time Pétain halted the battle on 6 August, Soissons had been recaptured and, importantly, the Allied line had been flattened. German casualties during this period were heavy – approximately 140,000 plus a further 30,000 prisoners. Faced by ever-growing numbers of US troops, it was Ludendorff's turn to ask his troops to dig even further into their depleted reserves of fighting spirit. In reality, however, the Second Battle of the Marne marked the beginning of the end for the German army on the Western Front.

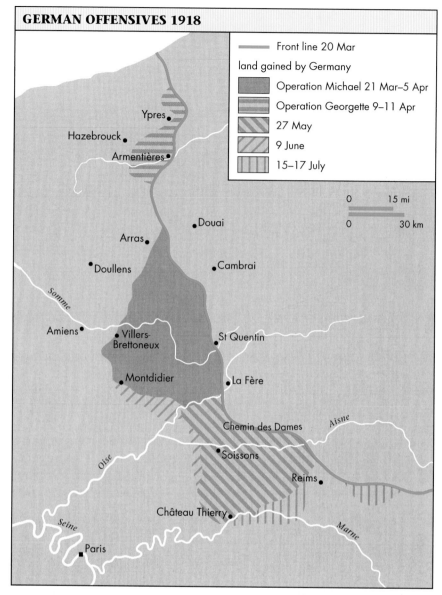

GERMAN OFFENSIVES 1918

Front line 20 Mar

land gained by Germany

Operation Michael 21 Mar–5 Apr
Operation Georgette 9–11 Apr
27 May
9 June
15–17 July

| 0 | 15 mi |
| 0 | 30 km |

Ypres
Hazebrouck
Armentières
Douai
Arras
Doullens
Cambrai
Somme
Amiens
Villers-Brettoneux
St Quentin
Montdidier
La Fère
Chemin des Dames
Aisne
Oise
Soissons
Reims
Château Thierry
Seine
Marne
Paris

The German Spring Offensives

21 March 1918: Operation Michael: devastating German offensive launched against the British Fifth Army on the Somme.

28 March 1918: the final push of Operation Michael is a failure, repelled by Allied forces, although Operation Michael as a whole has been a success.

9 April 1918: Operation Georgette: German thrust from Armentières to the La Bassée Canal seeking to capture the railway junction at Hazebrouk.

11 April 1918: Haig gives his famous Order of the Day to British troops: 'victory will belong to the side that holds out longest'.

12 April 1918: the Germans have managed to advance to within 5 mi/8 km of Hazebrouk, but the push is losing momentum.

25 April 1918: Mount Kemmel, the pivot of the Flanders defences, is lost.

30 April 1918: Ludendorff brings the slowing German offensive to an end.

27 May 1918: Germany attacks the French at the Chemin des Dames with vast success.

29 May 1918: German troops have advanced 40 mi/64 km and are nearing Paris.

June/July 1918: hundreds of thousands of US troops transported to France to help the Allies.

9 June 1918: penultimate German spring offensive.

14 June 1918: the attack ends inconclusively having met strong resistance from US troops.

15 July 1918: a final German attack on the Marne fails.

German Failure

The German spring offensives took a huge amount of ground between March and July 1918, but their success was only of a tactical nature, with no major objectives captured that might have changed the course of the war. In fact, Ludendorff's attacks had actually done far more to weaken the German position on the Western Front than to enhance it. In a deliberate move to ensure that the British were removed from the Allied equation before it was swamped by the weight of US numbers, all that had been achieved by Ludendorff was an uneven front line (double what it had been in March) for the price of about 1 million casualties. It is true that the Allies had suffered heavy casualties of their own, but they could sustain their losses, and the single fact that Britain had not been divided from the French and broken was a victory in itself. The Germans had lost the initiative with the failure of their spring offensives, and with tensions rising on the home front and resources becoming increasingly scarce on the fighting front, Ludendorff had little prospect of regaining it. The Allied summer storm was about to break.

CHAPTER 15
ALLIED SUCCESS

Buildings in Cambrai continue to burn following the Allied recapture of the town on 9 October 1918. British forces had launched an offensive on the previous day along a 32-km/20-mi front, and within 24 hours the German Hindenburg Line had been overrun along its whole length.

As the French counterattacks on the Marne came to an end on 6 August, it was obvious that there was still plenty of fight left in the German army, despite having lost the initiative. Indeed, Foch's strikes revealed that in sustaining their offensive operations, the French army had suffered similar problems to those of the Germans during the spring – the infantry out-running their artillery support and over-extending their lines of communication, while the defenders quickly deploy their reserves in order to prevent further exploitation. Moreover, in the wake of these French exertions (which cost considerable casualties), it became clear that the

'Our lines are falling back. There are too many fresh English and American regiments out there. There's too much corned beef and white wheaten bread. Too many new guns. Too many aeroplanes.

But we are emaciated and starved. Our food is bad and mixed up with so much substitute stuff that it makes us ill. The factory owners in Germany have grown wealthy; dysentery dissolves our bowels.

Our artillery is fired out, it has too few shells and the barrels are so worn that they shoot uncertainly, and scatter so widely as even to fall on ourselves. We have too few horses. Our fresh troops are anaemic boys in need of rest, who cannot carry a pack, but merely know how to die. By thousands... '
Erich Maria Remarque, *All Quiet on the Western Front*.

exhausted French army was in no position to put the enemy under the sort of continuous pressure required to shatter their cohesion fatally. Thus, if Ludendorff's troops were not going to be given the sort of breathing space that they so desperately required, the British would have to deliver the blows.

British Strengths

While the French were fighting on the Marne, the British were putting the finishing touches to an offensive that sought to relieve some of the pressure on their beleaguered communications centre of Amiens in the Somme region. This operation was not intended to be the decisive blow that knocked Germany out of the war, but it was to prove a watershed in British fighting methods.

Just like all armies that fought in World War I, the BEF constantly re-evaluated the way in which it fought – both offensively and defensively. The progress that was made between 1915 and 1918 was astonishing considering the nature of the British army at the time, and the administrative problems associated with learning lessons in the field. Nevertheless, the tactical and operational improvements that had been made by August 1918 put the BEF in a prime position to exploit the advantages that attrition had won over both the German army and the German nation throughout the course of the war. The '100 Days' of offensive action that culminated in the armistice was therefore conducted in a manner that was the product of a steep learning curve, and took immediate advantage of the efficiency of the munitions industry back in Britain. However, while it would be wrong to think of the BEF as a 'steam-roller' (it never had the manpower for that), it was capable of employing sophisticated fighting methods with the finesse required to attain victory.

The British army had clearly developed in many areas since Mons in 1914 and the clumsy offensives of 1915, but it is important to note that little could have been achieved had it not been for the copious amounts of weaponry available to it by late summer 1918. Hardware, and in vast quantities, was required at the fighting front in order for the military to be able to do its job. Thus, despite the setbacks of the spring, the British worked hard during the middle of 1918 not only to replace the guns lost in the German offensives, but to add to their number. They succeeded in this aim and also managed to produce a wide variety of shells for those guns in huge numbers. But the material requirements of the high command began and ended with the artillery, for it was recognized that, although vital, guns would not be enough to break the enemy. To defeat the Germans on the battlefield, the BEF would also need vast numbers of aircraft, tanks, and infantry weapons – together with plentiful combat-support resources. Haig received what he required in all of these areas: the home front had provided the foundation for a great victory.

German Weaknesses

The situation in which the BEF found itself in early August 1918 – well-armed and with the goodwill of the civilians bolstering its resolve – clearly revealed the close relationship between the ability of an army to achieve victory and stability on the home front. However, Germany had failed to strike a balance between civil and military requirements and this, together with the impact of Allied attrition, led to deep political, economic, and military difficulties. For example, the blockade not only had a serious deleterious effect upon production for the armed forces, but had also led to grave food shortages and social unrest. Ideally, the government would have intervened to ensure that such a situation was not allowed to continue, but in Germany the increasing hold that military leaders had over the decision-making process only aggravated the problems and exacerbated tensions on the home front. Meanwhile, the army, having failed to achieve the grandiose objectives set for them by Ludendorff in the spring, faced a huge and well-equipped Allied army bent on attack with depleted divisions and a widespread lack of munitions and vital weapons. The prospects for Germany and its army were not good. The parity of morale, resources, and fighting methods that for so long had led to stalemate on the Western Front had been broken, and all that was required now was for the Allies to exploit these circumstances.

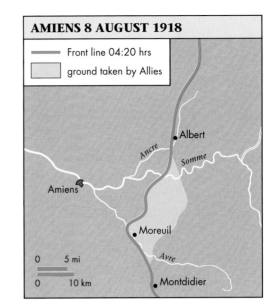

AMIENS 8 AUGUST 1918

― Front line 04:20 hrs

☐ ground taken by Allies

The Battle of Amiens

The Battle of Amiens was the first in a series of Allied offensives, and began at 0420 hrs on 8 August. Attacking on a 22.4-km/14-mi front, the British Fourth Army inflicted severe psychological damage on the defending Germans through the use of silent artillery registration, 530 tanks, and air attacks. Coordination of these assets was difficult, but the development of radio communications allowed for some rudimentary all-arms cooperation. Up to this point, reliance on land lines, visual signals, carrier pigeons, and runners had created all sorts of difficulties for commanders trying to coordinate offensive actions, but in early August 1918, radio sets proved themselves invaluable. While it must be remembered that infantry battalions, aircraft, and tanks were not linked, radio communications did mean that corps' headquarters could stay in touch with fast-moving

In the Battle of Amiens, 8 August 1918, German prisoners at Sailly-le-Sec prepare to evacuate stretcher cases from the front under the direction of Allied soldiers. This was the western limit of the German advance on the northern bank of the River Somme.

The Allies took large numbers of prisoners at the Battle of Amiens near Abbeville, August 1918, as the Germans were constantly being pushed back. On the 26th of the month, German forces withdrew 16 km/10 mi along a 88-km/55-m front, with Ludendorff deciding to try to defend the Hindenburg Line at all costs.

A carrier pigeon belonging to HM Pigeon Service leaves the trench with a message. Carrier pigeons were widely used to communicate between the trenches and forward military headquarters – they were fast, difficult to intercept, and avoided the high risk to human life that would have resulted had soldiers tried to convey such messages in person.

armoured and motorized units, and that aircraft could provide timely information upon which the artillery could act. Such developments allowed the British to advance 12.8 km/8 mi on the first day of the battle, inflict 27,000 casualties, and capture 400 German guns. These figures indicate that even in this period of mobility, attrition continued apace. Ludendorff recorded in his memoirs that, 'August 8th was the black day of the German army in the history of the war.' This might have been true, but the Germans did not collapse on that day and they fought on stoically while the British desperately struggled to sustain their offensive over the next four days – even at

A wireless room containing direction-finding apparatus used in night-bombing missions, 24 October 1918.

A tandem bicycle frame used by German forces to generate electricity for sending wireless transmissions in the trenches, Moislains, 5 September 1918. Electric power could be difficult to provide in remote front-line trenches, and ingenious contraptions such as this were ideal for use in intermittent communications.

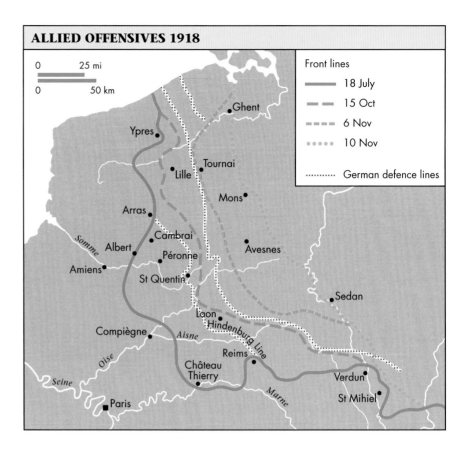

ALLIED OFFENSIVES 1918

Front lines
— 18 July
– – 15 Oct
- - 6 Nov
····· 10 Nov
········· German defence lines

Ghent
Ypres
Lille • Tournai
Mons
Arras
Cambrai
Albert • Péronne Avesnes
Amiens
St Quentin
Sedan
Laon
Compiègne Hindenburg Line
Aisne
Reims
Château Thierry Verdun
Marne St Mihiel
Paris

Somme
Oise
Seine

A captured German 5.9 gun and position on the Western Front, 10 August 1918. This was the third day of the renewed Allied offensive on the front, and 24,000 prisoners had already been taken by this point.

German prisoners from the front line march through the ruins of Sailly Laurette on 8 August 1918 during the Battle of Amiens. Stretcher-bearers from the Royal Army Medical Corps head in the opposite direction on their way to collect further casualties.

Patton, General George Smith (1885–1945)

Although he was better known as a bold and abrasive general during World War II, George Patton cut his teeth as an officer during World War I. As an aide to Gen Pershing during 1916, Patton followed the AEF commander to France in the following year. It was here that Patton became absorbed with armoured warfare and took command of a tank brigade in the St Mihiel battle (where he was wounded), and during the Meuse-Argonne offensive he formed the first US tank force and led it in action. It was in World War II, however, that Patton attained the fame that he so craved. Fighting in North Africa during 1942, Sicily in 1943, and as commander of the US Third Army in the northwest Europe campaign during 1944–45, he became a highly respected commander with a high public profile. He died in a car accident soon after the end of the war.

Bullard, General Robert Lee (1867–1947)

Robert Bullard trained at West Point, the US Military Academy and served in the Spanish-American War (1898) before crossing the Atlantic to France in 1917. He was a well-liked and gifted field commander of US forces, and was appointed to take command of the US 1st Division in late 1917. His success at Cantigny in May 1918 boosted his standing, and he became commander of III Corps in the Second Battle of the Marne from July to August 1918. He was made commander of the newly-created US Second Army in October 1918 in the Meuse-Argonne sector, but his troops had little opportunity to get involved in the fighting before the armistice. He retired from the army in 1925.

Gen Bullard, commander of the US First Army Division, in June 1918. At the end of May, US troops undertook their first major offensive of the war at Cantigny on the Somme, and this success considerably enhanced Bullard's reputation.

this late stage in the war, there were lessons to be learned. Indeed, the difficulty in maintaining momentum during the Battle of Amiens finally convinced Haig that more limited but achievable objectives were required if battles were not to degenerate perpetually into slogging matches. By advancing only as far as the artillery could provide fire support and the combat-support arms could maintain supply, the infantry did not become exhausted, and the conquered ground could rapidly be consolidated. In order to move forward again, the artillery had to be moved forward and the combat units rested, reorganized, and resupplied, but in order to keep the enemy under continuous pressure attacks were launched on other sectors of the front. In the wake of Amiens, these offensives became increasingly difficult for the Germans to defend against, as they were stretched increasingly thinly over the Western Front.

The Allies Roll Forward

The timing of the series of offensives that followed the British success on the Somme was all important, as commanders wished to ensure that they had adequate time to prepare for their assaults, but not so much time that the Germans were given the opportunity to reinforce their defensive positions. The fact that by the middle of September the British had reached the Hindenburg Line after a series of offensives launched by themselves and the French is testament to their success in maintaining operational tempo. It was during this period that US troups, who were deployed south of Verdun, launched an attack. On 12 September, the US First Army

The US Marines

When the USA entered the war in April 1917, the elite Marine Corps was approximately 14,000 men strong. During the war the marines were increased to a force of 75,000 men, but as a result of its strict selection procedure and stringent training, standards remained extremely high. The 5th Regiment was the first contingent of marines to cross the Atlantic for France, and over the following 18 months a further 30,000 made the journey, of whom nearly 3,300 did not return. The marines took part in a number of actions on the Western Front during 1918 (including the struggle at Belleau Wood and the Meuse-Argonne offensive) and they showed bravery, skill, and tenacity in each of them.

Men of the 5th Marines – the first US troops to cross the Atlantic for France – dig trenches in 1918. The first US army division entered the front line on 18 January, but was not initially involved in any offensive action. However, once the Germans found out they were there, they did their utmost to demoralize them by launching point attacks.

(including Douglas MacArthur and **George Patton**) attacked the St Mihiel salient and took 15,000 prisoners and 450 guns at the expense of approximately 7,000 losses themselves. This action was typical of the 'bite and hold' advances made by the Allies during the '100 Days' of their offensive action, but it was dwarfed by the enormity of the simultaneous advances made along the whole front during the last days of September.

Between 26 and 29 September, 217 Allied divisions attacked along the majority of the length of the Western Front: in Flanders; on the Somme; on the Aisne; and in the Meuse-Argonne sector. In this last area, a joint offensive was undertaken by US and French forces. In an amazing feat of redeployment, 600,000 of Pershing's troops were moved in just 14 days from St Mihiel to the Argonne, and a considerable degree of surprise was achieved as a result. Here 15 AEF divisions (enormous at 28,000 men a piece) and 22 French divisions (at about 9,000 men apiece) attacked. On the first day the 'Doughboys' advanced 4.8 km/3 mi, but as German resistance stiffened, US inexperience began to show, as they struggled to come to terms with the sort of defensive firepower that the British and French had been working against since 1914. These difficulties, together with poor staff work and immensely difficult terrain, made it impossible for the AEF to attain any useful momentum, and an advance of just 8 km/5 mi in 45 days was little to show for 117,000 casualties. The French fared little better, but despite the lack of an incisive breakthrough, 36 German divisions were pinned down in this area, and this was of great advantage to attacks on other parts of the front – including the British attempt to force the Hindenburg Line.

In its attack, the BEF had the extremely difficult task not only of breaching the Hindenburg Line, but also first crossing two defended canals. The fact that the British traversed the first of these, the Canal du Nord, in just 48 hours and followed it up with an advance of a further 9.6 km/6 mi, came as something of a shock to Ludendorff, who was increasingly of the opinion that an armistice should be sought before the army was totally defeated by the rampaging Allies. Nevertheless, he still had high hopes that the defences of the St Quentin Canal and the Hindenburg Line would hold out for long enough to give the British cause for concern – but he was to be severely disappointed. The crossing of the canal and the breaking of the first line of the Hindenburg defences was famously down to the efforts of the 46th (North Midland) Division. This attack – part of a much wider offensive that consisted of five British armies, two French armies, the Belgian army, and two US divisions serving with the BEF – culminated on 4 October with the breaching of the whole line. The British had broken through into open countryside – a great psychological boost for Haig and his troops – and although there was still over a month of hard fighting to come, victory was in their sights.

Men of the 52nd Division move forward in artillery formation to the bank of the Canal du Nord near Moeuvres on 27 September 1918. British forces managed to cross the well-defended canal in just a couple of days, but Ludendorff nurtured the hope that the St Quentin Canal and Hindenburg Line would offer a stiffer challenge.

Royal Engineers construct a bridge across the Canal du Nord near Cambrai on 28 September 1918. Arrangements at St Quentin on the following day were somewhat less elaborate, with soldiers apparently using lifeboats, ladders, and lifebelts taken from cross-Channel ferries to get across the canal.

Brig Gen J V Campbell, VC, CMG, DSO (third from left) with his staff at the breached Hindenburg Line at Bellenglise, 2 October 1918. His 137th Brigade had led the assault on the St Quentin Canal that was the prelude to the Line being overrun by Allied forces along a 48-km/30-mi length during the first few days of October.

Canadian troops advance through the ruined town of Cambrai on 9 October 1918 during the Allied push east of Arras. The town had been under German control for more than four years – since August 1914.

The Other Fronts

The likelihood of an eventual Allied victory in 1918 increased during the course of the year as Germany's allies collapsed one after another. Despite the numerous weaknesses in their army that so worried their high command in early 1918, the Austrians supported the waning German spring offensives in June with ill-conceived attacks on both the Trentino and Piave fronts. Operations on the Trentino were a complete failure and although some ground was taken on the Piave, the combined offensives not only cost the Austrians some 150,000 casualties but also its attacking capability. The Italians, however, were not well placed to exploit this situation immediately, as they were still smarting from the setbacks that they had suffered during the previous year, but on 24 October Gen Diaz did venture to attack across the Piave. The Austrians were in no position to mount a coherent defence, having been destabilized by over 400,000 desertions that summer and lacking many basic commodities – including food and ammunition – and the Italians, supported by British and French divisions, managed to successfully split the ailing enemy. The collapse of the army and the Austro-Hungarian empire followed rapidly and on 4 November, at the end of the Battle of Vittorio Veneto, the fighting came to an end on the Italian front.

The defeat of the Austrian army was not a great surprise considering the chronic weaknesses that riddled all parts of its organization, but the speed of that defeat was due at least in part to events in the Balkans. The Salonika front had been quiet since 1915, indeed the Germans joked that the area formed their largest internment camp, but the rapidly-changing face of the war altered all that in 1918. Commanded by the French general **Louis Franchet d'Esperey**, a 28-division force consisting of Greek, French, Serbian, British, and Italian divisions attacked Bulgarian and German divisions with a slight numerical advantage on 14 September; the results were impressive. With Serbian troops in the vanguard, and supported by an imposing array of guns, the attackers

Austrian prisoners carrying a stretcher across a pontoon bridge on the river Piave in Italy, November 1918. At the end of October, British and Italian troops managed to cross the Piave, and with Austrian soldiers refusing to counterattack, the Austrian emperor had no choice but to seek an immediate end to the war.

Franchet d'Esperey, General Louis (1856–1942)

A veteran of the French colonial wars, Louis Franchet d'Esperey was appointed commander of I Corps soon after war broke out, but took command of the Fifth Army on the eve of the Battle of the Marne in September 1914. Having enhanced his reputation during the first few months of the fighting, he rose to head up the eastern group of armies and then, in 1917, the northern group. In May–June 1918 his standing was badly dented by his reaction to the German offensives on the Chemin des Dames, during which his troops were pushed back 32 km/20 mi. As a consequence of his poor showing during these months, he was removed from the Western Front and was given command of the Allied forces in Salonika. Here he launched a major offensive beginning on 15 September that forced the Bulgarians to sue for peace. He was promoted to Marshal of France in 1922.

Italian troops march along the mountain road of Val d'Assa near Portule. The collapse of Austrian resistance at the end of October 1918 also led to the fall of the Austro-Hungarian empire a week later, with the Battle of Vittorio Veneto signalling the end of fighting on the Italian front.

'100 days' of Allied Offensive Action

12 September 1918: US First Army attacks the St Mihiel salient and takes 15,000 prisoners and 450 guns.

26/29 September 1918: 217 Allied divisions make attacks along the Western Front.

29 September 1918: Bulgarians forced to conclude an armistice.

October 1918: Turkey forced to conclude an armistice.

4 October 1918: Allied forces breach the whole of the Hindenburg Line. Central Powers make an offer of peace based on Wilson's fourteen points. Wilson's reply makes demands on the Germans that they are not prepared to accept.

October 1918: Allied offensive slows and Ludendorff is given the confidence to announce that the nation should fight on.

25 October 1918: after a bad reception of his announcement from the public and the Kaiser, Ludendorff resigns. Gen Wilhelm Gröner, his replacement, seeks an armistice at the earliest opportunity.

4 November 1918: the Austrian army is defeated by Italian forces and the Austro-Hungarian empire collapses. The poet Wilfred Owen is one of hundreds killed as lives are still lost in large numbers on the fighting front.

7/8 November 1918 (overnight): A German delegation crosses Allied lines to start discussions with the French.

9 November 1918: a republic is proclaimed in Germany.

10 November 1918: US Second Army begins its advance on Montmédy. The Kaiser flees to Holland.

11 November 1918: an armistice is concluded in a railway carriage in Compiègne. The guns fall silent at 11am.

managed to advance 128 km/80 mi in just 15 days having shattered the cohesion of the defenders. Indeed, such was the power of this offensive that on 29 September the Bulgarians were forced to conclude an armistice. The impact of this move by Bulgaria was to increase the pressure on an already fragmented Austria-Hungary at a time when they were already at breaking point; moreover, exhausted by Allenby's successes in the Middle East (see Chapter 5), it prompted Turkey to conclude its own peace with the Allies just four weeks later.

The Final Days

With the Hindenburg Line breached and their allies failing to stand up to the numerous Allied offensives launched on all fronts during 1918, German political and military leaders were compelled to think seriously about engaging the Allies in peace talks while they still held enemy territory. The Germans were hardly in a position to make demands, however, and even though the liberal Prince Max of Baden was made chancellor in an attempt to soften the face of the leadership, the Allies continued their imposing advance. The Central Powers made an offer of peace based on Wilson's Fourteen Points on 4 October, but the US president's reply made demands that the Germans were not ready to accept and an Allied push near Ypres and the capture of Cambrai

AMERICAN EXPEDITIONARY FORCE 1918

———	Front line July
●●●●●	Armistice line 11 Nov
	initial US activity
	main US advances

Night-time training at the machine gun school at Rombly in 1918. The teams continue to fire as a shell is exploded in front of them.

followed. German resistance grew weaker with every passing day, but as the Allied offensive slowed in mid-October, Ludendorff began to think that Germany still had a chance of turning the military tide on the Western Front and announced that the nation should fight on. Such views ran contrary to those held by both the army and civilians at this time, and with a very real fear that Germany would explode into revolution if made to fight on into 1919, the Kaiser made his anger known. Ludendorff resigned on 25 October and was replaced by Gen Wilhelm Gröner, who was more realistic in his appraisal of the situation and sought an armistice at the earliest opportunity. Meanwhile, the Allied offensive moved ever closer to Berlin as both Germany – where a republic was proclaimed on 9 November – and the German army were in a state of chaos. Lives were still being lost in large numbers at the fighting front, however (the soldier poet **Wilfred Owen** was just one of hundreds killed on 4 November), but on the night of 7/8 November a German delegation crossed the Allied lines to start discussions with the French. On 11 November, the day after the US Second Army began its advance on Montmédy, an armistice was concluded in a railway carriage in Compiègne. The guns fell silent at 1100 hrs on that day.

'I wouldn't dream of abandoning the throne because of a few hundred Jews and a thousand workers.'
The Kaiser, on being told that the people of Berlin were calling for the German monarchy to be abolished, on 1 November 1918. (On 10 November he fled, ignominiously, for neutral Holland.)

Owen, Wilfred Edward Salter (1893–1918)

Wilfred Owen was born in Oswestry and was educated at Birkenhead Institute and London University. He went to France in 1913 as a tutor, returning to England in 1915 to enlist in the infantry. In 1917 he was invalided home and sent to Craiglockhart War Hospital in Edinburgh where he met the soldier-poet Siegfried Sassoon, who encouraged his writing. Sent back to France as a company commander, Owen won the Military Cross, but was killed during the crossing of the Sambre Canal on 4 November 1918. Owen's literary work is among the most moving poetry of World War I and his death just a few days before the armistice added poignancy to his words about the horrific face of war and the waste of human life. When he died he left a draft of his first book of poems, and in the introduction he wrote, 'My subject is war, and the pity of war.' Sassoon published the book in 1920. Among Owen's best-known works are *Dulce et Decorum Est* and *Anthem for Doomed Youth*. Benjamin Britten used several of his poems in his 1962 War Requiem.

Wilfred Owen (left, in uniform), the British war poet. Having survived the rigours and dangers of front-line combat for much of the war, Owen was killed near Ors exactly a week before the Armistice while helping his men to try to bridge the Sambre Canal.

Winning the War

Douglas Haig was the architect of a great military victory on the Western Front in 1918, but today he is perceived by many to have been incompetent, unfeeling, and arrogant, and it is his name that is linked most often with the 'futile' battles of the Somme and Passchendaele. However, it is not widely recognized that to have fought in the way that the BEF did during the '100 Days' (and it must be remembered that by 1918 it was Haig's army that undertook the vast majority of the offensive work) the British had had to master complicated skills never anticipated in 1914 – and while they were in contact with the enemy too. Haig played an important part in this, as did many other senior officers who have been similarly derided. This is not to say, though, that Haig and the generals were without weakness or flaws, far less that there were not officers of similar quality in other armies.

British naval and French military representatives stand outside the train carriage in which the Armistice was signed in the Forest of Compiègne on 11 November 1928. Despite the negotiations conducted over several days, hostilities continued right up to the 11am deadline that was set for the end of the conflict.

Tenacity was required for the protracted nature of attritional warfare that played such an important part in the Allied victory, and it allowed the BEF – with its relevant fighting methods and new technology – to exploit the weaknesses that it had inflicted upon the enemy. Central to this strategy was the diminishing of the enemy's resources and the aggrandisement of one's own. If the blockade and fighting took care of the former for the Allies, then the role of the USA in the war was a great boost for the latter – both in terms of materials and manpower. But the war of attrition would never have been won and none of the great battles of the war would have been possible – not least those massive Allied efforts in 1918 – without men and women on the home front supporting the war effort and producing what was required to sustain the fighting troops. Allied politicians have to take much of the credit for understanding that the needs of civilians had to be catered for if the war was to be successfully prosecuted. The British acknowledged this early in the conflict, for they recognized that in a total war victory would only be achieved through a united effort while disrupting the enemy's unity and ability to sustain the war. The Allied victory was therefore as much dependent on the factory worker as on the trench fighter.

CHAPTER 16
ARMISTICE AND AFTERMATH

After over four years of extremely bloody and expensive total war, it was only to be expected that by November 1918 the belligerent nations and their populations were fundamentally affected by their experiences. The social, political, and economic landscape of the world had been altered forever by the war, and Germany was on the verge of revolution during the final months of the fighting. The signing of the armistice was not the end of the affair, however, for while a peace treaty still had to be discussed and agreed, there was still the issue of the former combatant states having to contend with the many vexing difficulties thrown up by the impact of the war and the outbreak of peace. The fighting may have ended in November 1918, but cleaning up was to prove a protracted and painful process for all concerned.

Civilian prisoners returning home, 9 November 1918.

Germany in Turmoil

During the last months of 1918, Germany was in a deep national trauma from which, it could be argued, the country took over 70 years to recover. The failure of the spring offensives, and the Allied '100 Days' that followed, set the seal on a war that had shaken Germany to its very foundations. For many months, demoralization and disillusionment had been ingraining themselves into the population's mental condition due to both shortages and military setbacks, but by the time these two unwelcome guests were accompanied by a mistrust of the political leadership, revolution loomed ominously on the horizon. A clear radicalization of politics, together with an increased militancy within the workforce and a mutinous military, caused the status quo not only to sit up and listen, but actively to make themselves a shelter for the coming storm. 'An armistice and an end to the monarchy' was the cry even of moderates during this period, but even more worryingly for the political elite were those growing voices that demanded revolution and drew great inspiration from what had happened in Russia a year before.

The reaction of the Kaiser in October was to agree to make Germany a constitutional monarchy with a government that had to answer to an elected parliament. This was the very least that could have been done to appease the masses, but it was not perceived by many as a solution to Germany's many ills. The mutiny of the sailors at Kiel in early November and the establishment of a number of revolutionary councils in several cities during that time provided yet more evidence – if more were needed

A large crowd of French women welcome the first French soldier to enter Lille on 18 October 1918. British forces had occupied the city the previous day without a shot being fired, and American forces also advanced at the same time on a 16-km/10-mi-wide front elsewhere in the region.

– that Germany could not continue to fight the war. In such circumstances the Kaiser's position became increasingly untenable and was further undermined when Gröner, who had taken over from Ludendorff as Deputy Chief of Staff on 26 October, made it clear that the army could not be relied on to take up arms against the revolutionaries. At first Wilhelm refused to abdicate, but after the seriousness of the situation had been pressed on him by the generals and advisers, he surrendered his throne on 9 November and fled to Holland.

The leader of the Deutsche Demokratische Partei (German Democratic Party) at the head of a demonstration that has just passed through the Brandenburg Gate in Berlin, on 29 December 1918. The march was a joint protest with the Majority Democrats against the Spartacists – the members of the extreme left-wing Spartacus League who were bent on revolution along the lines of the Russian model.

Two machine guns captured from Spartacists – the extreme left-wing revolutionaries in Germany at the end of World War I – are unloaded from a truck in a Berlin street on 7 December 1918.

For Germany the only logical next step was an armistice, and by the time that the Kaiser had abdicated, discussions had already begun with the Allies to bring the fighting to an end. Meanwhile, in Berlin, numerous political groups began vying to fill the power vacuum and form the new government. The Spartacus League, a group of extreme left-wingers bent on revolution and led by **Rosa Luxemburg** and **Karl Leibknecht**, even went as far as to seize the imperial palace and declare a new regime based on the Soviet model. This was premature, however, for the less extreme Social Democratic Party (SDP) had been courted by Prince Max of Baden, the chancellor, and power had been handed over to its leader, Friedrich Ebert. The status quo gave way to the moderates and, in an attempt to dismember the extremists, Gröner offered Ebert the support of the army to put down the Spartacists; Ebert accepted. The old guard were replaced by socialists but, importantly when future German politics is considered, it was them and not the army who were to negotiate and sign the armistice.

The Armistice

With political turmoil in Germany and disciplinary problems swamping the nation's armed forces, why did Germany continue to fight for so long? The answer lies not only in the discussions that needed to take place before an end to the fighting could be agreed, but also in the fact that the Allies were pressing ever closer to the German border with every passing day. There may well have been serious morale problems in Gröner's army, but there was still some motivation to fight. If this was the case though, with the

A US sailor, US Red Cross nurse, and two British soldiers celebrate the signing of the Armistice on 11 November 1918 near the Paris gate at Vincennes, Paris.

British sailors and the band from HMS Suffolk *take part in a peace parade through the Russian port of Vladivostock on a bright autumn day in November 1918.*

Germans clearly defeated strategically but still capable of inflicting numerous casualties, why did the Allies continue to fight? The answer lies in the Allies' desire to ensure that the German army was totally defeated and incapable of resuming the fighting if peace negotiations broke down. In the words of Foch, 'I am not waging war for the sake of waging war. If I obtain through armistice the conditions that we wish to impose upon Germany, I am satisfied. Nobody has the right to shed one more drop of blood.'

When discussions to end the fighting began, the Germans were in a poor position to demand anything due to their political and military situation – they may still have had troops fighting, but they had been totally defeated militarily and could no longer impose their will on the battlefield. Indeed, the

A vast crowd assembles in London outside Buckingham Palace and along The Mall on Armistice Day, 11 November 1918. Amid the evident relief that World War I had ended, few probably anticipated another total conflict starting just 21 years later.

German delegation had no option but to agree to the Allied terms, and so the armistice that they signed on the morning of 11 November not only brought fighting to an end but also pledged that they would hand over large numbers of weapons (including guns, locomotives, aircraft, battleships, and submarines), evacuate all occupied territories, and allow Allied troops into Germany. Such measures were clearly designed to thwart any German attempts to restart the fighting after the armistice and, in the same vein, the Allied blockade of Germany continued until the peace settlement was signed.

There was still a great deal of work to keep the diplomats and politicians busy, but the news that the fighting was to come to an end was greeted with great joy (and even an excitement to rival that seen at the outbreak of war in August 1914 in some places) across the Allied nations. In London thousands took to the street, waved flags, sang, and celebrated amid, according to one eye-witness, 'the wild noise of a world released from nightmare'. In Paris there were similar scenes, and one of the crowd later wrote, 'In the course of the morning the guns started firing, and Paris went charmingly off her head. Along the boulevards processions at once formed...the whole city resounds with cheers.' There was a carnival-like atmosphere in many cities, indeed *The Chicago Tribune* reported that, 'Harlequins danced beneath the street lamps in the arms of pretty girls dressed as men. Uncle Sam strode with dignity beside an uproarious Charlie Chaplin...[and] Hundreds of overloaded men reeled along the streets beside women reeling with hysteria.'

In the defeated nations, the mood was not anywhere near as jovial, but in many there was a feeling of relief that it was all over. In fact, elation was

'In November came the Armistice ... Armistice-night hysteria did not touch our camp much ... The news sent me out walking alone along the dyke above the marshes of Rhuddlan, cursing and sobbing and thinking of the dead.'
Robert Graves, *Goodbye To All That.*

The first train containing prisoners of war returns to Stuttgart after the Armistice in November 1918. By the final days of the war, having captured over 360,000 German soldiers, the Allies had taken a quarter of the German fighting force out of circulation.

ALLIES' DRASTIC ARMISTICE TERMS TO HUNS

The Daily Mirror

CERTIFIED CIRCULATION LARGER THAN THAT OF ANY OTHER DAILY PICTURE PAPER

No. 4,696. | Registered at the G.P.O. as a Newspaper. | TUESDAY, NOVEMBER 12, 1918 | One Penny.

HOW LONDON HAILED THE END OF WAR

The King and Queen appeared on the balcony at Buckingham Palace to acknowledge the cheers of the crowd that gathered to congratulate their Majesties on the victory.

Home on short leave, but now safe for always from the dangers of Hun bullet and steel.

How news of the armistice signature came over the wire to the newspaper offices. A facsimile of it as automatically printed on the tape machine. The cheers which greeted it were the first to be raised.

An historic message as it came over the wire. It is dramatic that the last British war communiqué should proclaim our forces at Mons.

"Now entitled to rejoice" and doing it. Daddy has beaten the Huns and is coming home.

Nothing gave greater satisfaction to all of us than the news that the cessation of hostilities found the British armies once more in possession of Mons, where the immortal

"Contemptibles" first taught the Huns what British valour and steadfastness could do. They left the town as defenders of a forlorn hope; they re-entered it conquerors indeed,

Commemoration

The need of the combatant populations to commemorate those who had laid down their lives during World War I was very important to their ability to come to terms with the trauma of total war. The impact that the conflict had on communities and individual families was enormous in every country that suffered heavy casualties; indeed, in Britain it was unusual for a household not to have lost a family member or a friend to the fighting. Thus, during the 1920s, the establishment of commemorative days was commonplace: Armistice Day in France and Britain; Anzac Day in Australia and New Zealand; and Memorial Day in the USA. During the same period memorials and monuments were unveiled to commemorate those who had lost their lives (and sometimes also those that had served) in their home communities and in capital cities. Memorials were also built by some nations on the battlefields themselves – the Menin Gate at Ypres and the Thiepval Memorial to the Missing on the Somme are two famous British examples – to commemorate the dead, individual actions, and fighting units.

The first released British prisoners to reach Tournai on 14 November 1918. These soldiers were luckier than some – not all prisoners-of-war were released so promptly, and many succumbed to the dreadful influenza virus that spread rapidly throughout Europe in 1918 and 1919.

'When I came out of hospital many months later the Armistice had been signed. I was just twenty-one years of age, but I was an old man – cynical, irreligious, bitter, disillusioned. I have been trying to grow young ever since.'
George F Wear, '17–21', taken from *True World War I Stories*, Robinson Ltd (1997).

short-lived even in the victorious nations, and there were numerous communities that greeted the news of an armistice with conflicting emotions. In many, sombre reflection took the place of elation, and a similar mood was experienced by the fighting troops. Although all were undoubtedly happy that the killing was at an end, the silence of the guns gave millions a chance to contemplate the future quietly and remember their dead – unfortunately, there were plenty of them to remember.

The grave of an unknown Canadian soldier on the Western Front. One of the features of the war in Western Europe was the huge number of dead soldiers from all sides who could not be identified, or whose bodies were never found in the sea of mud in which they were killed.

Gen Sir George Milne, Colonel Commandant of the Royal Artillery, salutes the war memorial he has just unveiled at Hyde Park Corner in central London in memory of World War I dead from the Royal Regiment of Artillery, 18 October 1925.

Reconstructing a damaged canal in 1919, on the former Western Front. With stretches of water (both natural and artificial) presenting a significant obstacle to advancing armies, it is understandable that they and any crossings built over them represented an ideal target.

Once the war was over and the peace treaty had been signed, the commemoration of those who had died was an important part of the warring nations' efforts to come to terms with the scale of the conflict and the implications of its outcome. In Belgium, the Menin Gate at Ypres (pictured here in 1930) remembers the soldiers of the British Empire who fought in the conflict, and particularly those who were killed and have no known grave.

'Here was the world's worst wound. And here with pride
"Their name liveth forever",
the Gateway claims.
Was ever an immolation so belied
As these intolerably nameless names?'
Siegfried Sasson, 'On Passing the New Menin Gate'.

Verdun in ruins in 1919, with the River Meuse in the foreground. After the intensive bombardments of the town during the course of the war, it was a wonder that any buildings were left standing at all.

The Wounded

The number of dead suffered by a nation during World War I does not give an accurate reflection of the degree of human suffering that occurred as a result of the fighting over the years. In most cases the number of casualties that the armed forces of any combatant country received in action was far in excess of the number of those who perished, and these men had to endure all sorts of hardships once back at home. In Britain 240,000 soldiers required total or partial limb amputations as a result of war wounds, but many more received no treatment of any kind for less visual injuries such as orthopaedic problems and mental distress. Even fit soldiers returning from the war faced an uncertain future, their sacrifices soon forgotten, and unemployment, financial hardship, and marital difficulties waiting where there had once been optimism and stability. In such circumstances the badly wounded found their reintegration into society all the more difficult.

Disabled German troops working with artificial limbs in the workshop of the hospital school in Hanover. The nature of trench warfare and the intensive bombardments that characterized the Western Front throughout the war meant that survivors had often lost one or more limbs.

An artificial limb specialist at the Roehampton limb workshop makes an adjustment to an artificial leg. The same workshop was to figure in World War II, fitting many amputees with artificial limbs – including the flying ace Douglas Bader.

Over the period 1914–1918, some 70 million men around the world were mobilized, and of that number approximately 13 million perished, while millions more suffered mental or physical scars: Russia lost 10 million casualties (dead and wounded); Germany 6.5 million; France 4.5 million; Austria-Hungary 7 million; the British Empire 3.25 million (of whom 2.5 million came from the British Isles); Turkey 3 million; Italy 2 million; and the USA over 325,000. It was therefore difficult to feel ecstatic when so many lives had been shattered.

The Treaty of Versailles

The formal end to the war came on 28 June 1919 with the signing of the Treaty of Versailles. The provisions of this peace treaty were understandably highly controversial as there were so many competing

German press representatives gather at the Paris Peace Conference, which began on 18 January 1919. The British prime minister, Lloyd George, became concerned that the severity of the peace terms being demanded of Germany could have implications in the future, but his worries went unheeded.

points of view from the victorious nations to consider. However, the overriding perception of the final document over the last 50 years has been that it was very harsh, and rather than providing the foundations for peace, merely stored up resentment for another war. But what is the evidence for such a view?

Considering that the treaty was formulated by the victors in the immediate wake of the war, harsh provisions should be expected, but what is often overlooked is the general tone of moderation encapsulated within the treaty. The main provisions were: the territorial annexations of Alsace and Lorraine to France, Eupen and Malmedy to Belgium, and a 'corridor' of land dividing East Prussia from the rest of Germany to the newly-

Young people demonstrate outside the Hotel Adler in Berlin against what were perceived as the harsh peace terms of the Paris Peace Conference, 14 May 1919. Although the resulting Treaty of Versailles might have seemed punitive, it made no attempt to undermine German unity or destroy its industrial infrastructure.

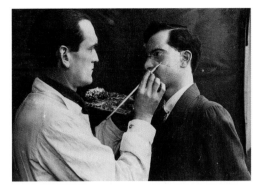

The English sculptor F Derwent Wood served with the RAMC during the war, and was responsible for the Machine Gun Corps memorial at Hyde Park Corner in central London. He also turned his hand to providing a constructive contribution to the war effort, producing copper masks for soldiers who had been badly disfigured facially in the trenches, and acting as the driving force behind the Masks and Facial Wounds department of the corps.

independent state of Poland; the reduction of the German army to a 100,000-men all-volunteer force, with no tanks and aircraft and a severely limited navy; and, controversially, reparations payments to the victorious powers. Underpinning all of this was a German 'war guilt' clause.

These provisions may seem severe at first glance, but the territorial aspects were in line with Wilson's Fourteen Points and, crucially, the treaty did not try to crush Germany's unity or industrial infrastructure. Unlike what happened to Germany after World War II, there was no division of the country as a result of Versailles, and even the Rhineland that was to be occupied by French forces for 15 years remained an integral part of Germany. In short, the nation was given every chance to reassert itself through peaceful means, as there was tacit recognition of the importance of a strong Germany to the European economy and the balance of power. It is true that the provisions affecting the armed forces and the limited French occupation were a source of great discomfort for the Germans, but even this was moderate in the circumstances as the French population sought revenge, and were desperate to undermine Germany's ability to take offensive action again.

However, of all the vilified aspects of the treaty, the decision taken to seek reparations has attracted the most criticism. Nevertheless, it must be remembered that while the principle was established at Versailles that Germany should pay an annual indemnity (eventually set over a period of

Remembrance Sunday

Known in Britain as Armistice Day until 1945, Remembrance Sunday is held on the second Sunday of November, and continues to be a national day of commemoration for those killed in both world wars and later conflicts. On this day ceremonies are held at the Cenotaph in Whitehall, London (the street in which the main British government departments are located), and in many other cities, towns, and villages around the country a two-minute silence is observed. Poppies are traditionally worn by the population in the week preceding Remembrance Sunday, and are sold in aid of war invalids and their dependants. This practice, together with The Royal British Legion, the charity that supports it, was established by Sir Douglas Haig in 1921.

The League of Nations

The League of Nations was proposed in Woodrow Wilson's Fourteen Points as part of the final peace settlement. The League covenant was drawn up by the Paris Peace Conference in 1919 and incorporated into the Treaty of Versailles. Established in Geneva, Switzerland, in 1920, the League included representatives from states throughout the world, but was severely weakened by the US decision not to become a member, and had no power to enforce its decisions. The member states undertook to preserve the territorial integrity of all and to submit international disputes to the League. Its subsidiaries included the International Labour Organization and the Permanent Court of International Justice in The Hague, the Netherlands, both now under the auspices of the United Nations. The League enjoyed some success in the humanitarian field (international action against epidemics, drug trafficking, and the slave trade), in organizing population exchanges after the Paris Peace Conference had established new national boundaries, and in deferring arguments over disputed territories and former German colonies by mandating a League member to act as a caretaker of administration for a specified period of time, or until a permanent solution could be found. Mandates were created for Palestine (Britain), Southwest Africa (South Africa), and the free city of Danzig (Gdansk). In the political and diplomatic field, the League was permanently hampered by internal rivalries and the necessity for unanimity in the decision-making process. No action was taken against Japan's aggression in Manchuria in 1931; attempts to impose sanctions against Italy for the invasion of Ethiopia in 1935–36 collapsed; no action was taken when Germany annexed Austria and Czechoslovakia, nor when Poland was invaded. Japan (in 1932) and Germany (in 1933) simply withdrew from the League, and the expulsion of the USSR in 1939 had no effect on the Russo-Finnish war. Long before the outbreak of World War II, diplomacy had abandoned international security and had reverted to a system of direct negotiation and individual alliances. The League of Nations was dissolved in 1946.

Expatriate Germans (identifying their countries of domicile by the way of banners) assemble in front of the Berlin Museum to listen to speakers protesting about the dictated peace terms of the Armistice, in March 1919. The principal speaker, Dr F Naumann, spoke against the fact that Germans were being expelled from a number of countries around the world and their assets being seized by governments.

30 years) to the victor nations for the damage that they had caused, the schedule of payments did not come until a later date. Reparations were not therefore formulated by the victors in a vitriolic atmosphere, but in a calmer environment that befitted such an important decision. In the end it was decided that Germany should pay for civilian damage (a broader term than the phrase might indicate) and, importantly, that the amount should be limited to Germany's capacity to pay. Thus, in January 1921 the Reparations Commission set the sum to be paid at £6.6 billion plus interest. The Germans found it difficult to finance even this amount, and the Dawes Plan and the Young Plan eased the reparations burden on Germany.

Rather than the Treaty of Versailles being overly harsh, it could therefore be said that it was a balanced and fair treaty. Indeed, it could also be argued that rather than the severity of the treaty being the root cause of so many later international problems, such problems were caused by the requirement of successive German governments to abide by the provisions and for the Allies to take action if they did not. As history reveals, neither happened.

The Aftermath

There is so much to be concerned about when considering the aftermath of World War I – whether the Treaty of Versailles was well conceived, whether its provisions could and should have been enforced – but it should not be forgotten in all this that disillusionment with the peace stemmed as much from unfulfilled 'promises' as anything else. World War I did not usher in a better or more just world, it did not make the world safe for

IMPERIAL WAR MUSEUM

"None of us can forget and this Museum will ever preserve the memory in future ages, that we owe our success under God not to the armed forces alone, but to the labours and sacrifices of soldiers and civilians, of men and women alike. It was a democratic victory, the work of a nation in arms, organised as never before for a great national struggle. We cannot say with what eyes posterity will regard this Museum, nor what ideas it will arouse in their minds. We hope and pray that as the result of what we have done and suffered they may be able to look back upon War, its instruments and its organisation, as belonging to a dead past. But to us it stands, not for a group of trophies won from a beaten enemy, not for a symbol of the pride of victory, but as an embodiment and a lasting memorial of common effort and common sacrifice through which, under the Guidance of Divine Providence, Liberty and Right were preserved for mankind."

George R.I.

An extract from the speech by King George V at the opening of the Imperial War Museum in June 1920. The king's apparent uncertainty as to how future generations would view the museum and World War I proved unfounded – more than 80 years later, the horrors of the conflict are still very much in the public consciousness.

Poster issued by the Belgian government reminding children that just because the war was over, it didn't mean there was no danger – unexploded ordnance would be a constant hazard for a number of years to come.

democracy, it was not the 'war to end all wars' and troops from the fighting front did not return home to find 'a land fit for heroes'. In the aftermath of war, the world desperately endeavoured to recapture its equilibrium after years of instability, but after years of economic instability, inflation, unemployment, and political turmoil, Europe once again descended into war in 1939. In such challenging circumstances it is no wonder that idealism – be it from Versailles or from more esoteric sources – was put through a series of punishing tests and, in most cases, found wanting.

(8 17 5) W6938—GD1389 5,000,000 10/13 HWV(P598)   Army Form Z. 18.

CERTIFICATE OF EMPLOYMENT DURING THE WAR.
(To be completed for, and handed to, each soldier).

A soldier is advised to send a copy rather than the original when corresponding with a prospective employer.

It is particularly important that an apprentice whose apprenticeship has been interrupted by Military Service should have recorded on this form any employment in a trade similar to his own on which he has been engaged during such Military Service.

Regtl. No. *Y 707*   Rank *L.*

Surname (block letters) *GREEN*

Christian Names in full *JOHN*

Regt. *KRRC*   Unit *5th Bn.*

1. Regimental Employment.

Nature of.	Period.
(a) *Duties*	From *28/8/14* To *Jany 1919*
(b)	" "
(c)	" "
(d)	" "

*2. Trade or calling before Enlistment (as shown in A. B. 64).

PLUMBER

3. Courses of Instruction and Courses in Active Service Army Schools, and certificates, if any.

(a) *Signalling Course B.S.S.I. passed 1st Cl.*

(b)

(c)

(d)

* The trade or calling must be filled in by the O.C. Unit from the Appendix to Special Army Order No. 6, of 21st October, 1918 (329 of November, 1918).

[P.T.O.]

4. Military qualifications as shewn in A. B. 64.

1st Cl. Signaller
1st Cl. Shot

5. **Special Remarks** as to qualifications, work done, or skill acquired during service with the Colours. This is required as a help in finding civil employment.

Has done very good work in France as a stretcher bearer.

Soldier's Signature (For identification purposes).   Sign *[signature]* (Rank)

Sgt J Green   *Capt*

Commanding *Comdg. No. 7 Coy.* (Unit)

6th K.R.R.

NOTES.—The object of this certificate is to assist the soldier in obtaining employment on his return to civil life. The form will be completed as soon as possible in accordance with Demobilization Regulations.

As soon as signed and completed it will be given to the soldier concerned and will remain his property. He should receive it as early as is compatible with making the necessary references in order that he can either send it home or keep it in his possession.

One form will be issued to each man, and no duplicate can ever be issued.

Soldier on left
J. Green
94
314
Given to me by wounded German after attending to his wounds

A collection of documents relating to an ordinary British soldier of World War I. John Green (shown photographed in his uniform) served his regiment throughout the entirety of the war, right from its earliest days in August 1914 until after the conclusion of the 1918 armistice. His certificate of employment, issued on his demobilization, was designed to aid reemployment in civil life and lists qualifications and work done throughout the war, as well as his pre-war occupation (a plumber). The small photo shown is a memento given to Green by a wounded German to whom he attended as part of his duty as a stretcher-bearer.

Index

Figures in italics indicate illustrations or caption text; figures in bold indicate feature boxes and figures in bold italic represent text within those boxes; *(d)* indicates a diagram or drawing; *(m)* indicates a map; *(q)* indicates a quote